ADVANCES IN STRATEGIC MANAGEMENT

Volume 2 • 1983

This volume is dedicated to Robert K. W. Lamb and Corinna N. E. W. Lamb

ADVANCES IN STRATEGIC MANAGEMENT

A Research Annual

Editor: ROBERT LAMB
Department of Management and Organizational Behavior
Graduate School of Business
New York University

VOLUME 2 • 1983

Greenwich, Connecticut *London, England*

36 Sherwood Place
Greenwich, Connecticut 06830

JAI PRESS INC.
3 Henrietta Street
London WC2E 8LU
England

ISBN NUMBER: 0-89232-409-0

Manufactured in the United States of America

CONTENTS

LIST OF CONTRIBUTORS

H. Igor Ansoff	European Institute for Advanced Studies in Management, Belgium
Henry Assael, Chairman	Department of Marketing, New York University
W. Graham Astley	The Wharton School University of Pennsylvania
Charles Fombrun	The Wharton School University of Pennsylvania
Kathryn Rudie Harrigan	Graduate School of Business, Columbia University
Charles W. Hofer	Department of Management, University of Georgia
Lawrence R. Jauch	Department of Administrative Sciences, Southern Illinois University Carbondale
Richard O. Mason	College of Business and Public Administration, University of Arizona, Tucson
Ian I. Mitroff	Graduate School of Business Administration, University of Southern California

Raymond Miles — Graduate School of Business Administration, University of California, Berkeley

Howard Moskowitz — Moskowitz and Jacobs, Scarsdale, New York

Samuel Rabino — College of Business Administration, Northeastern University

Paul Shrivastava — Graduate School of Business Administration, New York University

Charles Snow — Graduate School of Business Administration, Pennsylvania State University

J-C. Spender — Graduate School of Management, University of California, Los Angeles

PREFACE

Strategic management is a field that is groping for its identity. It is composed of coporate strategic planners in companies of all kinds, and of management consultants and academics, who are each feeling their way toward a set of common first principles, but are failing to engage in a meaningful dialogue.

Thus far most research in this field has been spotty, narrowly based, and inconclusive. The research approaches have been many, but have lacked a common core of beliefs or first principles.

In part, this failing is totally understandable as are the confusion and false starts typical of any field still in its infancy. However, in the next decade, strategic management practitioners and academics must struggle to come to terms with a painful reality.—Namely: many strategic planning systems in many actual corporations have failed.

Some have been too complex to be implemented. Some have been too simple minded to be relevant to any particular company. Some have been too unrealistic to bear directly on the company or industry that they were supposed to serve, whereas others have been too rigid, or too loose. Many have aimed at achieving the wrong goals.

Many unthinking critics have proposed that we simply discard strategic planning and abandon the concept of strategic management.

However, the reality is that today's corporate actions in countless international business arenas are simply too complex to permit companies to abandon strategic planning. Most top managers today are aware that the pace is too fast, the competitiveness too strong, and the variables too many to simply leave management decision making to ''seat of the pants'' guesswork. While such may have been the predominant mode of management in the past, the increasing risks of error, costly mistakes, and economic ruin have become important pressures causing professional managers to take seriously their need for strategic information and strategic plans in order to make the most of each of their potential competitive advantages.

Therefore, the answer is not to abandon strategic management because of its shortcomings, but instead to intensify the research and dialogue between managers and researchers in search of better methods for formulating and implementing strategy. Organizations need to develop a better fit between the company, its industry, its management and its system of strategy implementation.

Advances in Strategic Management is an ongoing series of volumes whose purpose is to permit a meaningful dialogue between corporate practitioners, management consultants and academics on the latest research in the field. Through these volumes, written from a variety of useful perspectives, it is hoped that the leading authorities in this field can become more knowledgeable. Gradually the underlying interrelation of quite different bodies of strategic management research will emerge, as it has in the interrelations of other sciences, such as physics, chemistry and biology. Thus the heavily quantitative statistical analysis of some researchers and the highly empirical case study analysis of others are not irrelevant to each other. But seen objectively the relationships between these quite different approaches have yet to be recognized, the bridges have yet to be built, the common denominators have yet to be agreed upon.

This series of volumes on *Advances in Strategic Management* is thus a first step in the building of bridges between different research methods, conflicting theories, and disparate schools of thought.

Robert Lamb
Series Editor

CORPORATE CAPABILITY FOR MANAGING CHANGE

H. Igor Ansoff

I. ABOUT THIS REPORT

After its introduction in the early 1970s, the technique of strategic management is now beginning to receive increasing attention from managers. Strategic management enlarges the scope of the earlier technique of strategic planning to include both the external strategic posture ("strategy") and the internal configuration ("structure") of the firm. Strategic planning, first introduced some 20 years ago, was built around a central concept of corporate strategy. As strategic management is introduced, an equally fundamental concept is emerging that is essential to matching the firm's structure to the demands of the environment. This is the concept of corporate capability—the ability of the firm's internal configuration to support its external strategic actions. This report explores the concept of corporate capability and presents a practical approach by which the capability of a firm can be matched to the turbulence of the external environment and to strategic opportunities as well as to its own internal complexity.

Advances in Strategic Management, Volume 2, pages 1–30.

ISBN: 0-89232-409-0

While the techniques for designing functional capability are well developed, the understanding of general management is still partial and incomplete. For this reason, discussion of functional capabilities will be limited to a brief historical review, from which may be drawn lessons transferable to general management. The bulk of the report will focus on general management.

II. BACKGROUND

A. Concept of Organizational Capability

A discovery made early in the history of the business firm, which was to become a key to its ultimate success, was that a firm runs smoother and more efficiently when the work of the firm is subdivided into distinct and internally coherent subtasks. When du Pont managers made this discovery early in the century, they called this subdivision "putting like things together." Later, the sets of "like things" became known as business functions.

Today, each functionally specialized unit produces a distinctive output. Production manufactures goods; marketing converts goods into sales; the innovative function generates products new to the firm. Each function has a distinctive and limited repertoire of tasks that it performs well. We shall refer to this repertoire as the capability of an organizational unit. Usually, the repertoire can be represented by what a mathematician would call a "step function." The response will be positive but variable over a particular range. Outside that range the response drops rapidly and usually becomes negative. For example, a consumer marketing organization will be effective over a range of responses aimed at consumer influence and selling; it will be marginally effective in industrial goods sales; but it will be useless for manufacturing the goods it sells. Historically terms like "production," "marketing," "purchasing," and so forth have emerged to describe the range over which an organizational unit can claim positive competence.

Another way to describe organizational capability is through the configuration of resources within the organization. This is determined by three components:

- The quality of the human, physical, technological, scientific, informational, and monetary resources within the unit. Thus, production workers have qualifications different from those of development engineers.
- The manner in which the resources are organized into a work system composed of the tasks, flows, and dynamics of the process. Thus, very similar production resources would be organized very differently, depending on whether the system is designed for mass production or for serial production.
- The social system of values, attitudes, rewards, and expectations within which the work of the unit takes place. Thus, the social system that makes production effective is based on stability and standardization and rewards

efficiency. The social system in the innovation function should encourage change and inventiveness and reward successful risk taking and venturing in new directions.

B. Concept of General Management

Another important discovery made early in the history of the firm was that after work was functionally subdivided it was necessary to integrate, coordinate, and direct the functional efforts toward common goals. The integrative and coordinating process became known as general management. Originally general management was the exclusive prerogative of the top manager in the firm; however, as firms grew larger, this individual increasingly had to share responsibility with others. Today general management is shared by members of the upper part of the organizational triangle, where the necessary visibility and span of control are available for directing the overall thrust of the firm.

Although it became apparent very early that different functions required different capabilities, it took more than 50 years of business history before an awareness began to emerge that the work of general management is more than a simple putting together of the functions, that general management required capabilities that are distinctive and different from functional capabilities. Because of this late recognition, the evolution of functional design technology progressed faster and further than did the technology of general management.

A great deal is known today about designing a complete function, such as a marketing organization, a production/distribution network, a research and development laboratory. This design includes acquiring and developing the appropriate resources, molding them into a smoothly functioning organization, and matching the capability to a particular repertoire of responses. By contrast, general management is still at a stage in which a great deal is known about such components as management development, the planning system, reward and incentive systems, and structure, but there is still no unifying "turnkey" expertise that combines and balances the components into an overall capability suited to a particular repertoire of behaviors. In fact, there is still little knowledge about matching the general management repertoire to the firm's environmental setting.

The historical development of functional capability can be traced through the evolution of three activities of the firm:

- The innovation activity, which invents new products or services, develops them, identifies customers for them, tests and establishes the products on the market, and eventually discontinues obsolete products.
- The operations activity, which acquires the necessary resources, inventories them, converts them into products or services, and distributes them to locations near sales outlets.
- The marketing activity, which promotes, advertises, sells, and delivers the products or services to customers.

Innovation is the firm's changing activity. It performs the important function of keeping products modern and up-to-date; thus, it creates and maintains the firm's profit potential. Operations and marketing convert the potential into actual profits.

At different points in the evolution of the firm, different activities assumed central importance. This process, in turn, caused a rapid evolution of the corresponding functional capability.

Innovation was critical to the creation of the modern enterprise. But most innovative acts were the product of individual inventors who made their discoveries prior to the organization of the firm. Thus, the creative activity of entrepreneurs lay in creating the productive mechanism for converting inventions into salable products, and in inventing what are now called marketing and distribution networks. Toward the end of the nineteenth century, and for some 50 years thereafter, in a majority of industries efficient low-cost operations became the key to success. As a result, attention was focused on developing and perfecting the productive mechanism: mass production technology in consumer industries, batch and continuous production in process industries, serial production in manufacturing of capital goods. Great progress was made in subdivision of work, plant layout, automation, timely equipment replacement, machine loading, inventory control, warehousing and distribution, and learning curve utilization. All this knowledge was brought together into a "turnkey know-how": timely and efficient creation of a complete operating production organization.

During the 1950s, while concern with operations continued, the focus of attention shifted to marketing. What had been a rather straightforward if vigorous sales activity during the first part of the century quickly grew to include market research, promotion, advertising, subliminal influence of customers, and, eventually, creation and shaping of new customer needs and tastes. The newly developed capabilities included sales analysis, consumer preference measurement techniques, salesmanship techniques, deployment of sales personnel, advertising and promotion, and, as in the case of operations, the concept of a balanced marketing organization.

The innovation function played a secondary role until after World War II, with the exception of some technology-intensive industries. During the first part of the century, research and development focused on improving production technologies, standardizing products, and making products reliable and durable. Major product innovations that occurred periodically were seen as episodic and long-lived. Thus, Mr. Ford's Model T lasted 30 years, and duPont's nylon patents survived unchallenged the period of protection provided by U.S. patent laws.

Starting in the 1930s, as the firm's attention increasingly focused on customer tastes and preferences, opportunities to serve novel needs with novel products became increasingly apparent. The focus of research and development began to shift from durability and standardization to product differentiation, annual model change, and artificial obsolescence. Innovation increasingly became a handmaiden of the marketing function.

After World War II innovation changed from a handmaiden to a leader. A torrent of technology unleashed by the war began to change the face of many industries, sent others into decline, and created new industries serving new social needs. The specter of an ungovernable "R&D monster" forced management attention to innovation. What was previously regarded as a secondary and essentially unmanageable province of inventors increasingly became the key factor to success that *had* to be managed. Innovation was progressively organized and structured; project selection, evaluation, and control techniques proliferated; budgeting and control of R&D were introduced; and leadership techniques for managing creative people and creative processes were developed.

Experience has shown that these three principal functions possess the same attributes across a wide range of industries. (The key attributes are shown in Table 1.) These attributes are determined by the basic nature of processes within the respective functions. Intrafunctional similarities are to be found both in the

Table 1. Attributes of Function Capability

Type	*Operations*	*Marketing*	*Innovation*
Process Management	Production Management Inventory Management Distribution Management Union Relations Operations Control Operations Planning and Budgeting Cost Control and Reduction Efficiency Leadership	Pricing Marketing Planning Sales Force Management Promotion and Advertising Long Range Planning Growth Financing Growth Leadership	Strategic Resource Allocation Project Selection Environmental Sensitivity Risk Taking Project Management Venture Management Leadership of Creative Personnel Charismatic Leadership
Logistic	*Plant *Machinery and Equipment *Inventories *Warehousing *Distribution Facilities Production/Process Knowhow Distribution Knowhow Work Study Equipment Replacement Plant Layout Production and Inventory Planning Control Systems	*Sales facilities Selling Promoting Advertising Customer Financing Customer Relation Sales Analysis Competitive Analysis Forecasting Planning System Design	*Laboratories *Equipment *Test Facilities *Model Shop *Research Knowhow Development Knowhow Project Evaluation Needs Analysis Environmental Surveillance Impact and Trend Analysis Risk Analysis

Source: SRI International.
*Capital-intensive attributes.

Table 2. Determinants of Functional Capability

Characteristics of Industrial Setting	*Production*	*Marketing*	*Innovation*
Nature of Production or Processes			
1. Size and Complexity of Firms	√√	√√	√√
2. Capital/Labor Intensity	√√		
3. Manufacturing/Fabrication Technology	√√	√	√√
Characteristics of Product Innovation			
4. Product Technology		√	√√
5. Technological Turbulence	√		
Characteristics of Demand			
6. Market Type Served by Firm		√√	
7. Market Structure		√√	
8. Competitive Behavior		√√	
9. Sociopolitical Intensity	√√	√√	√

Source: SRI International.

way a function is managed and in the character of the "shop floor" work. Thus, the design of a functional capability can start with building blocks common to most industries.

The content of the building blocks, however, is specific to the industrial setting. The characteristics of different settings are shown in the left-hand column of Table 2.

The entries in Table 2 show the importance of each characteristic in the design of the respective functions. Two checks indicate a determining influence and a single check a secondary one. For example, the design of the production function is determined primarily by the size and complexity of the firm, the capital/labor intensity ratio, the nature of the manufacturing technology, and the sociopolitical influences on the design and the conditions of work.

An important aspect that applies equally to each function as well as to general management is the systems character of organizational capability. This is another way of saying that capability is more than a simple sum of its parts. Experience with functional capabilities has underlined the following important systems properties:

- Overall capability is not stronger than its weakest component.
- Capability is determined by the manner in which the components are related to each other in workflow, space, and time. A set of fully satisfactory attributes, if poorly integrated, results in an unsatisfactory capability.
- Capability is also determined by the social climate within which cooperating individuals interact: the manner in which people are motivated, re-

warded, and treated, and the extent to which they fulfill their personal aspirations while fulfilling the objectives of the firm.

- Finally, the speed with which a new capability is built up, as well as the economic and social costs of the process, depend on the sequences of the buildup. For example, frictions and inefficiencies develop whenever people are assigned new tasks before they have developed the required skills and before rewards have been adjusted to motivate new performance.

Failure to recognize these important aspects of capability during change has resulted in inefficiencies and resistance to change in general management.

III. EVOLUTION OF CORPORATE STRUCTURE

Alfred Chandler in his book *Strategy and Structure* explained the process by which American firms adapted to a changing environment. He found that adaptation becomes necessary when a fundamental change, for example market saturation, makes the firm's existing strategy decreasingly profitable. Some time elapses before the firm recognizes that the problem is caused by a decline of the firm's markets. The typical response is a lengthy trial-and-error process that repositions the firm into a new field of opportunities. Also typically, the new strategic posture does not produce the anticipated profit recovery. As unsatisfactory performance continues to cumulate, management realizes that the problem is now inside the firm. This problem is identified as a mismatch between the old organizational structure and the new strategic posture.

The organization is restructured, but again the recovery is slow. Progressively it becomes evident that other changes must be made before the new structure begins to work: the information system must be adjusted to both the new strategy and the new structure, managers have to be oriented and trained to play new roles, new control and planning techniques must be introduced, and so forth. Chandler's work shows that, like the external adaptation, the internal changes are sequential, accomplished through trial and error, and time consuming. Thus, the total process of strategy and capability adaptation may take as much as 10 years.

Chandler traced this strategy–structure sequence for American firms during the first half of the century. Other researchers have duplicated Chandler's results by analyzing the postwar period both in the United States and in Europe. An interesting result of these studies is that the same structural adaptation pattern was followed in widely different firms and industries.

Within the time span covered by the studies, firms first developed the functional structure. This structure typically evolved at a time when the firm's strategic position was confined to a single major product line sold to a homogeneous coherent market. The challenge in the marketplace was to fill a rapidly growing demand for basic goods and services. Product offerings were not differentiated, and success went to the lowest-cost producer. Successful competitors used four tools to reduce and control costs: specialization and subdivision of work, automation, mass production, and economies of consolidated overheads. All these tools were incorporated into the functional form, which still remains the most efficient organization for mass production.

A pressure for structural change arose after both the firm's strategic complexity increased and the key to competitive success had changed. Firms diversified from a single product line to a multiproduct, multimarket strategic posture, and the key competitive factor shifted from production to marketing.

The multiplicity of products and markets strained the traditional functional structures. Economies of scale possible within a functional unit became limited. Different and frequently incompatible capabilities now had to coexist within the respective functions; these capabilities had limited interchangeability of specialties, capacities, and equipment. Internal competition among different product lines for resources and managerial attention clogged control and communication channels when the environment demanded faster and more attentive response to customers.

The structural response to these pressures by most manufacturing firms was "divisionalization" of the firm according to distinctive product–market lines. Strictly speaking, the functional structure was not abandoned, because each division was typically organized along functional lines. The economies of scale were not confined to divisions, but each division had a clearer view of its environment and a greater ability to respond to market demands and opportunities.

An early consequence of divisionalization that had an important impact on the evolution of general management capability was a trend to minimize the role of the corporate office by decentralizing a maximum of authority and responsibility to the divisions. The corporate office became small, concerned primarily with broad policy matters, selection and development of key executives, financing of the firm, and budgeting and monitoring divisional performance. The key strategic decisions about growth, expansion, and diversification of production markets were passed to the divisions.

A. Multistructure Forms

Continuing increases in strategic complexity and new environmental challenges have forced further changes in corporate structure. A major postwar development was internationalization of the developed country markets: the crossing of the Atlantic by U.S. firms, reduction of trade barriers within Europe, greater competition in world markets among U.S., European, and Japanese companies, the recent expansion of European firms to the United States and of both European and American firms into the rapidly growing developing countries.

The response to this new dimension of complexity came in two steps. The typical first step was the creation of an international division within the existing divisional structure. This was not a division in the same sense as a domestic one, because it served primarily as a channel for distributing and selling the products of the domestic divisions.

As firms diversified their manufacturing, purchasing, financing, and eventually research-and-development functions to many countries, a second step was to form a new multinational organization, which made possible management of the firm on a global basis. A typical multinational firm uses a ''cube-shaped'' structure whose principal organizing dimensions are usually product groups, countries, and functions.

An important but little discussed consequence of this structure was that it violated the traditional management principle of unity of authority and responsibility, which had been given justifiable credit for the historical successes of American management. Because of the (at least) three-way division of authority and responsibility—product, function, and country—it was no longer possible in a multinational firm to lodge complete profit/loss responsibility in any one office. Since coherence and accountability for decisions are as essential as ever, new arrangements for sharing authority and responsibility have developed within such firms. Thus the multinational structure can be viewed as a departure from a previously monolithic ''unistructure'' toward a ''multistructure.''

Most successful multinationals today use a variant of the multinational structure. But the time lag principle observed by Chandler is still observable, particularly in Europe, where many firms that need the multinational structure have recently adopted an international divisional configuration in which foreign activities are treated as subsidiary operations.

B. Project–Matrix Structure

Another change toward multistructure came about as the increased complexity of the firm multiplied and lengthened lines of decision and communication. This occurred when product life cycles became progressively shorter and competition became both global and more intense. The firm was caught in the dilemma of having to respond faster at a time when its ability to respond was becoming slower.

To resolve this contradiction firms in technologically and competitively turbulent industries invented the project–matrix structure. Properly speaking, the matrix structure is not an alternative structural concept but rather a structural mode that can be superimposed on any of the previously described structures in order to ensure rapid and efficient organizational response to special issues and challenges. The matrix structure permits selected groups (projects) within the firm to attend to episodic challenges, while the bulk of the work of the firm proceeds in accordance with a basic functional, divisional, or multinational configuration.

C. Dual Structure

Years of frustrating experiences, which we shall discuss in the next section, have shown that the organizational forms described above are not suitable for a comprehensive analysis of strategic posture. Saturation of basic demand in some industries, technology substitution in others, technology proliferation, new sociopolitical pressures on the firm, and basic structural changes in the behavior of economies—all these changes require the firm to address itself to a reexamination and a revision of the firm's strategic posture, not locally and episodically as in the matrix structure, but globally and continuously. As a result, another structural form is now emerging that extends the project–matrix concept. Within this new dual structure the entire firm shifts into an alternative organizational arrangement when the time comes to plan the firm's strategic posture. Since the ongoing work of the firm is not arrested, and since strategic planning and analysis typically consume a large portion of each year, the two structures effectively coexist side by side. An early pioneer of dual structure has been the U.S. General Electric Company with its apparently successful Strategic Business Unit (SBU) substructure, which operates side by side with GE's historical divisional structure.

General Electric's experience also points to another structural challenge. As a result of diversification and the proliferation of new technology-based industries, many firms find themselves today involved in several industries that are in different stages of growth. Some are in the emergence stage, some in the rapid growth stage, some in the saturation or decline stage. Recent experience has made it increasingly apparent that industries in different stages require not only different structural arrangements but also different management approaches.

It is not yet clear what impact this multidemand life-cycle mix will have on structure. One response used by several American firms has been the separation of the firm's life cycles into two groups: one containing the early life-cycle innovative activities and one containing established profit-producing activities. This has been labeled the innovative structure. A further extension of this type of dual structure to a multistructural configuration appears to be a logical possibility.

Another consequence of recent environmental challenges and of the increased complexity of the firm is a current trend toward revival of a strong corporate office. Although, superficially, the trend appears to be a reversal of decentralization, it reflects, in fact, an assumption by top management of new corporate responsibilities for balancing the firm's portfolio of life cycles, relating the firm to the new sociopolitical pressures, and balancing the intricate multiproduct, multicountry, multitechnology interdependencies and interactions.

Yet another environmental challenge is now clearly visible. This is the increasing likelihood of strategic surprises—momentous events such as the 1973/74 escalation of oil prices—that are impossible to foresee in time to permit advanced preparation and response yet that have major impact on the firm. This challenge will be difficult to meet because the firm has progressively evolved toward larger size and complexity, thus lengthening lines of communication and slowing down the firm's response. It may be that the increasing incidence of surprises will encourage the trend toward dynamic multistructure, reversing the historical strategy–structure sequence, and producing structural designs with much larger, more flexible repertoires of response than in the past.

The final dimension of complexity to be mentioned here is already a working reality in Europe but has not yet been fully translated into the inevitable structural consequences. This is the progressive redistribution of power within the firm in response to legislative and social pressures for codetermination and employee participation in management which is forcing managers to share their historical control over strategic decisions. All the previous structures evolved in response to complexity and turbulence in profit-serving activities over which management exercised exclusive control. A legally prescribed reorganization has already changed the composition and functions of supervising boards in Germany. The Swedish "full consultation" law will probably lead to similar structural rearrangements when the full impact of the law becomes clear.

Thus, the long trend of management-controlled structural evolution in response to profit opportunities is nearly at an end. The new trend will be toward conditions of shared power in response not only to profit opportunities but also to other social expectations and constraints.

Thus, corporate structures have evolved in response to the dual pressures of growing complexity within the firm and shifting environmental challenges. Table 3 summarizes the progression of these challenges and the structural responses. Although the table is presented as a historical summary, by ignoring the dates across the top, the management of a firm can use it as a quick diagnostic tool to identify the type of structure appropriate to the firm's strategic complexity and to its environmental challenges.

The evolution from unistructure to multistructure has been along two dimensions: a static dimension, in which several different structures are made to exist within the firm, and a dynamic dimension, in which the firm assumes different configurations according to the task to which it addresses itself.

Through most of the period examined, structure has evolved through trial and error in response to changes in the "strategy" of the firm. Moreover, structure has been treated as a key "independent variable," and only unhappy experiences with new structures showed that structure must change in concert with other key components of general management capability.

Table 3. Evolution of Corporate Structure

Time	*1900*	*1930*	*1950*	*1980*
Environmental Challenges	Satisfaction of Basic Demand Acceleration of Growth	Response to Customer Preferences Deceleration of Growth	Internationalization Technology Proliferation Saturation of Growth	Global Competition Stagflation Sociopolitical Pressures Limits on Growth
Critical Success Factor	Low Costs	Influence on Customer	Innovation, Diversification	Sociopolitical Awareness, Flexibility
Strategic Complexity of the Firm				
Single Product Line	Functional			
Multiproduct, Multimarket		Divisional Decentralized	Divisional	
Multiproduct, Multiculture			International	• Multinational
Frequent and Intensive				• Corporate Office
Strategic Change		Matrix	Dual Structure	
Multi-life Cycle				Multistructure
Response Slower than				Flexible Structure
Speed of Change				
Redistribution of Power				??
Within the Firm, New Social				
Expectations from the Firm				

Source: SRI International.

IV. EVOLUTION OF GENERAL MANAGEMENT SYSTEMS

Strategy–structure studies singled out organizational configuration as a key factor in a firm's adaptation to the environment. It is true that structural change occurred early in the internal adaptation, that it was dramatic and visible, and that the drama was accentuated by political realignments and changes in the personal fortunes of key individuals. But adaptation to a new strategic posture goes beyond organizational restructuring. Major changes in structure typically remain ineffective until such other components of capability as rewards and incentives, information, managerial skills, and management systems have been updated and realigned with the new structure.

Among these components, general management systems have become increasingly visible and, since the mid-1950s, have begun to precede and overshadow structural change.

Structure assigns roles and establishes relationship among them. Systems specify the dynamics of interaction within the structure, the timing, the sequence, the content of the roles, and the flows among them. It has already been mentioned that the evolution of functional capabilities spawned a profusion of systems for managing logistic work. Parallel with these developments, a succession of systems emerged on the general management level for guiding and controlling the total enterprise.

Differences in structure can be explained by the complexity of the firm's strategic posture and the increasingly turbulent challenges in the environment. Complexity has also been a major stimulus in the evolution of general management systems; in fact, it is the chief reason for the existence. As a firm grows large and complex, it becomes increasingly essential to systematize the many interacting streams of activity. Thus, as strategic posture becomes more complex, systems become more comprehensive.

A. The Impetus of Change

Whereas structure has been influenced by the changing nature and priorities of environmental changes, the evolution of systems has been propelled by the interplay between the speed and familiarity of change, on the one hand, and the time needed by the firm for an effective response, on the other. As change became faster, less and less time was available for response. But at the same time, the growing complexity of change (as well as growth in size and complexity of the firm itself) increased the time needed for recognition, development, and execution of an effective response.

Speed of change was not a problem early in the twentieth century. But in the 1920s, as economic growth accelerated and the shift to marketing took place, it was no longer safe to wait until the accounting system announced the arrival of an unwelcome result (some 15–30 days after the event). Increasingly, firms began to forecast their needs for capacity expansion, raw materials, and changes in products or in marketing strategies. This was typically accomplished by extrapolating past trends into the future.

In the 1950s, internationalization of business, product innovation, and saturation of growth made it necessary not only to extrapolate but also to anticipate discontinuities from the past trends. (In the business literature this became known as analysis of threats and opportunities.)

By the 1970s, competition became global, new technologies invaded traditional industries, and the relevant environment of the firm had expanded beyond the historical commercial boundaries to include major influences by governments, consumers, and unions. Increasingly, new trends arose and discontinuities occurred that could not be inferred from past trends. To respond effectively, the firm now had to search the environment for unfamiliar and novel trends and discontinuities.

In the late 1970s, it is becoming apparent that, because of their novelty and their speed, some of the new departures cannot be perceived in time for an effective response, even by the best surveillance techniques, unless the firm increasingly looks for early "weak signals" of their emergence. Moreover, it is becoming evident (exemplified by the "petroleum surprise") that even weak signal surveillance will fail to awaken management attention to some important environmental changes before their actual impact on the firm. Therefore, as in the military, no matter how good the radar system, the firm will increasingly need to be prepared for occasional strategic surprises.

B. Specific Systems

Table 4 illustrates the evolution of general management systems in response to the ever more rapid and discontinuous changes of the twentieth century. Across the top of the figure are summarized the progressive challenges that general management systems have had to be able to handle. Within the body of the figure the basic systems that evolved for coping with and changing environment are described.

An early general management system—the policy and procedures manual—was designed to routinize and standardize the handling of familiar and repetitive changes. As complexity and size increased, standard procedures no longer sufficed, and firms developed the financial control system, which analyzes the causes of nonrepetitive changes that have already taken place and develops corrective responses.

An important break occurred when firms shifted their time perspective from the past to the future. The shift started with budgeting, which extrapolated resource allocation into the future. Extrapolation of resource was soon supplemented by extrapolation of the desired results in what later became popular as the management-by-objectives system (MBO).

Table 4. Evolution of General Management Systems

Time		*1900*	*1930*	*1950*	*1980*
Environmental Challenges		Satisfaction of Basic Demand Acceleration of Growth	Response to Customer Preferences Deceleration of Growth	Internationalization Technology Proliferation Saturation of Growth	Global Competition Stagflation Socio-Political Pressures Limits on Growth
Strategic Information Perspective Time Horizon	Change				
Past	Stable	• Policy and Procedure Manual			
↓	Incremental	• Financial Control			
Future	Incremental	• Budgeting			
↓			• Management by Objective		
↓			• Long Range Planning		
↓	Familiar Discontinuities (Threat/Opportunity)			• Strategic Planning	
↓	Novel Discontinuities			• Strategic Management	
↓	"Weak Signals"			• Issue Management	
↓	Unpredictable Surprises			• Surprise Management	

Source: SRI International.

In the early 1950s budgeting and MBO were consolidated into the long-range planning system (LRP), which establishes goals, develops programs to accomplish the goals, and sets up budgets to support the programs. LRP relied heavily on extrapolation to predict the firm's future environment. Not long after the introduction of LRP, it became evident that extrapolation no longer described the firm's environment. Strategic planning was developed in response.

This system was another conceptual break in the firm's view of the environment. It departs from extrapolation and seeks to identify new trends and discontinuities to determine what the future of the firm should be.

Understandably, strategic planning is a much more elaborate and costly system than is long-range planning. It is also potentially more disruptive to a firm. For these reasons, long-range planning spread much faster than has strategic planning: it was not until the 1970s that strategic planning began to be used seriously by firms. By that time it had already become apparent that, when a firm confronted novel trends and discontinuities, external adaptation through strategic planning was only a part of the necessary response; an internal structural adaptation was equally essential.

To provide this more complete response strategic management is now emerging. This system pays simultaneous and equal attention to both external strategy and internal capability. It systematizes Chandler's sequence of organizational adaptation to environment and reverses the order of the sequence when the circumstances demand it.

But early forms of strategic management are showing shortcomings. They share two inherent limitations with preceding systems: they accept only a limited range of environmental signals, confined primarily to the information originating in the business environment, and they require strong signals, adequate for predicting outcomes and payoffs from the firm's responses. Yet the strategic environmental perspective is now moving to a scope much broader than the business environment, and the signals are becoming weak.

The first factor has already been recognized in business practice. It is safe to predict that issue management will be used increasingly as part of strategic management. It also appears that, after issue management, the next step will be incorporating means to deal with strategic surprises.

Just as with structure, systems have historically been addressed to planning the commercial activities of the firm under conditions of full control by management. Concern with the sociopolitical environment and new power distribution within the firm have already begun to enlarge the scope of managerial concerns and change the nature of the planning and implementation process. In the next 10 years general management systems will adapt further to these basic changes.

C. Interaction of Systems and Structure

As a comparison of their respective purposes will readily show, structure and systems are closely related and interdependent. Structure provides the architecture of the firm by specifying roles, authority, responsibility, tasks, and relationships among roles. Systems provide the "pattern for living" within the architecture by specifying how the tasks should be discharged within roles and how flows should occur among the roles. Structure and systems are, respectively, the static and dynamic components of the overall organizational configuration. For effective performance a firm needs both structure and systems, and they should be compatible and mutually reinforcing. If they are not, organizational dysfunctions will result.

This was discovered in practice during the first part of the century. After the initial structural adaptation took place, results were unsatisfactory until systems, as well as other components of capability, were brought in line with it. But since the adaptation process was by reaction, trial, and error, the obvious relationship between systems and structure was not perceived. Even in managerially sophisticated firms, there has historically been little communication between the corporate planner, charged with developing systems, and the organizational planner, charged with developing structure.

From 1950 onwards, as the environment demanded increasingly dynamic responses, firms began to use systems rather than structure as the first major step in adapting to new elements of turbulence. As the structure-system adaptation process began to reverse, the need for their compatibility became evident.

Long-range planning turned out to be readily compatible with most structures into which it was implanted, but strategic planning did not. A dramatic example of an early mismatch occurred in the U.S. Department of Defense when Secretary McNamara introduced a sophisticated strategic planning system called (PPBS) into a historically and politically entrenched structure. The structure was organized according to the functional specialties of the respective services and was not appropriate for perceiving and analyzing the potential threats and opportunities presented to the Defense establishment as a whole by the external environment.

To make PPBS work, McNamara introduced a second structure (which became known as the "mission slice structure") within which the strategic decisions were made. Once made, they were implanted in the functional structure.

McNamara's experience was not unique. Functionally organized business firms (for example, process industries) quickly found that an alternative organizational arrangement was necessary to permit effective strategic planning to take place. (In most such cases it turned out that execution of new strategy was difficult and the new structure was unstable, because of the mismatch of the new system-structure to the other essential components of capability. See the next section.)

At first glance, it seemed that strategic planning would be fully compatible with divisional structure, since both were invented to enhance the orientation of the firm toward the external environment. In practice, some firms were able to effect a happy marriage between strategic planning and the divisional structure. Typically these were firms whose respective divisions involved relatively narrow and homogeneous product–market scopes. But large firms with widely diversified divisions had difficulties both in making sense of the results of planning and in implementing these results. It has already been noted that when General Electric discovered that a divisional outlook on the environment did not give a clear view for developing strategy, it introduced a second structure into the firm (Strategic Business Unit Structure) through which it now performs its strategic analysis and planning. A growing number of firms are now adopting the same dual structure approach.

Table 5 presents an analysis of system–structure compatibility based on the systems and structures that have been discussed. The pluses and minuses indicate positive or negative fit between the respective systems and structures. The double plus entries indicate a ''natural marriage,'' situations in which the system helps the structure work, and vice versa. This situation exists, for example, for the functional structure and accounting control, MBO, budgeting, and long-range planning. When any of these four systems is used, authority, responsibility, and power relations within the functional structure are both clarified and reinforced. The resulting system–structure enhances the performance of the organization.

A similar match is observed in the lower right-hand corner, where the complexity of the matrix-, dual-, and multistructures is clarified and supported by the corresponding systems. (Recall that these structures, in fact, emerged to enable the firm to handle the new levels of turbulence without sacrificing the handling of complexity.)

It will be noted that strategic issue management works equally well in all structures because it is a flexible lightweight system that adapts easily to all structural forms.

The single pluses indicate situations in which there is neither reinforcement nor any basic system/structure conflict. For example, while LRP can be made to work in the multinational structure, it contributes very little to clarifying and resolving difficult conflicts of responsibility and authority that arise in that structural form.

Finally, minuses indicate situations in which system and structure can interfere with each other. Thus, early efforts to make strategic planning work within the functional structure typically came to grief. We entered both + and − for the match between strategic planning/stragetic management, on the one hand, and divisional, divisional international, and multinational structures, on the other, because in each case the success of the system will be inversely proportional to the complexity and homogeneity of the firm's product–market structure.

This table can be used both as a historical analysis and as a design tool for selecting compatible systems and structures. It is safe to predict that, as the relationship between systems and structure becomes better understood, the historical approach of treating the two as if they were unrelated will be replaced by a unified approach. The configuration of the firm will be increasingly described by

Table 5. Compatibility of Systems and Structure

	Accounting Control	*MBO*	*Budgeting*	*LRP*	*Strategic Planning*	*Strategic Management*	*Issue Management*	*Crisis Management*
Functional	++	++	++	++	–	–	++	–
Divisional	++	++	++	++	+–	+–	++	+
International	+	+	+	+	+–	+–	++	++
Multinational	+	+	+	+	+–	+–	++	+
Matrix	–	+	+	–	++	++	++	++
Dual Structure	–	+	+	–	++	++	++	++
Multistructure	–	+	+	–	++	++	++	++

++implies a natural and mutually reinforcing match.
+implies compatibility—structure and system do not interfere.
–implies incompatibility.
Source: SRI International.

sets of structure-systems, each of which will be designed to address a distinctive major task of the firm.

V. EVOLUTION OF THE CONCEPT OF GENERAL MANAGEMENT CAPABILITY

Systems and structure define the organizational configuration within which both the general management and the functions do their work. As we have already seen, it has long been recognized that, within this framework, each function must develop its own specialized configuration of capabilities. There has been much less clarity about the specialized capabilities required of general management.

Early in this century, the task of general management within the overall system-structure was viewed as "putting together" the respective functions, and reconciling conflicts among them to assure smooth coordination of their work. It appeared that this consolidation process required no additional knowledge or skills beyond those of the respective functions. Thus, the best way to qualify for a company presidency was to rotate through functional work assignments and then to understudy the incumbent president to get a "feel" for the complexity of such problems as setting prices, determining inventory and production levels, managing interfunctional conflicts, and developing key managers.

Business schools of the time reflected this perception of general management in their curricula. General management was treated as an "empty box" whose characteristics were totally determined by the inputs. A student was first exposed to the theory and knowledge of the respective functional skills and then to a series of general management cases. Later, when electronic computers emerged, instead of (or in addition to) the cases, the student participated in complex computer-assisted marketing–production–finance games.

Toward the middle of the century, it became increasingly evident that general management was more than a simple addition of functions. Just as designs of plumbing, structures, carpentry, electricity, heating, and air conditioning for a house do not constitute its architecture, neither do the functional capabilities constitute the architecture of the firm.

Design of systems and structures was recognized as a distinctive and an increasingly difficult skill. The problem-solving skills developed by functional management were seen as too stylized and convergent for the job of the general manager who must be a divergent creative problem solver. The key problem of the general managers was identified as relating the total firm to the outside environment and then harmonizing the internal capabilities with this new relationship. Increasingly general management needed skills, not developed through functional operations, of relating the firm to a multitude of noncommercial constituencies that increasingly demanded attention from the firm. Even the leadership skills and style of general management were recognized to be distinctive, requiring qualities of vision, risk taking, entrepreneurship, and statesmanship not developed by functional management experience.

Thus, general management capability progressed from being an "empty" to a very "full box." At the outset a view developed that it was also a "generic box" that could be transplanted from one division of the firm to another, or even to another firm.

Thus, a major U.S. company saw nothing wrong in transferring a successful manager of its U.S. consumer goods division to run a newly acquired computer subsidiary in a foreign country. This particular transfer did not succeed, not only because the business, the culture, and the social climate of the subsidiary were foreign to the manager, but also because he landed in the middle of a major political upheaval in the new country. But this incident was one of a growing series that eventually cast doubts on the "generic box" assumption. It became increasingly clear that problem-solving and leadership skills suitable to one environment may not only be inappropriate but self-defeating in a different setting.

In part, this new realization came from disappointments in diversification. Numerous companies, having diversified into attractive but unfamiliar fields of business, experienced difficulties in making the new subsidiaries profitable. Experience showed that frequently the failure was due to a misfit between the general management capability of the parent firm and the capability required by the new subsidiaries.

A second aspect of this realization is that different management capabilities may be necessary within a single firm at different stages of its life cycle. Thus, in the early emergence stage of a firm's life cycle, innovation is a critical management skill; in the rapid growth stage, management of expansion is key, and innovation must be controlled; in the mature/declining stage, controllership is key, and innovation is to be resisted.

As a consequence fo this awareness, General Electric has recently announced change from the concept of a generic general manager (in whose development GE was a pioneer) to a concept of a differentiated general manager. GE now seeks to identify and develop several distinctive types of managers to manage distinctive businesses within the firm.

VI. PROFILES OF GENERAL MANAGEMENT CAPABILITY

Having traced the evolution of the various systems of general management; it is now possible to construct a practical approach to establishing a management capability that is appropriate for a given firm. Developing a general management profile is the first step.

General management comprises three principal components: its culture, which characterizes the social system; its competence, which determines the repertoire of its tasks; and capacity, which measures the volume of work the general management can handle.

Of the three, general management capacity is the least understood component today because for much of the twentieth century it was held that best results are attained when the size of general management, in particular of top corporate management, is held at a minimum. So long as the principle was held valid, there was little inducement to measure the capacity of general management, nor to optimize its size. But the new workload brought about by postwar turbulence, size, and complexity forced a progressive increase in the size of general management.

One consequence has been the emergence of the multimanager corporate office to replace the single corporate officer. A second consequence has been growth of highly competent corporate staffs. Thus, while the minimal principle is no longer practical, techniques for measuring capacity and optimizing the size of management are still lacking.

The concept of general management culture, as we shall use it below, can be defined as both a propensity and a preference for a certain repertoire of organizational behavior. It can be described by means of the following attributes:

- The organizational *attitude toward change:* whether the organization is hostile, passive, or predisposed to change.
- The *propensity toward risk:* whether management avoids, tolerates, or seeks risks; whether it is only comfortable with familiar risks or whether it seeks novel ones.
- The *time perspective* in which management perceives its problems: whether it puts full reliance on past experience, prefers to deal with the present, or puts emphasis on the future.
- The *action perspective:* whether organizational attention and energies are focused on internal operations or on the external environment.
- The *goals of behavior:* whether it is stability, efficiency, effectiveness, growth, or innovation.
- The *trigger of change:* whether a crisis or accumulation of unsatisfactory performance is necessary, or whether the firm continuously seeks change.
- The *initiative* exercised by individual managers: whether they work passively within prescribed guidelines or seek to expand their "elbow room" and venture in new directions.

The third component, general management competence, can be defined as the effectiveness of management in supporting a certain repertoire of behavior. It can be described by the following attributes:

- The *problem solving skills* of individuals and groups: whether they are based on precedents, trial and error, optimization of available alternatives, or creation of new alternatives.
- *The problem solving process:* whether it is compartmentalized and hierarchical, or firm-wide and problem-centered.
- The *leadership skills* of managers: whether they are political, custodial, inspirational, entrepreneurial, or charismatic.
- The management *process* (formal and informal): whether it controls to past performance, anticipates familiar futures, or creates new futures.
- The *information* used in managing: whether it is derived from historical performance, extrapolation, or wide-ranging environmental surveillance.
- Organizational *structure:* the degree and type of complexity it is prepared to handle.
- The *rewards and incentives:* whether the firm rewards historical performance, growth, initiative, or creativity.
- The *job definition:* whether it is narrowly circumscribed or open, encouraging venture and initiative.
- The *technological aids to decision making* (computation procedures, rules, models, computer programs, etc.): whether they assist routine and repetition or innovation and change.

An examination of the ranges of the respective attributes of both culture and competence suggests three conclusions. The first is that the culture and the system can each be internally consistent—a condition in which the values of respective attributes are mutually supportive; or discordant—a condition in which conflict exists among the attributes. The second conclusion is that, in relationship to each other, culture and competence as a whole can be either discordant or mutually supportive. The third conclusion is that several mutually supportive profiles of culture and competence are possible and that the respective supportive profile sets are best suited to different repertoires of organizational behavior.

VII. BUILDING CORPORATE CAPABILITY

A. The Capability Profile

The following hypothesis can be used to generalize from Chandler's environment strategy–structure relationship: "For a given level of environmental turbulence and complexity, there is a particular combination of culture, competence, and managerial capacity that will produce the most effective behavior by the firm."

This hypothesis can be used to construct a practical method for selecting the most appropriate managerial capability for a particular firm.

Establishing a scale of environmental turbulence is the first step. The following five levels are used, based on Table 6.

- Environment in which change is infrequent and the appropriate time perspective is past experience.
- Environment that is past-dependent, but in which important changes are incremental to past experience.
- Environment in which change is incremental and the appropriate time perspective is the future.
- Environment is which important changes are discontinuous from extrapolated trends.
- Environment in which new trends are emerging and change is both novel and discontinuous from the past.

Each turbulence level is linked with an appropriate, consistent profile of general management culture, as shown in Table 6. Shown across the top of the table are the five levels of turbulence and, in the respective columns underneath, the elements of culture appropriate to each level.

The five management culture profiles show that the respective cultures describe what sociologists and systems theorists would refer to as the degree of the firm's openness to the environment. At one extreme a "fully open" culture has the propensity to focus on the environment, to seek out threats and opportunities and even actively to shape the environment. At the other extreme, a "fully closed" culture is introverted, focused on internal activities, and hostile to change. In contradiction to much sociological literature, optimal performance is not always achieved in fully open states. Instead, the table suggests a conclusion that supports Ashby's requisite variety theorem found in the cybernetic literature: for successful performance, the openness of the firm must match the level of turbulence in the environment.

The bottom line of the culture profiles shows that respective cultures work best under different power structures within the firm. Thus, the introverted, stable "don't rock the boat" culture works well in a firm where power and control are exercised from the top; the future-oriented anticipating culture works best when decentralized power supports and encourages initiative. In discontinuity-supporting cultures, decentralization of initiative must be complemented by a strong direction from top management that encourages risk taking, while also insisting on an environmental search consistent with the firm's objectives.

The management competence profiles in Table 7 show profiles of competence appropriate to the respective levels of turbulence. Line six is starred to indicate that, although the organizational structures shown are compatible with the respective states of turbulence, they may not be compatible with the level of the

Table 6. Management Culture Profiles

Time Perspective	*Past*			*Future*	
Change	Stable	Incremental	Incremental	Familiar Discontinuous	Novel Discontinuous
Components					
(1) Attitude Toward Change	''Don't Rock the Boat''	''Roll with the Punches''	''Plan Ahead''	''If It's New It's Good''	''Create the Future''
(2) Risk Propensity	Avoid	Accept	Seek Familiar Risk	Seek Unfamiliar Risk	Seek Novel Risk
(3) Time Perspective	Past	Present	Familiar Future	Perceivable Futures	New Futures
(4) Action Perspective	← Introverted →		← Extroverted →		
(5) Goal of Behavior	Stability and Survival	Efficiency	Synergistic Effectiveness	Global Effectiveness	
(6) Change Trigger	Crisis	Unsatisfactory Results	Threats and Opportunities	Continued Search for Change	
(7) Initiative	''Don't Volunteer''	''Follow the Rules''	''Run with the Ball''	''Be a Self Starter''	
(8) ''Congenial'' Power Structure	← Centralized →		Decentralized	← Decentralized + Strong Corporate Office →	

Source: SRI International.

Table 7. Management Competence Profiles

Time Perspective	*Past*			*Future*	
Change	Stable	Incremental	Incremental	Familiar Discontinuous	Novel Discontinuous
Components					
(1) Problem Solving Skills	← Trial and Error →		← Choice of Best Alternative →		Creativity
(2) Problem Solving Process	← Hierarchical, Compartmentalized →		Hierarchical	← Problem Centered →	
(3) Leadership Skills	Political/Custodial	Controllership	Firm-Wide Goal Achievement	Entrepreneurial	Charismatic
(4) Management System	Policy and Procedure Manuals	Financial Control, Capital Budgeting	Long Range Planning	Strategic Planning, Strategic Management	Strategic Management, Strategic Issue Analysis, Crisis Management
(5) Information System	Informal Precedents	Past Performance	Extrapolative Forecasting	← Environmental Surveillance →	
(6) Organizational Structure	← Functional →		← Divisional →	Multistructure, Matrix	
(7) Rewards and Incentives	Length of Service	Past Performance	Multinational Contribution to Growth	Contribution to Innovation	
(8) Job Definition	Specific and Narrow	← In Terms of Functional Responsibility →		← In Terms of Missions →	
(9) Technology	Work Study, Environment Repl. Maching Loading, etc.	Ratio Analysis, Capital Invest. Analysis	Forecasting, Operations, Optimization	"What if Analysis," Acquisition Analysis, Scenarios, Delphi, etc.	Synectics, Brainstorming
(10) "Congenial" Function	← Operations and Finance →		← Marketing and Corporate Planning →	← Innovation, R&D, New Ventures →	

Source: SRI International.

firm's strategic complexity or with its technology. For example, in many process industries even the strongest culture–competence profiles can be found to coexist with the functional structure.

At the bottom of the competence profiles are the principal functions best supported by the respective types of competence.

These two profiles (Tables 6 and 7) can be used for two practical purposes. The first is to diagnose the internal balance of a firm's culture or competence. This is done by diagnosing the state of the respective attributes and joining them by lines to obtain the competence and culture profiles. If the profile is a vertical straight line, the culture (or competence) is well balanced and the components are mutually supportive. If the profile zig-zags widely, the culture is internally discordant and measures must be taken to balance it. Further, if the culture and competence profiles center on different columns, there is a conflict between the culture and the competence and they must be brought in line.

The second use of these profiles is to determine whether the firm's capability is matched to the turbulence of the environment. First, the state of the environment (the first two lines of the tables) is diagnosed separately from the two profiles. Then the competence and culture profiles are determined. Third, the gaps between the present culture and capability attributes and the desired state are identified. Fourth, programs are developed to close the gaps.

The preceding discussion suggests a conclusion of great importance for practical purposes: the desired state of capability can be determined directly by analyzing the capability profiles and the environmental turbulence, without recourse to the analysis of strategy. It is this conclusion that makes possible a planned reversal of Chandler's sequence.

B. Dynamics of Planned Capability Change

The environment–capability relationship developed in the preceding section permits a planned systematic approach to adapting the firm's capability to environmental change. But planned approaches have a mixed history. On many occasions they have induced resistance and were rejected by organizations, in ways reminiscent of a human body rejecting a foreign transplant. On other occasions, introduction of planned approaches failed to produce the anticipated results.

Demonstrably the trial-and-error adaptation has worked in the past. Many of today's distinguished firms have gone through Chandler's sequence early in the century. But history shows that the process was slow and inefficient and that it generated resistance to change, political confrontations, and crises. Thus, contrary to the notions of some sociologists, organic, reactive "muddling through" is more like spreading the pain over time than avoiding it. Certainly there is evidence that historical trial and error was less efficient and more costly than a carefully preplanned and executed process. Thus, planned capability change can be advocated on the grounds of time saving, efficiency, and not necessarily higher social costs.

But today the strongest argument for planned anticipatory capability change is that reactive unplanned change requires more time than the environment permits. In the past, the total adaptation cycle has frequently lasted as long as 10 years. Even in the less turbulent environment of the first half-century, the adaptation cycle frequently was not completed until after the environmental change had already made necessary the next adaptation. This situation occurred, for example, in the duPont Company, where the functional structure was not perfected until after the environment created a need for the divisional structure. Another example, discussed previously, has been the belated adaptation of the divisional structure in Europe at a time when the multinational structure was already needed.

With accelerated rates of change since the 1950s, the time span of an environmental change cycle is now typically shorter than the time needed by large and complex firms to complete a reactive sequential strategy–structure adaptation. This places the firm in danger of never having a capability that is responsive to the current needs, a situation analogous to a squirrel in a cage that always chases but never succeeds in catching its own tail.

Thus, today there is a compelling argument not only to take the planned approach but also to abandon the strategy–structure sequence in favor of either a reversed or a parallel sequence. (In fact, this approach is one of the key concepts that distinguishes stragetic management from strategic planning.) But how to assure acceptance and to minimize this pain?

C. Influence Strategies

Acceptance can be promoted by recognizing that the more drastic the capability transformation, the more threatening and unwelcome it will appear to many managers who may lose power and job security and may appear incompetent to cope with the new realities. Therefore, it is important that change be introduced in a clear and unambiguous way, and that an appropriate influence strategy be carefully selected and consistently applied.

Among influence strategies observed in practice, four are commonly used: coercion, contagion, learning, and crisis. In coercion strategy the superior authority and power of top management are used to enforce change. This strategy has been commonly used in the past for introducing long range and strategic planning into business firms. The procedure has been to get the top management to declare itself unequivocally in favor of planning (without any additional effort to help other managers understand why planning is necessary or how it can help them in their own work), to distribute the planning formats, and to trigger the planning process according to a prescribed schedule.

The coercion strategy has the advantages of simplicity and speed. It is the fastest way to force changes of behavior.

Its disadvantage is that it invariably induces organizational resistance and friction. Further, unless coercion is maintained for a long time, behavior reverts to earlier modes once the management's attention is diverted elsewhere and the coercive pressure is relieved.

In contagion (or imitation) strategy, top management picks a unit of the firm that has either already gone through a process of planned adaptation or is ready and eager to do so. This unit is given resources, encouragement, and rewards. Typically, other units will begin to imitate the chosen group, and change will gradually spread throughout the firm.

The advantage of the contagion strategy is that it requires the least amount of effort and initiative on the part of top management. A disadvantage is that the diffusion may be too slow compared with the rate of environmental change. The major disadvantage is that a potential "showpiece" group may not exist within the firm.

Learning strategy exposes managers at all levels to the realities of their own environmental predicament. In the Philips Company this has been called creating a "strategic mentality" within the firm. As managers perceive the need for change in their own situations, they begin to accept it. They are then provided with the necessary concepts and tools for planning and conducting their own capability transformation.

This strategy is slower than coercion and faster than contagion. It is visibly costly. (The coercion strategy is typically more costly because of frictions, resistance, and subversion, but these remain hidden and do not appear in the budgets.) Experience shows that learning produces a lasting change as well as positive feelings and attitudes toward environmental realities.

The crisis strategy uses a threat to organizational survival to spur the organization into accepting change. In cause and effect it is similar to the coercion strategy, except that it does not require top management to be either powerful or aggressive.

Of the four influence strategies, the contagion strategy results in a change process that appears serendipitous, unguided, and "organic." The learning and coercion strategies are, by definition, planned and guided. The crisis response is typically turbulent, disorganized, and voluntary. But it need not be so, if top management perceives the crisis in advance and plans the response.

The last question to be explored is how to minimize the cost and the pain of implementing appropriate capabilities. One answer is that, whichever influence strategy is used, top management must understand the nature of the process, remain consistent in the application of the strategy, and anticipate and deal with foreseeable obstacles and resistance.

A second answer is a recognition that there are natural sequences in capability transformation, in which every preceding step prepares and reinforces the following one and that there are also resistance-generating sequences, in which a step reinforces the resistance to further change.

To illustrate both the natural and the conflict-generating sequences we can

Table 8. Types of Capability Attributes

	Items from:	
Categories	*Management Culture Profiles*	*Management Competence Profiles*
Values	1,5,6,7	
Information	3,4	9
Systems		4,5,7
Structure	2,6,8	8

Source: SRI International.

aggregate the attributes of the capability vector of the management culture and management competence profiles into the categories shown in Table 8. A natural change sequence in which each step prepared and reinforces the following one is:

Values → Skills → Capacity → Information → Structures → System

A resistance-generating sequence that has frequently been observed in the introduction of strategic planning into business firms is:

System → Skills → Information → Structure → Capacity → Values

In this sequence, managers are first asked to act outside their competence and to use irrelevant information within a structure that does not encourage the new system. As the deficiencies are uncovered through failure and frustration, remedies are introduced one by one. Little wonder that strategic planning has encountered so much resistance!

A key result of this analysis is that capability needs can be determined directly from the environment, without the intermediate determination of strategy. Thus, it is possible to change capability before, or in parallel with, the change in the firm's strategy. Another key result is that the influence strategy used to introduce change is as important to success as the change itself. These concepts will enable a firm to effectively match its capabilities to its strategic environment while avoiding costly trial-and-error methods and organizational resistance.

ACKNOWLEDGMENT

This was an internal report for the Stanford Research Institute. It has not been publicly published. Reprinted with permission from SRI.

A TELEOLOGICAL POWER-ORIENTED THEORY OF STRATEGY

Richard O. Mason and Ian I. Mitroff

I. INTRODUCTION

It is commonplace to say that the field of strategic planning necessitates a marriage of behavioral science and economics. It is still far from being commonplace, however, to recognize that the field requires the marriage of many more diverse disciplines as well. This paper argues that not only are behavioral science and economics indispensible to the field of strategic planning, but that ethics and epistemology are as well. Even further, we argue that a concept of aesthetics is also absolutely indispensible.

These "nontraditional" concerns pose the most severe challenge the field has to face. It is clear that the unification of such a wide array of disciplines and concerns cannot be accomplished by traditional means, such as by mathematical, statistical, or structural models alone. Instead, a new concept and meaning of unification is called for.

Advances in Strategic Management, Volume 2, pages 31–41.

ISBN: 0-89232-409-0

The paper points to a new concept of unification. It is based on the fact that social systems are fundamentally teleological in the sense that they are composed of teleological entities. Teleological systems are characterized by uncertainties in our ability to know the entities which compose such systems and in our ability to describe accurately the properties of the components themselves. If the attainment of certainty is a precondition for strategy making, our task is doomed to failure unless we can develop a concept of strategy making that is founded on the clear appreciation, recognition, toleration, and use of uncertainty. We offer a teleological power-oriented theory in response to their need.

II. A CONCEPT OF STRATEGY

Strategies are plans for acquiring power. Power in this context refers to the human control of the energies necessary to achieve human purposes, whatever those purposes may be—survival, profitability, prestige, growth, efficiency, equity, or social responsibility. This kind of organizational power includes power over other human beings, exercised with or without their consent, with or against their "will," and with or without their knowledge or understanding. Thus, the power harnessed by a strategy may be used either for good or for evil. Ethical strategies, of course, are those which employ power in morally justifiable ways.

This power-oriented definition of strategy has much in common with the more traditional definitions which, drawing on notions of organizational Darwinism, define strategy as the "basic characteristics of the match an organization achieves with its environment . . ." (Hofer and Schendel, 1978, p. 4). By biological analogy the successful organizations are those whose strategies ensure the "survival of the fittest." These surviving organizations find nourishing niches in their environment. That is what fitness and, hence, power is all about.

Power is also the fundamental construct underlying some of the practical methodologies for making strategy. For example, the typical evaluation of the internal strengths and weaknesses of an organization as they relate to the external opportunities and threats has implicit in it the question "does this organization have enough power—excess of strengths over weaknesses—to ward off its threats and avail itself of its opportunities?"

So, if this power-oriented definition of strategy is so similar to the other definitions, what is its advantage? The principal advantage is that it shifts the focus of the strategist's attention away from responsive behavior toward proactive behavior. That is, the responsive process of *matching* is replaced by the anticipatory process of *creating enabling* conditions. Power is a logical prerequisite to positioning. Once an organization is enabled with power it can become an effective matchmaker.

This subtle psychological shift also yields some fruits in analysis. The concept of power can be analyzed in terms of a means/ends schema, which in turn has direct application to the development and execution of a strategy. Drawing on the philosophy of Singer (1959), Churchman (1971, 1979), and Ackoff and Emery (1974), we propose that the enabling conditions of organizational power and, hence, of an effective strategy are:

1. The ability to change purposes (ends) and create new purposes (Aesthetic Dimension). We refer to this as the "Change and Creativity" dimension.
2. The ability to acquire and mobilize adequate resources (means) (Political, Economic Dimension). We refer to this as "Business—Political and Economic Function(s)."
3. The ability to discover and develop resources and to allocate the right resource, in the right amounts, to the right organizational component at the right time; that is, the ability to relate means to ends effectively (Knowledge, Information Dimension). We refer to this as "Information and Communication."
4. The ability to sustain cooperation and to eliminate conflict among all stakeholders so that the purposes are achievable (Ethical–Moral Dimension). We refer to this as "Ethical, Moral, Cooperative."

In essence these four criteria describe a successful strategy as one which provides for good goals and objectives, adequate resources, effective management information and scientific information, and cooperative efforts among the people involved. Notice that if a strategy fails by one of these four criteria it will be unsuccessful. Thus, each criterion is necessary for success. Moreover, satisfactory performance on all four criteria implies success for the strategy as a whole. Thus, collectively the satisfaction of these criteria is sufficient. Any strategy that satisfies these four criteria augments the power of an organization and therefore will be successful.

Organizational power for us is a teleological concept because power is defined in terms of the purposes that are to be achieved. Consequently we describe the enabling conditions for power as they relate to the teleological entities—we call them *stakeholders*—which comprise a teleological system. Our teleological theory of organizations and strategy may be summarized by 11 key propositions.

III. ELEVEN KEY PROPOSITIONS

1. An organization is a collection of internal and external *stakeholders*.
2. A stakeholder is a distinguishable entity which has resources, its own purposes and "will," and is capable of volitional behavior. That is, it has vitality.
3. There is a network of interdependent *relationships* among all

stakeholders. Some relationships are *supporting* in that they provide movement toward the organization's purposes. Some relationships are *resisting* in that they serve as barriers of encourage movement away from the organization's purposes.

4. A new strategy changes one or more of these stakeholder relationships.
5. A strategy results in more power for the organization when it provides for a greater flow of purposeful achievement through the supporting relationships than flows through resisting relationships.
6. Relationships with each stakeholder may be changed in one or more of the following ways:
   a. *Convert* (change) the stakeholder by means of:
      (1) *Commanding* him through the exercise of power and authority
      (2) *Persuading* him by appealing to reason, values, and emotion
      (3) *Bargaining* with him by means of exchange
      (4) *Negotiating* with him to reach "give and take" compromises
      (5) *Problem solving* with him by means of sharing, debating, and arriving at agreed-upon mutual conversions
   b. *Fight* the stakeholder and *politic* to overpower him by means of:
      (1) Securing and marshaling the organization's resources
      (2) Forming coalitions with other stakeholders
      (3) Destroying the stakeholder
   c. *Absorb* aspects of the stakeholder's demands by incorporating them in a process of *cooptation* which imparts changes to some of the organization's goals.
   d. *Coalesce* with the stakeholder by forming a *coalition* with joint decision-making powers.
   e. *Avoid* or *ignore* the stakeholder.
   f. *Appease* the stakeholder by giving in to some of his demands.
   g. *Surrender* to the *stakeholder*.
   h. *Love* the stakeholder by forming an emotional bond and union with him.
   i. *Be* or *become* the stakeholder by transforming the organization into the stakeholder through merger, imitation, idolatry, or role modeling.

   Strategies must be implemented through one or more of these change-oriented activities. Hence, all strategies presuppose the presence of the power necessary to employ the relevant methods of bringing about change.
7. The state of the organization at time T will be the result of confluence of the behavior of all the organization's stakeholders as it flows through the network of relationships from the beginning up to time T.
8. Therefore a strategy undertaken at time T in order to achieve outcomes in time T + t is based on one or more assumptions about (1) the properties

and behavior of the stakeholders, (2) the network of relationships which binds them to the organization, and (3) the organization's power to change relevant relationships.

9. *Leaders* are those stakeholders who create new strategies for an organization.
10. *Managers* are those stakeholders who allocate resources among the set of stakeholders and control their employment so that the purposes of the strategy are achieved.
11. *Operators* are those stakeholders who perform the tasks necessary to achieve the purposes of the strategy.

All stakeholders are operators to some degree. Which stakeholders are leaders and/or managers depends on the pattern of authority and responsibility relationships established within the organization. A dictatorship has a single leader. In a pure democracy all stakeholders function as leaders.

Having asserted these basic propositions, we next propose the enabling condition for strategic power based on the means/ends schema described earlier. In parenthesis following each condition are some of the key management concepts which relate to that condition.

IV. ENABLING CONDITIONS FOR STRATEGIC POWER

A. *Change and Creativity*
   1. The leaders of the organization must have the *inspiration* and creativity necessary to reevaluate the organization's current missions, purposes, objectives, and goals and to conceptualize new purposes (leadership, statesmanship, goal setting, missions, MBO).
   2. The managers must have *capability* for translating new purposes into programs of action. (innovation, creativity, management of change, organizational change, invention, patents, copyrights, flexibility, changeability).
   3. All stakeholders must have the *spirit, dedication,* and *commitment* necessary to secure the new purposes (motivation, incentives, satisfaction, promotions, careers, personal values, renewal, catharsis, energy, drive).

B. *Business—Political and Economic Functions*
   1. The total resources held by the collection of stakeholders must be adequate to accomplish the purpose (capital availability, recruitment, capital budgeting, finance, purchasing, energy, mergers, acquisitions, plant location, working capital, cash flow, inventory, dividend policy).

2. The managers must reallocate the resources from stakeholder to stakeholder so that each receiving stakeholder possesses the amount of resources necessary to carry out his tasks at the right time and place (budgeting, decision making, resource allocation).
3. The stakeholders must employ the resources they have effectively and efficiently when executing their tasks in order to ensure that the maximally useful output is produced (productivity, production, work assignment, organizational structure, materials handling, design of jobs).
4. The managers must distribute the output effectively to all relevant stakeholders (marketing, sales, distribution, sales force, sales training, advertising, customer relations).

C. *Information and Communication*
1. The collection of stakeholders must have the capacity to acquire or produce basic knowledge—scientific, industrial, and operations—about the organization's products, technology, operations, finances, markets, and customers (R&D, accounting, MIS, market research, operations research, corporate intelligence, planning, library).
2. The managers must ensure that the right information is transmitted to the right stakeholder at the right time (communications, organization, reporting, dissemination, education, training, advertising, public affairs, auditing, storage and retrieval, telecommunications, teleconferencing).
3. Each stakeholder must have the capacity to use the knowledge and information he receives to make effective decisions (management systems, knowledge utilization, applied research, participation, boards of directors, policymaking structure, authority, responsibility, accountability, cognitive style, intuitive decision making, decision processes).

D. *Ethical, Moral, Cooperative*
1. Each stakeholder must have the peace of mind within himself to be fully effective in his organizational life and all other aspects of his life (midlife crisis, quality of work life,human potential, satisfaction, health and safety, stability, fringe benefits, stress, psychic energy).
2. There must be a minimum of conflict between the internal stakeholders—individuals, groups, departments—that function within the organization (organizational development, role clarification, conflict resolution, leadership, dissension, goldbricking).
3. There must be a minimum of conflict between the organization and its external stakeholders such as governments, public interest groups, social activists, unions, and competitors. (public relations, government relations, labor relations, ethics, morality, social responsibility, product safety, SEC, EPA, EEOC, OSHA, OPEC, issues management, freedom of information, antitrust).

V. METHODOLOGY

What methodologies, then, are appropriate for the process of strategy making if one accepts the power-oriented theory of strategy? How is the strategist to define the strategic problem, to study it and to forge an action plan? The key we believe lies in proposition number 1, namely, the assumption that "an organization is a collection of internal and external *stakeholders.*" As we describe in our recent book *Challenging Strategic Planning Assumptions* (Mason and Mitroff, 1981), the first step in the strategic planning process is to identify the full range of relevant stakeholders.

Stakeholders are woven together in a producer/product web. The outcome—that is, *effect*—of the strategy will be the result of the collective behavior of all the stakeholders—that is, *cause*. No one stakeholder acting alone can *cause* the outcome to result. However, a stakeholder's actions can be necessary, although not sufficient, for achieving the desired result. The more power a stakeholder has—in terms of purposes, resources, knowledge, and cooperation—the more influencial its contributory role in achieving the outcome. An illustration will help make this point clearer.

Some years ago Heublein, Inc., embarked on a strategy intended "(1) to make Smirnoff the number one liquor brand in the world; (2) to continue a sales growth of 10% a year through internal growth, acquisitions, or both; and (3) to maintain Heublein's return on equity above 15%" (Steiner and Miner, 1977, p. 541). The achievement of these goals will depend upon the collective actions of Heublein's stakeholders—customers (largely, relatively prosperous young adults), competitors, suppliers, stockholders, creditors, employees, franchisors and distributors, salesmen, labor unions, local communities, investment bankers, government agencies, the corporate management and staff, and a host of others. Each of these stakeholders' supportive behavior is necessary to the accomplishment of the goals. Any one of them can "pull the plug,"as it were, by withdrawing support. However, each of these stakeholders also has its own purposes, its own strategy, its own power position, that is, its own vitality. By definition, not all of its goals will be consistent with those of Heublein. Some of each stakeholder's goals will reflect its own inique existence. This difference in purposes between Heublein and its stakeholders means that some stakeholder behavior will be nonsupportive, resistant, or opposed to Heublin's strategy. Thus, Heublin functions in a field of stakeholder forces which are unavoidable and to some extent uncontrollable. This leads us to the conclusion that the success of Heublein's strategy for achieving its three goals depends inevitably on the assumptions it makes about its stakeholders and their behavior.

The strategic assumption surfacing and testing technique (SAST) we have developed (Mason and Mitroff, 1981) is designed to help organizations identify their stakeholders and to elucidate the assumptions underlying their strategy. The task, of course, is formidable due to the immense number of stakeholders any organization has. Indeed, the task would be overwhelming were it not for one key notion: stakeholders and the assumptions being made about them are not all equally significant. Some stakeholders' assumptions are more crucial to the success of the strategy at any point in time than are others.

John R. Commons had great insight into this problem. He classified stakeholder forces as either complementary—generally supportive of the goals—and limiting. "The limiting factor is the one whose control, in the right form, at the right place and time, will set the complementary factors at work to bring about the results intended" (Commons, 1961, p. 628). For any given strategy there are relatively fewer limiting factors—let us call them *strategic assumptions*—than there are other forces in the stakeholder force field. Strategic power consequently depends on having purposes, resources, knowledge, and cooperation necessary to control the limiting factor. For this reason, the SAST process forces the strategist to rate the stakeholder on a scale of *importance*.

Heublein, for example, made the crucial assumption that the relatively prosperous young adult market would buy vodka. They acted on that assumption by advertising Smirnoff intensively in that market, including the portrayal of women in its advertisements and the launching of the Smirnoff Mule for the discotheque set, and their strategy paid off. Ford made similar assumptions about young adults' willingness to buy the Edsel and, of course, it failed. Clearly Ford's assumption was important but it was wrong.

So, SAST requires that a second question be asked of any assumption. How *certain* are you of the validity of this assumption? The strategist is required to rate each assumption on a scale of *certainty*. The result of the two ratings—importance and certainty—is a two-dimensional plot that reveals the strategic status of each assumption at the point in time it was plotted.

There are some important concerns that flow from having rated an assumption as to its certainty, especially if it is an important assumption. The basic concern is "what is our current state of knowledge about this assumption?" We have found that an effective way to respond to this question is to submit the assumption to argumentation analysis. We have drawn on and modified the work of Toulmin (1958) and Rescher (1976) to create a model of argumentation analysis for strategic decision making. Its basic question are:

1. What is your best judgment as to the assumption to make about a stakeholder and the ratings of importance and certainty you assign to that assumption? The response is treated as a *conclusion* in an argument.
2. What *facts* do you base your judgment on?
3. What *warrants*—interpreting assumptions—are required to interpret the facts as supporting evidence for the conclusion?
4. What are the *rebuttals*—conditions under which your conclusion does *not* hold?

5. How *plausible* are your conclusions, facts, warrants, and rebuttals?

The answers to these questions may be processed through a logical mechanism to determine their relative epistemological status (Mason and Mitroff, 1981).

As a strategist considers a potential limiting factor assumption, the results of argumentation analysis take on additional significance. If the strategist's knowledge is inadequate and time permits, he may want to engage in business intelligence and management information systems activities in order to improve his knowledge and understanding of the assumption. In an article entitled "Creating the Manager's Plan Book" (Mason et al., 1980) we identified three modes of inquiry that might be used at this stage:

1. empirical, scientific, and other research methods,
2. dialogue, reflection, and other intuition- and judgment-supporting methods, and
3. monitoring methods.

The effective use of any of these methods will increase the power of the organization to achieve its goals, especially if the inquiry effort is directed toward limiting factors.

Monitoring takes on special significance throughout the strategic history of an organization. Strategic assumptions tend to have a "half life." Through time stakeholders flow in and out of the relevant network. The forces they exert in the field change. And, of course, the purposes and goals of the organization change as well. By dint of new external forces or the successful management of a limiting factor, the force field shifts. Some new stakeholders and the assumptions being made about them emerge as crucial; others move down to a less compelling status. Consequently, we recommend that the importance/certainty rating graph be updated periodically and that strategic information systems be instituted to provide the necessary background data. These systems need to report on the current state of power of each stakeholder in the relevant force field in terms of its purposes, resources, knowledge, and degree of cooperation. All strategic assumptions made about stakeholders ultimately relate to the power they potentially can exert in the organization's force field, that is, within the relevant network of stakeholders.

This leads us to the final stage in strategy—action taking or, in the language of strategic planning, implementation. SAST provides guidance for action taking by focusing attention on the limiting factors and the stakeholders who control them. These stakeholders have power, so does the organization, and their forces interact through a relationship of mutual dependency. A new strategy inevitably requires changing one or more of these power-based stakeholder relationships. The planning of change, then, as Warren Bennis and his associates reminded us years ago (Bennis et al., 1961, 1969), is fundamental to the successful implementation of strategy. In principle, a strategy should have an action plan for each stakeholder, although in practice the major emphasis should be directed toward those stakeholders controlling the limiting factors in the force field. The planned change involves the processes of converting, destroying, absorbing, coalescing, avoiding, appeasing, surrendering, loving, and becoming, as outlined in proposition 6 earlier. The processes that are finally chosen depend on the power profiles of the organization and the stakeholder involved.

It should be noted that this broad stakeholder force field analysis subsumes many contemporary approaches for analyzing industries such as Michael Porter's *Competitive Strategy* (1980) approach. Concern with such factors as threats to entry, intensity of rivalry, product substitutability, product substitutability, buyers' power, suppliers' power, and the like all relate to the kinds and direction of power that a stakeholder might exert within the stakeholder force field. The strategist must assess that power and develop an action plan accordingly. Distinctive competence in this context refers to the class of purposes an organization's power permits it to achieve.

All of the foregoing indicates why the aspects of power identified in Section III are so important. These are the crucial dimensions of organizational power in a strategic situation. An organization's power and hence its ability to achieve its purposes is based on the four key components identified—ability to change, resources, knowledge, and cooperation. Each of these four components has three or four logical subdivisions which help define their scope. Collectively these enabling conditions form a skeletal framework for evaluating an organization and its stakeholders at any point in time and for guiding the development of a successful strategy. Also, based on the theory of teleological systems and an ends/means scheme, we propose that the set of conditions is necessary and sufficient for success. One need only take this broad set of conditions and apply it in more refined detail in conjunction with SAST and argumentation analysis to the strategic problem at hand.

REFERENCES

Ackoff, R. L. and Emery, F. (1974), *On Purposeful Systems,* Chicago: Aldine-Atherton.

Bennis, W. G., Benne, R. D., and Chin, R. (1961), *The Planning of Change* (1st ed.), New York: Holt, Rinehart, and Winston.

Bennis, W. G., Benne, K. D., and Chin, R. (1969), *The Planning of Change* (2nd ed.), New York: Holt, Rinehart, and Winston.

Churchman, C. W. (1971), *The Design of Inquiry Systems,* New York: Basic Books.

Churchman, C. W. (1979), *The Systems Approach and Its Enemies,* New York: Basic Books.

Commons, J. R. (1961), *Institutional Economics,* Madison: University of Wisconsin Press.

Hofer, C. W. and Schendel, D. (1978), *Strategy Formulation: Analytic Concepts,* St. Paul: West Publishing.

Mason, R. O. and Mitroff, I. I. (1981), *Challenging Strategic Planning Assumptions,* New York: Wiley.

Mason, R. O., Mitroff, I. I., and Barabba, V. P. (1980), "Creating the Manager's Plan Book," *Planning Review,* July.

Porter, M. E. (1980), *Competitive Strategy,* New York: The Free Press.

Rescher, N. (1976), *Plausible Reasoning,* Amsterdam: Van Gorcum.

Singer, E. A. (1959), *Experience and Reflection,* Philadelphia: University of Pennsylvania.

Steiner, G. and Miner, J. B. (1977), *Management Policy and Strategy,* New York: MacMillan.

Toulmin, S. E. (1958), *The Uses of Argument,* Cambridge, England: Cambridge University Press.

ROVA:
A NEW MEASURE FOR ASSESSING ORGANIZATIONAL PERFORMANCE

Charles W. Hofer

I. INTRODUCTION

Much of the early research in most areas of management, including business policy/strategic management, organizational theory, organizational behavior, and marketing, was descriptive or comparative in character. As a consequence, such studies usually contented themselves with describing the phenomena under investigation in terms of the processes by which the phenomena took place, the systems which facilitated these processes, and the inputs to these systems. Seldom were output measures used, and, in those instances in which they were, they were usually either subsystems measures related directly to the subject under study, such as employee satisfaction in some organizational behavior studies, or very crude measures of total systems performance, such as organizational survival or comparative growth rates.

Advances in Strategic Management, Volume 2, pages 43–55.

ISBN: 0-89232-409-0

As management research has evolved, however, it has become more normative and hypothesis-testing in character. And with this change in character has come an increased focus on assessing overall organizational performance, especially relative organizational performance. Still, the measures used have varied by schools of thought and fields of study, as Table 1 indicates.

In the early 1970s there was some concern about this multiplicity of organizational performance measures, as well as much discussion about which performance measures were "best." More recently, most researchers have acknowledged the fact that the differences in the performance measures utilized in different fields appropriately reflect the different purposes that these fields are pursuing.

Within each field, however, the questioning of appropriate performance measures has continued to a greater or lesser degree. At the same time, such questioning has taken on a substantially different focus. Rather than being concerned primarily with whether there is one "best" measure of organizational performance for all purposes, such questioning has focused instead on the various "measurement" problems associated with the different performance indices used in each subfield, such as those listed in Table 2, and, more recently, on a key issue which all organizations must face—that of goal tradeoffs.

The major reasons for such questioning of the quality, desirability, and usefulness of different measures of organizational performance has been the increasing volume of normative research in all fields of business over the past two decades. At the present time, several conclusions seem appropriate. First, it seems clear that different fields of study will and should use different measures of organizational performance because of the differences in their research questions, as well

Table 1. Performance Measures Used by Various Research Disciplines

Research Area	*Typical Performance Measures*
Accounting	Current Ratio, Quick Ratio, Net Working Capital, Cash Flow
Economics	Profits, Sales Growth
Finance	Stock Price, EPS, Net Income, ROI
Marketing	Sales Growth, Market Share, Brand Awareness
Organizational Behavior	Employee Satisfaction, Turnover Rate, Span of Control
Production	Cost/Unit, Inventory Levels, Reject Rates, Output/Direct Manhour
Strategic Management/ Business Policy	Sales Growth, Net Profits, ROI

Table 2. Some Problems Associated With Different Measures of Organizational Performance

Measure	*Some Typical Problems With These Measures*
Dollar Sales	Inflation Problem.
Unit Sales	Why Growth for Its Own Sake?
Market Share	How Does One Define the Market?
	What If the Market is Declining/Dying?
Net Profits	Problems of Different Accounting Conventions.
	Problem of Setting Appropriate Targets.
Net Profits/Dollar Sales	How to Standardize for Variations among Industries?
	Problems of Different Accounting Conventions.
ROI	How Should Investment Be Defined?
	Short-Run vs. Long-Run Tradeoff Problems.
ROE	How to Standardize for D/E Variations Among Industries?
	Should One Be Concerned with Only *Stock*holders?
EPS	Impossible to Compare Across Firms or Industries.
Stock Price	Is the Stock Market Rational?
	Impossible to Compare Across Firms or Industries.
Dividends/Share	May Vary by Stage of Organizational Evolution.
	Subject to the Whims of Top Management and/or the Board of Directors.
Reject Rates	May Vary Because of Different Strategies.
Output/Direct Manhour	Will Vary According to Capital Intensity and Organizational Strategy.
Employee Satisfaction	Are the Employees the Only *Stake*holders in the Organization?
Brand Awareness	Will Vary According to Business Strategy.
Current Ratio	Should Vary by Organizational Size, Business Strategy, and Industry Involved.

as in their ultimate purposes. Second, it also seems clear that several different measures of performance will be used within each field because of the various difficulties associated with almost all of the currently used performance indices, and, more importantly, because organizations themselves quite legitimately seek to accomplish a variety of different objectives by their actions. One other point also seems clear, though. It is that little attention has been given to the question of what measures of organizational performance make sense. Stated differently, there has been little research done as to what constitutes appropriate measures of overall organizational performance. Instead, the vast majority of the research studies done over the past two decades have relied almost exclusively on performance measures that have been "handed down" from industry practice. This does not mean that these measures are totally inappropriate for the purposes for which they have been used. They are not! In fact, most have been tested repeatedly over time. Nonetheless, almost all of them were developed for different purposes than for doing academic research on the relative performance of organizations and the relative effectiveness and efficiency of different organizational strategies, structures, and processes.

The principal purpose of this paper is to address the latter question of what constitutes appropriate measures of effective organizational performance for the strategic management/business policy area. In this context, in the next several pages I shall: (1) review the performance measures used in most of the strategic management/business policy research studies done to date, (2) describe a new measure of organizational performance that might usefully be used for such research, (3) examine the strengths and weaknesses of this proposed new measure, and (4) suggest some possible directions for new research on organizational performance measures for the strategic management/business policy area.

II. PERFORMANCE MEASURES USED IN STRATEGIC MANAGEMENT RESEARCH

Table 3 lists the performance measures used in a number of normative strategic management/business policy studies done in the past few years. Several patterns emerge from an examination of this table. First, studies of the effectiveness of formal strategic planning systems have used the greatest number and variety of measures. Second, studies dealing with the content of business strategy were a distant second with respect to the number and variety of measures used, while studies of the content of corporate-level strategy used the fewest performance measures among these three types of normative studies, though not many less than those dealing with business strategy. Perhaps even more significant, however, are the facts that: (1) few recent studies of strategic processes other than those on the use of formal planning systems have been normative in character, and (2) even among those studies that have been normative in character, almost none have used management objectives as a measure of organizational achievement in spite of theoretical arguments, such as Kirchhoff's (1977), in favor of such measures. Moreover, except for Patten's 1976 research, no studies have explicitly addressed the question of trade-offs among various organizational objectives. There is also one other singular characteristic of these studies as a group or, more precisely, as a set of four groups that bears on the discussion here. It is that almost none of the researchers involved paid great attention to the choice of measures that they used. In fact, only a few researchers discussed the various limitations of the measures they used at all. And even in these cases the discussions were almost always very short. Moreover, when a later study questioned the findings of an earlier one, it almost always did so in terms of factors such as poor research design, limited sample size, and poor questionnaire structure. Never did it say that the results of the earlier study were invalid because it used inappropriate measures of organizational performance.

There seem to be three reasons for this circumstance. First, as noted by Hofer (1973), most measures of overall organizational performance tend to move together and reasonably strongly so. Thus, a separate focus on different measures seemed unnecessary as long as one was willing to group organizational performance into three broad categories: (1) superior, (2) average, and (3) poor. Second, few studies attempted to look at goal trade-offs or to examine situations in which such tradeoffs were necessary. Finally, most of the studies used either matched pairs of firms or drew their samples primarily or exclusively from one industry.

Nevertheless, there are a number of problems with the existing measures of organizational performance, as noted in Table 2. One of the most serious of these is the lack of comparability across industries, a factor which has never really been adequately compensated for even in matched pair studies.

III. SOME NEW MEASURES OF ORGANIZATIONAL PERFORMANCE

The problem of finding appropriate measures of overall organizational performance is an empirical one, not a theoretical one, as there are at present no theories that describe any characteristics or features of organizations that might remain invariant across different industries.

To find such invariant measures of overall organizational performance, one could proceed in two different ways. First, one could try to find transformations of currently existing measures that are invariant across industries. Or, one could seek entirely new measures that possess this characteristic.

An example of the first approach might be to calculate the percentage deviation of the various traditional measures of organizational performance on a normalized scale rather than using the current absolute scales. Thus, rather than measuring sales growth in either absolute or percentage terms, one might examine the number of standard deviations by which either the absolute or, even better, the percentage growth rate of the organization in question differs from that of the average of the industry in which it competes. The question of whether the statistical distributions of traditional performance measures can be normalized across different industries is, therefore, an empirical one that can be answered through further research.

The focus of this paper, though, is on the second approach, i.e., on trying to identify new measures of overall organizational performance that are invariant across different industries. In this regard, three measures are suggested for assessing different characteristics of overall organizational performance and one—Return on Value Added (ROVA)—is examined in greater detail with respect to its degree of invariance across several different industries. Table 4 lists three of

Table 3. Performance Measures Used in Recent Strategic Management/Business Policy Research Studies

Types of Research Studies Involved	*Growth*			*Profitability*			*Asset Utilization*		*Contributions to Stockholders*				
	Dollar Sales	*Unit Sales*	*Market Share*	*Net Profits*	*Net Profits / Dollar Sales*	*Cash Flow*	*ROI*	*ROE*	*EPS*	*Stock Price*	*Dividends Per Share*	*Management's Objectives*	*Other Measures*
STUDIES ON THE EFFECTIVENESS OF STRATEGIC PLANNING													
Thune & House (1970)	X			X			X	X	X	X			
Ansoff et al (1970)	X			X			X					X	
Herold (1972)	X			X			X	X	X	X			
Rue & Fulmer (1973)	X			X			X						
Sheehan (1975)	X			X			X						
Karger & Malik (1975)	X			X	X	X	X	X	X	X	X		
Woods (1977)	X			X			X						
Kudla (1980)									X	X			
STUDIES ON BUSINESS STRATEGY													
BCG (1968)					X	X							
Chevalier (1972)							X						
Fruhan, Jr. (1972)			X										
Hunt (1973)	X		X	X						X			
Newman (1973)	X		X	X						X			
Hatten (1974)	X		X				X						X
PIMS (1974)						X	X						
Biggadike (1976)	X					X	X						X
Kirchoff (1976)							X					X	
Patten (1976)	X			X			X						
Porter (1976)	X		X		X					X			
Christensen (1977)	X					X	X						

Lenz (1978)	X	X	X							
Soukup (1979)		X								
Harrigan (1979)	X	X								
Woo (1980)				X	X					
Galbraith (1981)		X		X	X					
STUDIES ON CORPORATE STRATEGY										
Gutmann (1964)	X		X		X					
Kitching (1967)			X							
Hanna (1968)	X		X				X	X		
Hofer (1973)	X		X		X					
Rumelt (1974)	X		X		X					
Schendel & Patten (1975)	X		X							
Hammermesh (1976)			X	X				X	X	X
Montgomery (1980)	X				X	X	X			X
STUDIES ON THE NATURE OF STRATEGIC DECISION MAKING										
Berg (1964)										X
Aharoni (1966)										X
Carter (1970)									X	X
Allison (1971)									X	X
Dory (1973)										X
Gilmour (1973)								X	X	X
Trevelyan (1971)									X	X
Miller (1976)	X	X								X
Bryson (1978)									X	X
Bourjois (1978)	X	X								X
Jemison (1978)									X	X
Hambrick (1979)									X	X
Spender (1980)	X	X							X	X
Duhane (1981)								X	X	X

Table 4. Some Measures of Overall Organizational Performance

Performance Characteristic	*Some Traditional Measures of These Characteristics*	*The Proposed New New Measures*
Growth	Dollar Sales, Unit Sales Dollar Assets, # of Employees	Value Added*
Efficiency	Gross Margin, Net Profits, Net Profits/Dollar Sales	ROVA**
Asset Utilization	ROI, ROE, EPS	ROI/ROVA

*Value Added = Dollar Sales − Cost of Raw Materials and Purchased Parts.

**ROVA = Return on Value Added = $\frac{\text{Net Profits Before Tax}}{\text{Value Added}} \times 100\%$.

the major characteristics of overall organizational performance examined by most strategic management/business policy studies, some traditional indices used for measuring those factors, and the three new measures proposed there.

As with the first approach, there are no a priori theoretical reasons why the proposed new measures should be more useful than traditional ones from an organizational perspective. From a societal perspective, however, there are some positive aspects of the new measures, which will be discussed more fully later. The principal questions about the usefulness of the new measures, at least presently, are therefore primarily empirical ones.

IV. ROVA: A QUASI-INVARIANT MEASURE OF ORGANIZATIONAL PERFORMANCE?

When one examines ROVA as a possible measure of organizational performance for different types of organizations, it appears that it has the desirable property of being quasi-invariant across industries, as is indicated by the statistics in Table 5.

These figures need to be evaluated with several notes of caution. First, they all correspond to either average firms or slightly better than average firms in their respective industries. Thus, leading firms may often have better results (higher ROVAs) than reported here, while lagging firms may have poorer (lower) and perhaps even negative results (ROVAs). Second, the net-profits-to-dollar-sales figures represent normal years for the industries involved. Consequently, these figures may vary substantially during good or bad years, depending on the industry involved. Third, the companies examined were all in industries that were in the maturity or saturation phases of their life cycles during the periods from which these figures were taken. Different results may be obtained for different time periods. For instance, in the case of the aerosol manufacturer, ROVAs of 22% to 25% were earned earlier in the life cycle. Finally, the sample

Table 5. The ROVA for Average Firms in Various Industries

Type of Firm	*Net Profits/$ Sales (in percent)*	*Value Added/$ Sales (in percent)*	*ROVA (in percent)*
Aerosol Manufacturer	3.2	20	16.0
Light Aircraft Manufacturer	7.2	45	16.0
Appliance Manufacturer	10.0	60	16.7
High Intensity Lamp Manufacturer	6.5	50	13.0
Grocery Store	2.3	15	15.3
Auto Parts Wholesaler	5.0	33	15.0
Auto Manufacturer	13.0	75	17.3
Management Consultant	14.5	85	17.1

of firms represented in Table 5 is very small. One should, therefore, be especially careful about generalizing these results to a broader population of firms.

In spite of the above qualifications, however, the data seem to indicate that ROVA may a far more invariant measure of organizational performance than most, if not all, other measures currently in use for evaluating overall organizational performance. In this regard, analysis of divisional performance by two major *Fortune 500* multi-industry firms have indicated that the ROVAs for their average and slightly above average divisions typically range from 12% to 18%, with the higher end of the range corresponding to divisions that have high engineering content, or unique products, or use highly skilled labor forces, while the lower end of the range corresponded to divisions with low engineering content, nondifferentiated products, and unskilled workers. To the extent that these observations are accurate, it would mean that the variation among intraindustry ROVAs (i.e., the ROVAs of different firms within the same industry) would be far greater than the variation of interindustry ROVAs (i.e., the ROVAs of firms in different industries which have roughly the same position within their respective industries in terms of overall performance). And this is just the characteristic one needs to be able to assess relative organizational performance across industries! Thus, if larger samples corroborate the initial pattern of results described above, ROVA may represent a measure that could be used to make effective cross-industry comparisons without the necessity of seeking matched pairs of firms or of making careful adjustments for the different characteristics of the industries involved.

V. SOME FURTHER OBSERVATIONS ON ROVA AS A MEASURE OF ORGANIZATIONAL PERFORMANCE

One might naturally ask why ROVA has the characteristics described above. At this time, it is a bit premature to speculate too much because additional testing is needed to indicate whether the preliminary patterns described above will hold up under further investigation. One line of thought is most provocative, however. It stems from two points.

1. That Value Added is the most direct measure available of the contribution that an organization makes to society. Dollar sales, for example, could vastly overstate that contribution for firms that assemble parts and components manufactured by others, while dollar assets fails to reflect the different time consumption patterns of current and fixed assets, as well as the differences in technologies across industries. Value Added, by contrast, incorporates all of these considerations and others too.
2. That the variations in Value Added for the average firms within an industry tend to stabilize to a far greater extent after the shakeout phase of industry growth is completed.

Taken together, these points would seem to suggest the possibility that ROVA is a reflection of the contribution that each organization makes to society and that society, in turn, values such contributions approximately equally (though with some small variations to reflect high quality or other unique contributions) once it has had sufficient time to assess them as part of a total societal system of products and services, i.e., once the products or services and the technologies that produce them have reached some degree of maturity.

VI. SUMMARY AND CONCLUSIONS

The increasing emphasis on normative research in the strategic management/business policy area as well as in other areas of management has made necessary the use of various measures to assess relative levels of overall organizational performance. To date, most such research has used various traditional measures of organizational performance either individually or in combination. While this is not totally inappropriate, such measures have been derived primarily to help management assure the survival and continued profitability of the organization. As a consequence, it is difficult to make cross-industry comparisons using such variables even though they can be used reasonably well for intraindustry comparisons. In the future, though, interindustry comparisons will be needed to an increasing degree to assess the relative performance and contributions of organizations in different industries. There are two basic approaches to trying to make such comparisons. One is to try to develop variations of existing measures, such as the degree to which they deviate from normalized multi-industry means, as performance measures. The second is to try to develop new measures of performance that are invariant across industries. This paper has examined one such new measure—ROVA (Return on Value Added)—that does indeed seem to be invariant across several substantially different kinds of industries and for reasons that, if true, would permit it to be used as a basic measure of the contribution of various organizations to society. Moreover, because of the consistency of the initial data, it would seem that ROVA holds substantial promise as such as measure. However, the data examined to date are also very limited in scope. Consequently, it would seem that the next steps should be to test the ROVA concept as a measure of organizational performance across a larger sample of industries, while at the same time exploring various variants of this measure that might be used to compare other characteristics of organizations, such as growth and utilization of assets, across different industries.

ACKNOWLEDGMENT

This article was originally copyrighted by Charles Hofer, 1982, although this is the first publishing, all copy-right permissions, requests for reprinting, or publication should be made directly to Charles W. Hofer.

REFERENCES

Aharoni, Y. (1966), *The Foreign Investment Decision Process,* Boston, MA: Harvard Business School Division of Research.

Allison, G. (1971), *Essense of Decision: Explaining the Cuban Missle Crisis,* Boston, MA: Little Brown.

Ansoff, H. I., R. G. Brandenburg, F. E. Portmer, and R. Radosevich (1971), *Acquisition Behavior of U.S. Manufacturing Firms: 1945–1965,* Nashville, TN: Vanderbilt University Press.

Berg, N. (1964), "The Allocation of Strategic Funds in a Large, Diversified Industrial Corporation," Doctoral Dissertation, Harvard Business School.

Biggadike, R. (1976), "Entry Strategy and Performance," Doctoral Dissertation, Harvard Business School.

Boston Consulting Group Staff *Perspectives on Experience* (1968), Boston, MA: The Boston Consulting Group.

Bourjois, J. (1978), "Strategy Making, Environment, and Economic Performance: A Conceptual and Empirical Investigation," Doctoral Dissertation, University of Washington.

Bryson, J. M. (1978), "A Contingent Approach to Program Planning," Doctoral Dissertation, University of Wisconsin-Madison.

Carter, E. E. (1970), "A Behavioral Theory Approach to Firm Investment and Acquisition Decisions," Doctoral Dissertation, Carnegie-Mellon University.

Chevalier, M. (1972), "The Strategy Spectre Behind Your Market Share," *European Business,* Vol. 34: 63–72 (Summer).

Christensen, H. K. (1977), "Product/Market and Company Influences Upon the Profitability of Business Unit and R & D Expenditures," Doctoral Dissertation, Columbia University.

Dory, J. (1973), "Scanning for Domestic Diversifying Acquisitions," Doctoral Dissertation, Harvard Business School.

Duhaune, M. (1981), "Influences on the Divestment Decisions of Large Diversified Firms," Doctoral Dissertation, University of Pittsburgh.

Fruhan, W. E. Jr. (1972), "Pyrrhic Victories in Fights for Market Share," *Harvard Business Review,* Vol. 50:100–107 (September/October).

Galbraith, C. (1981), "A Heteromorphic Model of Business Strategy: Empirical Analysis of Consumer and Industrial Products," Doctoral Dissertation, Purdue University.

Gilmour, S. D. (1973), "The Divestment Decision Process," Doctoral Dissertation, Harvard Business School.

Gutmann, P. M. (1964), "Strategies for Growth," *California Management Review,* Vol. 6:31–36 (Summer).

Hambrick, D. (1979), "Environmental Scanning, Organizational Strategy, and Executive Roles: A Study in Three Industries," Doctoral Dissertation, Pennsylvania State University.

Hammermesh, R. G. (1976), "The Corporate Response to Divisional Profit Crises," Doctoral Dissertation, Harvard Business School.

Hanna, R. G. C. (1968), "The Concept of Corporate Strategy in Multi-Industry Firms," Doctoral Dissertation, Harvard Business School, 1968.

Harrigan, K. R. (1979), "Strategies for Declining Industries," Doctoral Dissertation, Harvard Business School.

Hatten, K. J. (1974), "Strategic Models in the Brewing Industry," Doctoral Dissertation, Purdue University.

Herold, D. M. (1972), "Long-Range Planning and Organizational Performance," *Academy of Management Journal,* Vol. 15:91–102 (March).

Hofer, C. W. (1973), "Some Preliminary Research on Patterns of Strategic Behavior," *Proceedings of the Business Policy and Planning Division of the Academy of Management,* Paper No. 5 Boston, Academy of Management, August.

Hunt, M. S. (1972), "Competition in the Major Home Appliance Industry: 1960–1970," Doctoral Dissertation, Harvard University.

Jemison, D. (1978), "The Strategy Making Influence of Boundary Spanners," Doctoral Dissertation, University of Washington.

Karger, K. and Z. A. Malik (1975), "Long-Range Planning and Organizational Performance," *Long Range Planning,* (December).

Kirchhoff, B. A. (1975), "Empirical Analysis of Strategic Factors Contributing To Return on Investment," *Proceedings of the National Meeting of the Academy of Management,* New Orleans, Academy of Management, (August) pp. 46–48.

Kirchhoff, B. A. (1977), "Organizational Effectiveness Measurement and Policy Research," *Academy of Management Review,* Vol. 2:346–355 (July).

Kitching, J. (1967), "Why Do Mergers Miscarry," *Harvard Business Review,* Vol. 45:84–101 (November/December).

Kudla, R. J. (1980), "The Effect of Strategic Planning on Common Stock Returns," Doctoral Dissertation, University of Pittsburgh.

Lenz, R. T. (1978), "Strategic Interdependence and Organizational Performance; Patterns in One Industry," Doctoral Dissertation, Indiana University.

Miller, D. (1976), "Strategy Making in Context: Ten Empirical Archetypes," Doctoral Dissertation, McGill University.

Montgomery, C. A. (1980), "Diversification, Market Structure, and Firm Performance: An Extension of Rumelt's Model," Doctoral Dissertation, Purdue University.

Newman, H. H. (1973), "Strategic Groups and the Structure Performance Relationship: A Study with Respect to Chemical Process Industries," Doctoral Dissertation, Harvard University.

Pattern, R. (1976), "A Simultaneous Equation Model of Corporate Strategy: The Case of the U.S. Brewing Industry," Doctoral Dissertation, Purdue University.

Porter, M. E. (1976), *Interbrand Choice, Strategy, and Bilateral Market Power,* Boston, MA: Harvard University Press.

Rue, L. W. and R. M. Fulner (1973), "Is Long Range Planning Profitable?" *Proceedings of the*

Business Policy and Planning Division of the Academy of Management, Paper No. 8, Academy of Management, (August).

Rumelt, R. (1974), *Strategy, Structure, and Economic Performance,* Cambridge, MA: Harvard University Press.

Sheehan, G. (1975), "Long Range Strategic Planning and Its Relationship to Firm Size, Firm Growth and Firm Variability," Doctoral Dissertation, University of Western Ontario.

Schendel, D. E., and R. G. Patten (1975), "An Empirical Study of Corporate Stagnation and Turnaround," *Proceedings of the National Meeting of the Academy of Management,* New Orleans, Academy of Management, (August), pp. 49–51.

Schoeffler, S., R. D. Buzzell, and D. F. Heany (1974), "Impact of Strategic Planning on Profit Performance," *Harvard Business Review,* Vol. 52: 137–145 (March/April).

Soukup, W. R. (1979), "Strategic Responses to Technological Threats," Doctoral Dissertation, Purdue University.

Spender, J. C. (1980), "Strategy Making in Business: Coping with Uncertainty in the Organizational Design Process," Doctoral Dissertation, University of Manchester.

Thune, S. S. and R. J. House (1970), "Where Long Range Planning Pays Off," *Business Horizons,* Vol. 13:81–87 (August).

Trevelyan, E. W. (1974), "The Strategic Process in Large Complex Organizations: A Pilot Study of New Business Development," Doctoral Dissertation, Harvard Business School.

Woo, C. (1980), "Strategies for Low Market Share Business," Doctoral Dissertation, Purdue University.

Woods, R., Jr. (1977), "An Analysis of the Strategic and Operational Planning Systems in Large United States Banks," Doctoral Dissertation, University of Tennessee.

DEMAND CRITERIA FOR NORMATIVE MARKET SEGMENTATION:

A RETROSPECTIVE VIEW

Henry Assael

In rereading Wendell Smith's original paper (1956), I was struck by the fact that he clearly established the basis for normative market segmentation theory. By normative market segmentation theory, I mean the demand criteria for optimally allocating resources to alternative segments. Smith was concerned with market segmentation as a strategic alternative to the more prevalent strategy of product differentiation and as a means of improving the efficiency of marketing resource allocation. The focus in the literature on analytical methods for defining market segments (Wind, 1978) sometimes causes us to lose sight of this emphasis on the allocation question and the underlying demand criteria for allocation. I thought I would focus on these key aspects of the concept of market segmentation by

Advances in Strategic Management, Volume 2, pages 57–65.

ISBN: 0-89232-409-0

considering demand criteria for segmentation and showing how Smith's original work set the stage for subsequent approaches to market segmentation.

Specifically, I will focus on three demand criteria for segmentation: first, brand utility; second, the level of demand; and third, demand elasticity. I will be using Table 1 as a basis for discussion by considering these three demand criteria, their applications in marketing, and their degree of utilization. I will then focus on response elasticity as the most important criterion for allocation across market segments and consider why use of this criterion has been so rare. I will also consider some recent challenges to the notion that grouping consumers by response elasticity represents the optimal criterion for segmentation. And, finally, I will provide some thoughts as to where we are heading with these three approaches.

Before getting into these issues, let us first consider a key statement in Smith's work that underlies normative segmentation theory, namely that "segmentation is based upon developments on the demand side of the market and represents a rational and more precise adjustment of product and marketing effort to consumer requirements." Although the statement is not startling, remember it was written in 1956 and is important for three reasons: first, it was a direct application of the emerging marketing concept; second, it represented a logical extension of the theory of imperfect competition; and third, it led to a consideration of the demand criteria for segmentation strategies that I just mentioned. Let me consider each of these three points in turn.

The relation between market segmentation and the marketing concept is clear since segmentation is directed to satisfying diverse consumer needs. The concept of market segmentation can be considered the result of the post–Korean War buyers' market. Sometime around 1953/54 it became clear that consumers were holding back on expenditures for durables despite sufficient purchasing power. This was partly due to a stocking up at the start of the Korean War and to a greater sophistication in shopping habits. It became apparent that strategies of convergence of resources on a limited number of offerings could not be sufficient to gain a competitive advantage. Moreover, by 1954, marketing institutions were sufficiently developed to permit greater diversity in product offerings. Smith defined this need for diversity in meeting consumer needs.

In addition to the marketing concept, a second underpinning of market segmentation is the theory of imperfect competition. Smith cited the works of Robinson (1948) and Chamberlin (1946) because of the importance of recognizing diversity in demand in a buyers' market. In the early 1930s Robinson and Chamberlin began moving away from the prevailing concept of an aggregate demand curve for a given product category by recognizing heterogeneity in demand and the possibility of several demand curves for separate markets. They saw that the likelihood of administered pricing rather than the market-derived price of pure competition could produce the possibility of maximizing profits through price discrimination. The vehicle was pricing based on differences in demand elasticities among consumer groups. Therefore, the concept of imperfect competition recognized different demand curves at the individual consumer level. In the words of Joan Robinson (1948, p. 186):

> The total demand of the market is made up of the demands of individual buyers. If the elasticities of demand are different, he (the manufacturer) will first divide all individual buyers into two classes such that the highest elasticity of demand in the one class is less than the least elasticity of demand in the other class.

Robinson then goes on to say that if, after dividing consumers into two groups, there are differences in elasticities, then "each sub-market will be split into two on the same principle as before, the parts will again be subdivided, and so forth until the point is reached at which each sub-market consists of a single buyer or a group of buyers whose elasticities of demand are the same" (p. 186). Thus, Robinson has given us a very explicit criterion for defining market segments: disaggregate up to the point where elasticities of a group are the same. This criterion for maximization can easily be translated in clustering terms to mean a minimization of within-group variance in elasticities and a maximization of between-group variance (see Assael and Roscoe, 1976; Claycamp and Massy, 1968; Frank et al., 1972).

Now this may be regarded as a disaggregation or aggregation criterion, depending on the starting point. Given such a disaggregation of the market, Robinson also states an appropriate allocation criterion as follows (1948, p. 181):

> He [the manufacturer] can increase his profit by selling less in those markets where the elasticity of demand is less and the marginal revenue smaller, and selling more in those markets where the elasticity of demand is higher and the marginal revenue greater. He will therefore adjust his sales in such a way that the marginal revenue obtained from selling an additional unit of output in any one market is the same for all the markets.

In other words, the optimal allocation criterion is to distribute marketing effort to segments so that the ratio of incremental revenue to incremental costs is the same for all segments. The important point here is that the theory of imperfect competition provides a basis for identifying the optimal aggregation and allocation criterion for a normative theory of market segmentation. Later I will return to this distinction between aggregation and allocation criteria.

It was Wendell Smith who recognized the importance of these theories for marketing strategy. And that brings me to my third point, the development of demand criteria for segmentation strategies. Smith makes a statement that links market segmentation with the writings of Joan Robinson. He says, "[S]egmentation is disaggregative in its effects and tends to bring about recognition of several demand schedules where only one was recognized before." The recognition of several demand schedules produces two demand criteria in addition to response elasticity. First, segments can be defined by differences in utilities (that is, needs). This criterion defines what the demand curve is characterizing in the eyes of the consumer, namely, a bundle of utilities that represents a brand. Second, segments can be defined by the position of the demand curve, that is, by the level of demand. And third, as noted, segments can be defined by response elasticity, that is, by the shape of the demand curve.

Since Wendell Smith's basic work, market segmentation has followed three broad approaches characterized by these three demand criteria. One approach has been clearly related to brand attribute utility. It has been referred to as benefit segmentation and is characterized by grouping consumers by similarity in the needs and/or brand attributes considered most important. The newer approaches involving conjoint analysis (Green and Wind, 1975) and componential segmentation (Green, 1977) clearly fall into this category.

The next two approaches can be generally referred to as behavioral, as distinct from benefit, segmentation (Assael, 1973). Segmenting by the position or the shape of the demand curve requires utilizing a behavioral rather than a perceptual criterion. (I would include purchase intent under behavioral segmentation even though it is a perceptual variable since it does define a predisposition to act.)

Segmentation by the position of the demand curve relies on the criterion of quantity purchased. Reference to heavy vs. light buyers or the "heavy half" is typical. Segmentation by brand purchased also is in this category despite the fact it is dichotomous since, on the aggregate level, the percentage of consumers in a segment buying the brand is a reasonable proxy for volume. Typically, these criteria have been used as dependent variables with demographics, life-styles, or brand attitudes used as descriptor variables. Whereas benefit segmentation has been used primarily for new product development and positioning, segmenting by level of demand has been used to describe existing markets.

The third criterion, segmentation by response elasticities, is the only one that provides guidelines for resource allocation along the lines proposed by Joan Robinson. If elasticity can be determined on the individual level, then segments can be defined based on similarity in elasticities and resources allocated accordingly. Segmentation by price elasticity has its limits because of the obvious restrictions regarding price discrimination. But there could be direct applications to marketing strategy for deal, coupon, or sales promotional elasticities, all of which are related to price; and defining advertising elasticities would have direct implications for the level of marketing effort to each segment.

By the way, I have been referring to elasticity as the optimal aggregation criterion and will soon be referring to a study that challenges this view. Other bases for aggregating consumers could be considered, such as marginal response, or response function coefficients. But they all have one thing in common; they require measurement of consumer responses to marketing stimuli on the individual level.

The three approaches to segmentation I just referred to, their applications and their degree of utilization, are summarized in Table 1. As noted, the most

Table 1. Three Demand Criteria for Market Segmentation

Demand Criteria	*Applications*	*Amount of Past Use*
1. Needs; Utilities (Benefit Segmentation)	New Product Development; Product Positioning	Heavy
2. Level of Demand (Behavioral Segmentation)	Description of Characteristics of Target market; Selection of Components of Marketing Mix	Heavy
3. Response Elasticities (Behavioral Segmentation)	Level of Marketing Effort and Allocation to Market Segments	Light to None

important applications of benefit segmentation have been in the area of new product development, and utilization has been heavy. Segmentation by level of demand has been used to develop and adjust the components of the marketing mix. The demographic, life-style, or attitudinal characteristics of heavy users, brand loyalists, or regular brand users are identified and media, advertising, and distribution strategies are developed accordingly. Utilization here has also been heavy. Segmentation by response elasticities has been applied to establishing the level of marketing effort between segments. Utilization of this approach has been very light to nonexistent.

The lack of utilization of response elasticity as a segmentation criterion is certainly not due to shortcomings in terms of strategic relevance. It is due to the difficulty of measuring elasticity. If the optimal aggregation and allocation criteria are to be utilized, elasticities must be measured on the individual level. But how? Table 2 shows some methods. Controlled store experiments could be run in which consumer responses to changes in in-store conditions are tracked. Simulated in-store facilities could be used such as Yankelovich's LTM service or Elrick and Lavidge's COMP. But small-sample experiments may be insufficient to establish aggregation criteria for a number of segments that would then be generalizable to the total market. Paper and pencil tests could be used to assess the consumer's perceived sensitivity at various price levels. Woodside and associates' (1979) Dollarmetric approach is an example. But the validity and reliability of these perceptual measures are questionable.

Consumer panel data could also be utilized to attempt to establish elasticities on the individual level. But here the problems are even more serious. There is no provision for controls to ensure that response is due to changes in the marketing stimulus. Also, as Smith states, demand should be measured on a selective rather than on a primary basis, meaning that brand not product category elasticities should be measured. It then becomes difficult to assess whether a switch from one brand to another is a function of the marketing stimulus under study or some other variable. Variations in repurchase cycles add to the difficulty of measuring

Table 2. Methods for Measuring Response Elasticities on the Individual Consumer Level

Method	*Problem*
1. Controlled Store Experiments	• Reliability of Controls • Projectability • Small Sample for Aggregation
2. Simulated In-Store Facilities	(Same as 1)
3. Self-Report (E.G. Dollarmetrics)	• Validity of Data • Reliability
4. Consumer Panels	• No Controls • Interpreting Behavior

consumer response to marketing stimuli since the researcher cannot distinguish between a "no purchase" decision and a "normal" interval in the purchase sequence. Finally, variations in package size confound attempts to measure consumer responses to changes in marketing stimuli.

On the other side of the coin, the "new technology" may assist researchers in measuring elasticities on the individual level. Controlled experiments could be run in stores with scanners. Panels of consumers who shop in such stores could be tracked to determine changes in purchase behavior as a result of changes in in-store conditions. As scanner data becomes widespread, such experimentation could provide a more reliable base for aggregation and allocation criteria. Split cable TV could provide a more reliable basis for measuring advertising elasticity. Matched samples of consumers could be tested with different frequencies of exposure. As cable TV becomes more widespread, such testing could also provide a more reliable basis for marketing allocations.

The difficulty of utilizing elasticity criteria is demonstrated by the paucity of results in the literature. The few attempts to segment by elasticity have predefined segments by some other criterion and then determined elasticity on the aggregate level within the segment. Massy and Frank (1965) were among the first to do so. Writing in 1965, they first state the classical criterion of optimization, in this case regarding advertising elasticities, as follows: "The within group variances for the *individual* purchase promotional sensitivities should be small and the between group variance large." Having stated that promotional elasticities should be measured on the individual level, they then predefine segments by demographic criteria and measure elasticities within segments on an aggregate basis.

There are two additional problems in utilizing criteria of elasticity for purposes of segmentation. First, theoretically, maximization of profits is achieved if the marketer is free to allocate resources to individual consumers. This of course assumes there are no economies of scale in marketing, an invalid assumption.

But it must be recognized that, in the process of aggregation from the individual consumer level, some point will be reached where further aggregation will reduce profits. To my knowledge, only one study has come close to establishing a criterion for defining the point where the decrease in marginal revenue from further aggregation is just balanced by the reduction in marginal costs from economies of scale. I will be citing this study shortly (Tollefson and Lessig, 1978).

Second, assuming segments have been defined by some criterion of elasticity, is the optimal allocation criterion reliable? Such a criterion would require comparing the marginal revenues of segments to given levels of marketing stimuli. Presumably, if segments can be defined by elasticity criteria, then their marginal responses and marginal revenues can be determined. But are the underlying causes of marginal revenues comparable across segments? Can one be assured that responses in all segments are equally a function of sensitivity to the marketing stimulus under consideration? Assume that a given segment has a higher ratio of marginal revenue to marginal advertising expenditure than other segments. Is it not possible this segment is reacting to other conditions (e.g., greater sensitivity to word-of-mouth information)?

Let me add one other wrinkle to the problems of utilizing individual elasticities as an optimal criterion for segmentation. I mentioned the need for establishing an aggregation and an allocation criterion. Recent doubt has been expressed whether elasticity is in fact the optimal criterion for defining segments. I am referring to an article in the August 1978 issue of the *Journal of Marketing Research* (the special market segmentation issue) by Tollefson and Lessig (1978). Tollefson and Lessig suggest that the optimal criterion for segmentation is to combine aggregation and allocation into one criterion for profit maximization. As noted, the theoretical ideal for allocation is to treat each consumer as a separate segment and allocate according to their marginal response, assuming no economies of scale. Tollefson and Lessig state the optimal aggregation criterion is to combine two segments so that the consequent profit reduction is minimized. Further, they suggest that the aggregation criterion is contingent on the allocation criterion since their optimal aggregation criterion requires defining individual consumer reactions to various sets of marketing variables. This proposal appears logical and is theoretically superior to traditional views that separate the aggregation and allocation criteria and define optimal aggregation based on similarity of elasticities. But if there are problems in operationalizing the criterion of elasticity on the individual level, consider the problems in operationalizing Tollefson and Lessig's optimal criterion. To operationalize their segmentation criterion requires one to know how each segment or individual will respond to various levels of marketing activity. Implementation requires knowing not only optimal response and allocation levels but also near-optimal levels, and then estimating the profit consequences of aggregating two or more consumers. Such complete knowledge of one's market is rarely if ever available. Thus, although theo-

Table 3. Future Advances in Market Segmentation

Method	*Future Applications*
Benefit Segmentation Segmentation by Level of Demand Segmentation by Response Elasticities	Componential Segmentation Segment Congruence Analysis 1. Improvements in Measurement • Scanner Data • Cable TV 2. Improvements in Aggregation Criteria • Marginal Response or • Response Coefficients or • Elasticities

retically sound, the information requirements of the Tollefson and Lessig criterion make its implementation impractical.

I started out by defining segmentation by elasticities on the individual level as the optimal segmentation criterion. I expressed serious reservations about the practicality of such an approach. I then cited a challenge to this traditional view and a definition of an optimal criterion based on minimization of profit loss in the process of aggregation, but expressed even more serious reservations about the feasibility of such an approach. Where does all this leave us? Where do we go from here? Table 3 provides a perspective on future applications. It seems that we have a handle on benefit segmentation. Traditional approaches to defining homogeneous groups based on similarity in needs will continue to be relevant. Further, methodologies for concept formulation and testing through conjoint analysis will be strengthened with the application of componential segmentation techniques (Green, 1977). These techniques seek to combine product features and consumer characteristics in the analysis of attribute utilities. An orthogonal array of consumer types and product features is developed, and a product-by-consumer matrix is submitted for analysis. Predictions can then be made of the optimal product characteristics for any combination of consumer characteristics.

We also have a handle on segmenting by level of demand. Again traditional approaches defining the characteristics of behavioral segments by life styles, attitudes, demographics, and needs will continue. The primary focus here will also continue to be on methodological issues, for example, the treatment of multiple dependent variables or the introduction of interactive variables for behavioral predictions. But more work is likely to be needed on comparing the bases for segmentation. Here, segment congruence analysis (Green and Carmone, 1977) holds some promise as a means of comparing classes of descriptor variables so as to guide the researcher to the most powerful descriptor set.

We have gone a long way regarding benefit segmentation and segmenting by level of demand since Wendell Smith's original article. But we have not gone very far in utilizing normative criteria for segmentation. Yet it seems these are the criteria that Smith was emphasizing because he continuously refers to the problems of marketing resource allocation in the context of market segmentation. I believe more work will be done in analyzing consumer response functions to marketing stimuli, particularly the very important issue that Tollefson and Lessig raised, the nature of the optimal aggregation criterion. In some sense, it may be too early in the state of the art of market segmentation to raise the issue whether aggregation should be by elasticity, marginal response, or response function coefficients. We have to overcome the problem of data collection so that consumer responses can be linked to marketing stimuli over time. Therefore, it is likely that more refined attempts at experimentation utilizing simulated environments, scanner stores, and cable TV will be attempted in the future.

REFERENCES

Assael, Henry (1973), ''Segmenting Market Segmentation Strategies and Techniques,'' *European Research,* 1 (September) 190–194; and 1 (November) 256–258.

Assael, Henry and A. Marvin Roscoe Jr. (1976), ''Approaches to Market Segmentation Analysis,'' *Journal of Marketing* 40 (October), 67–76.

Chamberlain, E. H. (1946), *Theory of Monopolistic Competition* Cambridge, Mass: Harvard University Press.

Claycamp, Henry J. and William F. Massy (1968), ''A Theory of Market Segmentation,'' *Journal of Marketing Research,* 5 (November), 388–394.

Frank, Ronald E., William F. Massy and Yoram Wind (1972), *Market Segmentation,* Englewood Cliffs, New Jersey: Prentice-Hall.

Green, Paul E. (1977), ''A New Approach to Market Segmentation,'' *Business Horizons,* 20 (February), 61–73.

Green, Paul E. and Yoram Wind (1975), ''New Ways to Measure Consumers' Judgments,'' *Harvard Business Review,* 53 (July–August), 107–117.

Green, Paul E. and Frank J. Carmone (1977), ''Segment Congruence Analysis: A Method for Analyzing Association Among Alternative Bases for Market Segmentation,'' *Journal of Consumer Research* 3 (March) pp. 217–222.

Massy, William F. and Ronald E. Frank (1965), ''Short Term Price and Dealing Effects in Selected Market Segments,'' *Journal of Marketing Research,* 2 (May), 171–185.

Robinson, Joan (1948), *The Economics of Imperfect Competition* London: MacMillan.

Smith, Wendell R. (1956), ''Product Differentiation and Market Segmentation as Alternative Marketing Strategies,'' *Journal of Marketing,* 21 (July), 3–8.

Tollefson, John O. and Parker Lessig, (1978), ''Aggregation Criteria in Normative Market Segmentation Theory,'' *Journal of Marketing Research* 15 (August), 346–355.

Wind, Yoram (1978), ''Issues and Advances in Segmentation Research,'' *Journal of Marketing Research* 15 (August), 317–337.

Woodside, Arch, Alok K. Sharma and William O. Bearden, (1979), ''A Dollarmetric Approach for Estimating Consumer Brand Loyalty,'' Presentation at the American Marketing Association's 10th Attitude Research Conference.

ENTRY BARRIERS IN MATURE MANUFACTURING INDUSTRIES

Kathryn Rudie Harrigan

ABSTRACT

New measures of entry barriers are proposed and tested because traditional ones seemed inadequate in a sample of mature industries. Entry opportunities are found to be most attractive for fringe firms where labor-to-capital ratios are high and excess capacity is low.

I. INTRODUCTION

Entering a mature industry is seldom expected to be easy. The entry barriers, which can indicate the attractiveness of investment in a particular setting, may be relatively high (Porter, 1980). Yet some firms have earned good returns when they entered industries which had already matured. Because knowledge of the

Advances in Strategic Management, Volume 2, pages 67–97.

ISBN: 0-89232-409-0

nature of entry barriers can be helpful in suggesting whether the "strategic window" is open (Abell, 1978), study of them would be helpful for strategists contemplating entry. (This "window," or market opportunity, closes when competitive conditions have reduced an industry's attractiveness as a candidate for entry.)

A means of estimating the height of entry barriers would be of particular interest to outsider firms evaluating a seemingly attractive entry candidate because overcoming such barriers can make an industry so costly and risky to enter that the likelihood of successful new entry is reduced or the price of acquiring an existing firm which has hurdled these barriers would be increased (Bain, 1956; Bass et al., 1978; Orstein et al., 1973; Scherer, 1980). Yet firms seeking to obtain the cash-generating attributes of an established market environment may not only pay the price of entry but also seek to insulate the industry from subsequent penetration by new and sizable firms if they better understood its structure.

II. ENTRY AND MATURE INDUSTRIES

This inquiry concerning entry barriers reviews the theory and evidence supporting their existence and proposes a new way of thinking about them in the context of mature manufacturing industries. The study of barriers in a mature setting is particularly interesting because the environment is one which is widely assumed to be inhospitable to enter. Yet entry does occur and should be studied to understand whether ongoing firms in mature industries can take actions to protect their market positions.

A. A Definition of Entry Barriers

Entry barriers are forces that discourage firms from investing in a particular industry (or niche of an industry) which appears to be attractive.[1] Because entry barriers can represent substantial disadvantages for many types of potential entrants, they suggest that higher-than-average profits may be difficult to attain not only due to size or timing advantages enjoyed by existing firms but also due to the willingness of these firms to lower prices to the "limit price," that is, to the price level that will limit new entry) in order to discourage other firms from trying to enter (Collins and Preston, 1969; Gaskin, 1971; Spence, 1977, 1979). Industries characterized by such high entry barriers have generally been considered to be more profitable in the long run (Bain, 1956, 1972; Modigliani, 1958; Stigler, 1958) and increasingly have become the targets of those large domestic firms or foreign entrants which can afford to overcome such entry deterrents (Gorecki, 1976).

In addition to these dynamic sources of entry barriers, economic theory has argued that entry barriers derive from static advantages due to (a) economies of scale, (b) lower absolute costs, or (c) product differentiation (Bain, 1956; Needham, 1975). This study expands and clarifies the list of entry barriers and proposes measures of their heights.

High entry barriers are a necessary *but not sufficient* condition for long-term industry profitability. High entry barriers are necessary because without them plant expansions (a strategic investment which is difficult to reverse) could rapidly outpace demand. The pressures created by underutilized plant capacities could precipitate price wars which may drive out some firms (provided the exit barriers they face are low; see Harrigan, 1981) but will ruin profit margins for all (Chamberlain, 1962; Fellner, 1949; Vernon, 1972).

However, high entry barriers alone are not sufficient to create conditions that enhance industry profitability. The steel industry, for example, possesses extremely high capital barriers yet is only marginally profitable. The presence of one or more traits such as high exit barriers, a fragmented structure of nonhomogeneous firms, commodity-like product traits or other characteristics all reduce an industry's profitability potential, as in the case of steel.

Firms which already hold a stake in the health of an industry may seek to erect protective barriers around their markets. If they are highly determined to do so, they may even hold a portion of their own plant capacity idle as a warning against entry, thereby signaling their willingness to fight a war of attrition to prevent entry (Esposito and Esposito, 1974; MacMillan, 1980). By studying an industry's history, other such patterns may become apparent.

What is needed is a framework for evaluating markets which the firm might enter, particularly for firms wishing to avoid traps where their resources would be wasted in trying to overcome the combination of high entry barriers and competitors' resistance. Pre-entry analysis of these barriers, such as this paper suggests, might prevent firms from committing resources to battles that cannot be won cheaply.

B. Mature Industries

Although entry may be more difficult in mature industries, typologies of industry traits frequently overgeneralize this difficulty and the nature of other traits describing mature environments. Briefly, models such as the product life cycle—which describe "mature" industries as those which generally grow slowly (less than 10% annually in real terms), where demand is frequently inexpansible and where product traits are generally familiar to consumers or users—oversimplify conduct within specific industries. They underplay, for example, the possibility that product modifications may occur which retard them from growing commodity-like in some mature industries. They also de-emphasize findings (such as those in Utterback and Anthony, 1975) suggesting that, although technology may have been generally stable within mature industries, process innovations and new technological configurations could compete alongside the relatively aged (and frequently capital-intensive) assets which have been generally expected to populate such industries. Finally, although the competitive structure may be expected to remain reasonably stable in mature industries, there are expections to these (and the aforementioned) industry traits.

Entry does occur in mature industries. Although the new firms more frequently occupy the fringes of a competitive landscape, some late entrants do make significant inroads to the core of competition.[2] Among these firms, process innovations are particularly likely to be a key to capturing substantial market share when entering mature industries because those firms which enter late and seek a sizable share of sales would need some advantage to succeed. Because firms operating the conventional technologies of a mature industry are more likely to be far down existing experience curves and would have exhausted the cost-saving benefits of many easy operating innovations, new firms seeking entry would be more likely to introduce radical process innovations.

Arguments that different marketing approaches or production technologies might characterize competitors within a particular industry are consistent with the concept that industries are populated with different strategic groups of firms. Although the number of such groups might be fewer in maturity, differences among competitors exist and are relevant when evaluating opportunities for entry. This study of entry barriers uses the distinction between leader firms (which have pursued large market share objectives), specialist firms (which have pursued lucrative, unique niches), and firms which appear to be trapped between either extreme in constructing its sample.

C. Tracking the Entry Phenomenon

This study investigates *de novo* entry by fringe firms, not entry by acquisition,[3] although the large numbers of merger inquiries undertaken by regulatory bodies, such as the Federal Trade Commission, suggest that entry through acquisition of ongoing firms—through horizontal, vertical, or conglomerate forms of foothold merger—has been viewed by aspiring entrants as being the less risky method of diversifying into new markets. The study focuses on the net result (whether entry was achieved or not) rather than on the processes associated with entry.

Further limiting this study's scope, it does not probe the causes of population changes within the industries studied nor the methods (such as product innovations, technological improvements, obsolescence, or other evolutionary forces (including luck) used to achieve entry. The controversy regarding whether entry into a new business and subsequent successes is a matter of luck or strategy was revived by Rumelt and Wensley (1980).[4] Stochastic simulations of industry life and death as well as random entry rates, growth rates, and exits were used in Ijiri and Simon (1964) and Simon and Bonini (1958), where *random* models predicted industry populations with relatively high accuracy. The issue of how successfully firms entered is not treated herein.

The dependent variable denotes whether entry occurred within a particular industry in a given year.[5] Entry was deduced by counting the firms listed in Dun & Bradstreet indices and corroborating that count with *Census of Manufactures* reports of firms in operation. Entry was indicated as a binary code (where "1" indicated entry occurred). Unless a horizontal merger occurred (and the merged firms consolidated their operations), acquisitions would not indicate an additional firm had entered or exited.

The construction of independent variables which indicate influences upon the likelihood that fringe firms will enter requires special commentary as well. The financial data (from COMPUSTAT®) used to construct the independent variables exemplied the market postures of firms which may be considered to be the "core" competitors. Entry, by contrast, was expected to occur in the "fringes" of an industry. Therefore, information about the core firms and the environment they created are used to infer patterns of entry behavior among fringe firms. By standardizing the available information describing leading firms, measures describing the environmental variables new entrants would face were constructed. (Industry average information was available from *Census of Manufactures,* the National Science Foundation, and *Leading National Advertisers* studies. The COMPUSTAT® industries examined were relatively undiversified, thus offering information about firms which approximated that of the single business firm.) The influences of these variables upon entry behavior are described later. A list of the firms comprising this sample is discussed there also.

III. FACTORS AFFECTING THE ENTRY DECISION

This section presents the independent variables and links their derivation to the literature of industrial economics and corporate strategy. In mature industries the most important influences upon entry behavior are (1) technical factors and (2) competitive conduct variables. The technological variables included: (a) capital requirements; (b) changes in average scale economies; (c) changes in the age of an industry's productive capital (physical plant and equipment); (d) the balance of labor intensity to capital intensity predominant in an industry's technology; and (e) variability in the average R&D expenditures of a particular industry. The competitive behavior variables included: (a) previous entries (designated by counting the number of firms); (b) changes in the dispersion of market shares; (c) industry advertising outlays; and (d) average levels of excess productive capacity. Two measures of industry attractiveness (explained in the following section) were also included in the model. Exhibit 1, which summarizes these variables, is explained below. It stands in notable contrast with Biggadike's work (1976), where the PIMS database of strategic business units which were parts of multi-

Exhibit 1. Construction and Discussion of Independent Variables' Expected Effects Upon the Entry of Fringe Competitors

Variable Name and Construction [Denomination]	*Mean*	*Standard Deviation*	*Expected Effect on Entry*	*Explanation*
1. *Capital Requirements*: (1/M * total value of industry plant, property, and equipment$_{t-1}$) where M equals the number of establishments responsible for 50% of the industry's value of shipments [Dollars per plant, thousands]	67.21	133.83	Negative	If the capital requirements for effective competition are relatively high and if leading firms possess this requisite critical mass, fringe firms are less likely to attempt entry.
2. *Changes in Average Scale Economies*: (1/LOG (Capital turnover ratio)$_{t-1}$ less (1/LOG (capital turnover ratio)$_{t-2}$ divided by the average industry scale measure [Dollars per plant, thousands]	4.22	17.71	Negative	If scale economies are rising (due to technological changes) entry at less than minimum efficient scale would result in substantial cost disadvantages which should discourage entrants not undertaking these changes.
3. *Percentage Change in Relative Age of Physical Plant*: (Net plant/gross plant)$_{t-1}$ less (Net plant/gross plant)$_{t-2}$ divided by the industry average change in age of physical plant measure [Relative percentage, decimal]	0.13	0.19	Negative	Increases in the net to gross physical plant ratio could indicate leading firms are making technological improvements or simply replacing their capital stock. Both explanations indicate that leading firms expect their particular market niches to become more attractive in spite of overall industry maturity. Expectations that a market opportunity exists would encourage some firms to attempt entry. However, the reinvestments leading firms made raises the height of entry barriers, reducing the likelihood that successful entry will occur.

4. *Labor to Capital Ratio*: Number of employees divided by gross book value of physical assets$_{t-1}$ [Percentage]	0.15	0.20	Positive	High proportions of labor to capital represent opportunities for technologies using high degrees of capital substitution. Fringe firms entering with technologies that obsolesce older processes might do so with greater likelihoods of success.
5. *Variability of Average R & D Expenditures*: (R & D expenditures/sales)$_{t-1}$ divided by average R & D/sales measure$_{t-1}$ [Relative percentage, decimal]	0.05	0.20	Negative	High levels of R & D variability indicate some competitors are expending larger amounts to improve their products or processes. Although the existence of these expenditures indicates some differentiation, it also represents high R & D entry barriers which few fringe firms could afford to overcome.
6. *Entries in Previous Periods*: Number of firms in industry$_{t-1}$ less number of firms$_{t-2}$ [Net change]	−1.13	7.83	Negative	Because each entering firm represents additional productive capacity, entries in previous periods should discourage entrants in the present period unless growth in demand is unusually rapid. (Exists in previous periods should relieve excess capacity and permit profit levels to rise, thereby encouraging new entrants unless growth in demand has been stagnant.
This measure was also lagged for an additional period	−2.31	6.34		
7. *Changes in the Dispersion of Market Shares*: (Sales/industry sales)$_{t-1}$ less (sales/industry sales)$_{t-2}$ divided by industry average market share changes [Relative percentage, decimal]	.004	.056	Negative	A market structure characterized by high market shares among leading firms indicates they enjoy absolute cost and scale advantages, a condition fringe competitors would find difficult to overcome. Sizable changes in these market shares indicate aggressive growth strategies are pursued by these firms.

continued

Exhibit 1—Continued

Variable Name and Construction [Denomination]	*Mean*	*Standard Deviation*	*Expected Effect on Entry*	*Explanation*
8. *Average (Industry) Advertising Outlays*: Advertising expenses divided by average expenses (Total advertising expenditures divided by number of firms_{t-1} [Relative percentage]	111.94	15.96	Negative	High levels of advertising indicate some competitors are creating entry barriers through product differentiation activities. Although an entry by a differentiated product the market values could be successful, the high advertising barriers should discourage many fringe firms from entering.
9. *Excess Capacity*: MOS plant utilization less level of capacity that was employed_{t-1} [Average percentage, decimal]	.08	.18	Negative	High levels of excess capacity represent unstable pressures on prices which could result in price-cutting, a condition that is unattractive to fringe firms. Low levels of excess capacity represent the need for more plants, a condition which could be satisfied by fringe firms which enter.
10. *Relative Sales Growth*: Changes in competitors sales_{t-1} (deflated by GNP growth) divided by deflated industry sales growth [Percentage, decimal]	−0.0069	0.095	Positive	Mature industries where market segments are growing faster than GNP growth should appear to be more attractive to fringe competitors. Mature industries where no market segments are growing relatively faster than GNP would appear less attractive to such firms.
11. *Industry Attractiveness*: Relative returns on capital $\text{expenditures}_{t-1}$ capital turnover ratio divided by (industry average capital turnover ratio multiplied by the percentage of industry capital expenditures made by four largest competitors_{t-1}) [Relative percentage]	1.18	1.57	Positive	Industries where higher than average (1.00) returns were earned on additions to capital should encourage fringe competitors to attempt entry.

business firms constituted the sample and entrants were defined in terms of their relationships with their parents. The framework used by Biggadike considered "entered market traits" to be composed of (a) buyer concentration, (b) seller concentration and dispersion, (c) product differentiation, and (d) stage of life cycle, and predicted that entry within mature industries would occur in oligopoly markets. This proportion could not be tested rigorously, however, because Biggadike included only six firms in mature industry settings.

A. Scale-Related Variables Affecting Entry

Mature industries can be penetrated if entrants can use improved technologies to obtain superior operating economies. Aspiring entrants could also enter by buying the cumulative wisdom of existing firms (see Boston Consulting Group, 1968; Henderson, 1974). The scale economy variables include capital requirements, ages of physical plant and equipment, capital-to-labor ratios, and changes in scale economies. Research and development (R&D) and advertising expenditures are absolute cost advantages which may be captured through sizable expenditures.

1. *Capital Requirements*

Capital requirements have long been identified as entry barriers (Bain, 1956). The heights of such barriers were estimated by multiplying 1/M by the gross value of industry plants. (M, the number of establishments responsible for 50% of the industry's value of shipments, was obtained from the *Census of Manufacturers.*) This construction approximates the cost of a minimum efficient scale plant (Scherer, 1973; Shepard, 1967, 1972; Stigler, 1978). High capital requirements were expected to act as entry barriers for fringe firms.

2. *Changes in Average Scale Economies*

Changes in scale were estimated by the difference in consecutive periods of the reciprocal of the logarithm of the capital turnover ratio (Ornstein et al., 1973; Rosenbluth, 1957). Positive changes in scale were expected to represent increases in the height of entry barriers. Small firms (the "fringe") which were expected to be unable to enter with plant sizes that were at least of the new minimum efficient scale sizes were expected to incur significant cost disadvantages which would hinder their efforts to earn acceptable returns or gain market share (Caves et al., 1976).

3. *Changes in the Average Plant Age*

Changes in the ratio of net to gross plant values were compared to industry averages to determine whether the trend of these assets indicated either technological improvements or high commitment to continued investment in the industry by ongoing firms. Large relative increases in the balance of net to gross plant were expected to signal expectations that an industry would be attractive in the future and to encourage fringe firms to attempt entry.[6] But because the impetus for entry is investment behaviors by leading firms, much of the response to improved or new business opportunity will have been made by existing firms. Accordingly, the height of entry barriers for fringe firms will have been raised. The net effect of this variable upon entry behavior would be negative.

4. *Labor-to-Capital Ratio*

Estimates of capital intensity (gross plant to sales) and labor intensity (number of employees to sales) were used to construct an estimate of the relative proportions of labor to capital which characterized the technologies of leading firms. Industries where existing firms' technologies were already relatively capital intensive were expected to represent relatively less attractive opportunities for fringe firms to offer superior technologies as a means of achieving entry.

B. Cost Advantages Affecting Entry

Fringe competitors (or potential entrants) seeking sizable shares of their market are most likely to attain success through process or produce innovations. Both are strategies which require fringe firms to overcome entry barriers based upon absolute cost advantages.

Absolute cost advantages originate from access to scarce resources which new entrants cannot develop as inexpensively as earlier entrants did, if at all. Examples include access to distribution channels, ownership of a uranium mine, or other factors which would be more costly to replicate when entering late. This cost disadvantage would be due in part to inflation and in part to the limited nature of the resources possessed. New entrants would be obliged to spend heavily in order to match the access to scarce raw materials, vertical relationships, or patents which constitued these advantages. Although some experience curve advantages can be replicated through accelerated spending programs, a few are not attainable by late entrants except by acquiring existing firms.

1. *Variability of Average R&D Expenditures*

Research and development outlays offer the first path to penetrating the established market positions of earlier entrants. In order to match patents or licensing advantages enjoyed by leading firms which relied upon heavy R&D expenditures in the past, potential entrants must spend heavily to obtain new skills or draw upon research skills which may have been developed previously in other industries they served (Kamien and Schwartz, 1975; Mueller and Tilton, 1969). In this study, high levels of relative R&D expenditures were interpreted as representing high barriers (absolute cost advantages). Few potential entrants were expected to be capable of undertaking the types of expenditures necessary to overcome this particular type of entry barrier because the risks would be generally unacceptable. (There is no guarantee that those fringe firms which do undertake R&D to enter will generate the necessary patents to overtake the existing market leaders.[7])

Calculation of the "variability of R&D expenditures" variable used as a denominator represents National Science Foundation estimates of industry totals divided by the number of firms within an industry. This variable indicates the relative range of leading firms' R&D outlays (individual to industry average).[8] High values indicate that some competitors can belong to a strategic group which is substantially more R&D intensive than the industry average. High values also indicate a market opportunity for firms which can afford to overcome this particular entry barrier or are equipped to do so due to preexisting research and development competencies.

2. *Average Industry Advertising Outlays*

The creation of demand for a branded product is the other major means for potential entrants to penetrate a mature industry setting. However, if a product is not yet a commodity but the market is mature, it is likely that buyer loyalties exist toward the incumbent businesses, thus raising barriers to entry because the product is older and many ways to differentiate the existing generic products have been employed. But product innovations may permit entrants to challenge the core of industry competition (seize large market share) due to customer crossovers from the obsoleted product.

Measurement of product differentiation is a problem, however. The strategic implications of product differentiation seem to be treated least effectively in industrial economics. (For example, a useful measure of this critical phenomenon has not yet been developed.) Yet the implications of competing in environments where products can be differentiated (as compared with environments where products are commodity-like) can be critical in evaluating whether entry should be attempted. Tactics such as branding, advertising, quality variations, or other differentiating maneuvers might be employed effectively to dominate a desirable market segment within noncommodity businesses. Because emulating the tactics which captured those customers in the past would be quite costly, firms desiring to do so must be able to withstand the several years of losses which are required to erode the barriers successful firms have erected to gain entry. In this context, the advertising expenditures fringe firms must make to overcome the customer loyalties attained by ongoing firms (a variable with *is* measurable although it is scarcely a global estimate of the extent of product differentiation) may be considered to be a form of entry barrier.

Much of the controversy concerning whether advertising acts as such a barrier has been due to an incorrect understanding of this factor, however. (See Comanor and Wilson, 1967; 1974; Demsetz, 1979; Mueller and Rogers, 1980; Reddy, 1980; Schmalensee, 1976, 1978; Wright, 1978.) Scholars have used an adjusted advertising-to-sales ratio to approximate the relative height of this type of entry barrier in the past. They expected its effect to be negative. But if high advertising expenditures are indicative of an industry environment where many different configurations of a product could satisfy consumers' needs, they indicate also that some competitors (representing a particular strategic group) have been supported in these expenditures by the market's response. High advertising outlays can indicate a market opportunity for firms which can afford the cost of advertising campaigns which were intended to match or capture existing firms' marketing advantages. Accordingly, the sign of an advertising variable could be positive or negative when tested in a model of entry behavior.[9]

Estimates of the average advertising expenditures variable in this study were calculated using industry advertising information as the denominator (*Leading National Advertisers* data divided by the number of competitors). High average expenditures suggested the cost of differentiating a new product or of building a rival distribution network would be sizable, and high costs were expected to act as entry barriers.

In summary, scholars have held that entry barriers are created by large capital requirements, scale economies, and product-differentiating activities. (Previous exploratory research has also posited that R&D and advertising expenditures affect the height of entry barriers.) The need for this paper is to develop a better set of variables by drawing upon a number of data sources. Thus, the variables defined in the preceding section of this study build upon the foundations of the economic studies cited and improve upon their measurements by creating new variables which better capture the nuances of industries which are not homogeneous in nature. A brief explanation of the need for these revisions is in order.

3. *An Example of the Shortcomings of Earlier Studies*

The early studies of entry barriers were inconclusive, yielding ambiguous results. An example of these models is presented in Exhibit 2, using the dependent variable and data of this study and independent variables suggested by these earlier economic studies. Since there are a large number of mature industries in the U.S. economy, one would expect results similar to those in Exhibit 2 if data for other mature industries were substituted.

Exhibit 2 has focused on traditional measures of the variables used in economic literature with pretty poor results. The most notable result shown in Exhibit 2 is that the value of the intercept term (.494) approximates closely the actual mean value of the dependent variable (.500). The independent variables' coefficients add relatively insubstantial information to the predictive power of this model. (The coefficients are not large.) The signs of the coefficients are

Exhibit 2. A Model of the Relationship of Traditional Static Economic Variables to the Likelihood of Entry

	Capital Requirements	*Scale Economies*	*Relative Advertising Expenditures*	*Intercept*	*R^2 Coefficient of Multiple Determination*	*F-Statistic Test of Significance of the Multiple Determinant Coefficient*
(1) Parameter Estimates	−.002	−.002	.000	.494	.0200	3.56*
	(−1.00)	(−1.86)	(2.45) *	(22.06)**	n = 524	
(2) Standardized Coefficients	−.043	−.080	.106	.000		

Notes: (Figures in parentheses indicate students' t-statistic testing the null hypothesis that the parameter equals zero.)
*Significant at the 5% confidence interval.
**Significant at the 1% confidence interval.
Average likelihood of entry = 50%
n = degrees of freedom.

consistent with economic theory, although the most statistically significant coefficient value (that of advertising expenditures) has been the most controversial in theory building with respect to its expected sign. Given these ambiguities, more meaningful models were needed when the precepts of this topic were translated into questions of interest to scholars of strategic management.

The section which follows tests a model of the likelihood of entry by fringe competitors using the technological variables constructed in the previous section, but, first, competitive behavior and industry attractiveness variables are posited and constructed below. The model of entry behavior tested incorporates these improved variable specifications which are summarized in Exhibit 1.

C. Competitive Behaviors Which Create Entry Barriers

The results of firms' previous investment decisions and competitive conduct can also create conditions which function like entry barriers. The competitive behavior variables discussed below include: (1) previous entries; (2) changes in the dispersion of market shares; and (3) average levels of excess productive capacity. A fourth behavioral variable, industry advertising outlays, has been discussed in the section describing absolute cost advantages because it has been one of the variables posited and tested in previous economic studies. The new variables proposed below are specified and related to the theory of entry barriers in this section.

1. *Previous Entries and New Entry*

This variable approximates changes in concentrating within each industry over time by counting the number of firms in the industry. (Four firm concentration ratios were not available for each year under study.) Increases (or decreases) in the number of competitors represent two effects: (1) increases (or decreases) in the number of plants in operation[10] and (2) expectations concerning the nature of future demand. Although favorable expectations might encourage entry by firms seeking to pursue a ''me-too'' business strategy, the net economic effect of multiple entries in previous periods will be a more fragmented market structure. (Fragmented market structures are generally unattractive because they are subject to a greater likelihood of price warfare, even in industry maturity.) The net effect on entry (of entry in a previous period) should be negative.

2. *Changes in the Dispersion of Market Shares and Entry*

This variable indicates the stability of market shares among leading firms. It is calculated by comparing the changes in leading firms' shares with average industry changes. (The variable is based upon the COMPUSTAT® firms' market share changes divided by average market share changes taken from *Census of Manufactures* estimates of total industry shipments.)

Sizable changes in share (relative to average industry market share changes) suggest that some competitors are pursuing growth objectives. Since market share points are quite difficult to gain in mature industries, the presence of large relative changes should signal a volatile environment which discourages entry. Moreover, firms possessing high market shares would be expected to enjoy relative cost advantages (due to the distance they have traveled down the industry's experience curve). New firms entering this type of environment would be less likely to succeed unless they can insulate themselves from these cost pressures by exploiting a technological innovation.

3. *Average Levels of Excess Productive Capacity and Entry*

This variable indicates the average excess capacity present in an industry by subtracting the practical (dollar) capacity utilized in a particular year from MOS, "optimal," or engineered capacity. (The *U.S. Census of Manufactures* estimates of engineered capacity provided the denominator. MOS is an estimate of the percentage of total designed plant capacity at which facilities are most likely to be operated when "fully utilized.") The difference between practical and engineered capacity provides "percentage excess capacity" when divided by MOS.

High levels of excess capacity should discourage new entry because existing firms would likely cut prices to fill their underutilized plants. Firms should expect market share to be difficult to capture and losses to be high if they try to enter when excess capacity is high.

D. Industry Attractiveness and Entry

New firms will be attracted to industries where there appear to be opportunities to enter easily and earn acceptable profits. The more attractive candidates for entry would be those industries where growth in demand is outpacing ongoing competitors' abilities to satisfy it (for example, where excess capacity is low). Two industry attractiveness variables, sales growth and an index of capital investment productivity, are proposed, and their construction is explained below.

1. *Relative Sales Growth and Entry*

This variable indicates whether the market segments served by some firms seem to be growing faster than the average rate of sales growth. The relative sales growth variable is calculated by comparing the difference in competitors' sales volumes (deflated by GNP figures) in two consecutive periods with average (deflated) industry sales growth ($[\text{sales}_t - \text{sales}_{t-1}]/\text{sales}_{t-1}$). Fringe firms would be attracted to market segments where demand is growing more rapidly than average rates.

2. *Relative Attractiveness of Leading Firms' Performance*

This variable indicates the relative capital productivity of leading firms by dividing firms' capital turnover ratios by an industry average composed of the average capital turnover ratio multiplied by the percentage of industry capital expenditures made by industry's four largest competitors. (The capital expenditures data in the denominator may be found in *Census of Manufactures* special reports.) High returns on additions to capital which were enjoyed by leading firms could indicate high returns (or productivity) for fringe competitors, as well. Attempts to enter an industry which appears to be attractive would increase if these returns were high.

In summary, the traditional model of entry behavior could be improved by developing conduct variables which reflect the diversity of a particular industry setting. The following section presents the results of a model of entry which used these improved measures.

IV. THE MODEL AND RESULTS

A. The Sample

Entry behavior was studied within five industries by pooling financial time series data. The data described industry behavior and firms' performance, and were constructed by merging the contents of several years of COMPUSTAT® tapes with firms' annual reports. These data were supplemented by *Census of Manufactures* and Federal Trade Commission data[11] as well as information gathered from published articles and private studies of competition concerning each industry. The industries in the sample were meat-packing, distilled liquors, tobacco products, hydraulic cement, and aircraft manufacture. Exhibit 3 lists the firms examined. Transformations made for corrections of the heterogeneity, serial correlation, and lagged structure are explained in the Technical Appendix. The observations used to test the models which follow spanned a decade (the differences of nine intervals). These were pooled (and corrections made) to yield a total of 540 data points.

A Comment Regarding the Sample Industries. These industries were examined because: (1) they provided a useful contrast between industries whose products are generally considered commodity-like or differentiated; (2) they provided a control over phase of industry development (all were mature industries), which facilitated investigation of the differing growth rates which may be associated with firms possessing differing strategic postures; and (3) due to extant Federal Trade Commission investigations of these industries, they were already known to differ with respect to attributes such as capital requirements, differing degrees of reliance upon advertising or R&D, or other industry factors which this study argues may act as entry barriers. The choice of these industries,

Exhibit 3. List of COMPUSTAT® Firms Used in Study of Entry Behavior*

Amcord Inc.	Halco Products	National Distillers
American Distilling	Heublein	Neuhoff Bros. Packers Inc.
B.A.T. Industries	Hormel (Geo.)	Northrup Corporation
Bayuk Cigars	Ideal Basic Industries	Northwestern States Portland Cement Corporation
Beech Aircraft Corporation	Illini Beef Packers Inc.	OKC Corporation
Bluebird Inc.	Imperial Group Ltd.	Oregon Portland Cement Co.
Boeing Company	Iowa Beef Processors	Publicker Industries
Brown-Foreman Distillers	Kaiser Cement Corporation	Puerto Rican Cement Company
Cagle's Inc.	Kane-Miller Corporation	Rath Packing
California Portland Cement	Keystone Portland Cement Co.	Seagram
Cessna Aircraft	Ligget Group	Southdown Inc.
Conwood Corporation	Lockheed Corporation	TFI Companies
Culbro Corporation	Lone Star Industries	Tobin Packing
Federal Company	Louisville Cement	U.S. Tobacco
Gates Learjet Corporation	Mayer (Oscar)	United Aircraft Products Inc.
General Portland	MBPXL Corporation	Universal Cigar
Giant Portland & Masonry	McDonnell Douglas Corporation	Valmac Industries
Glenmore Distillers	Medusa Corporation	Verit Industries
Glover Inc.	Mickleberry Corporation	Walker (Hiram) Goorham & Wort
Grumman	Montfort of Colorado Inc.	Whitehall Cement Mftg. Co.

Comments: The selection of firms was based upon Standard Industrial Classification categories. However, highly-diversified firms such as Esmark or American Brands were deleted to produce a sample of relatively undiversified firms. Missing values were plugged using industry average data. Because most of the variables were constructed to reflect distributions around industry averages, these plugs did not bias the sample in either direction.

*COMPUSTAT® data were supplemented by *Census of Manufactures*, Federal Trade Commission, *Leading National Advertisers*, and National Science Foundation reports as well as annual report data.

which were known to possess a priori differences with respect to important environmental factors, provided a basis for investigating the effects of these contrasts upon entry behaviors.

Exhibit 4 indicates the zero-order correlation matrix for the variables tested (before they were corrected by first differencing procedures explained in the Technical Appendix). Recalling that the sample is a pooled cross section of time series data, it would not be surprising to discover some serial correlation among the observations which constituted a partical time series. Autocorrelation problems limit the number of variables which can be included in any specification to $n - 1$, where n is the number of years in the time series being pooled. Yet there should be $(m + 1)$ variables where m is the number of industries being pooled.

In this sample, arithmetic relationships created few collinearity problems. Those which seemed significant could be circumvented by not using the collinear variables together in the same specifications of the entry model. (Thus, several

Exhibit 4. Correlation Coefficients of Predictive Variables Used in Studying the Likelihood of Entry by Fringe Competitors

	1	2	3	4	5	*6a*	*6b*	7	8	9	*10*	*11*
1 Capital requirements$_{t-1}$	1.000											
2 Changes in average scale economies$_{t-1}$	−.010	1.000										
3 Percentage of change in relative age of physical plant$_{t-1}$	−.019	.014	1.000									
4 Labor to capital ratio$_{t-1}$	−.008	−.180	.173	1.000								
5 Variability of average R & D expenditures$_{t-1}$	.204**	−.051	.221**	.842**	1.000							
6a Entries in previous periods$_{t-1}$	−.076	.057	.115	−.109	−.049	1.000						
6b Entries in previous periods$_{t-2}$	.004	.079	−.068	−.146	−.067	.166	1.000					
7 Changes in the dispersion of market shares$_{t-1}$	−.001	−.063	−.095	−.010	−.039	−.000	.003	1.000				
8 Average industry advertising outlays$_{t-1}$	−.055	.052	.015	−.051	−.035	.141	.299**	−.003	1.000			
9 Excess capacity$_{t-1}$	−.019	.152	−.012	−.270**	−.091	.109	.214**	−.003	.372**	1.000		
10 Relative sales growth$_{t-1}$	.002	−.102	−.116	−.010	−.036	−.004	−.007	−.116	.019	−.023	1.000	
11 Relative industry attractiveness$_{t-1}$	−.003	−.098	−.004	.083	−.095	−.006	−.096	−.009	−.035	−.236**	.001	1.000

Notes:
**Probability > .001 under H_o: $\rho = 0$
n = 540, 60 firms, nine years

alternative models are presented below.) After imposing the constraint against particular combinations of variables, few significant problems remained.

B. Results and Discussion

The models which explained the greatest amounts of variance in entry behavior are of the generalized least-squares form presented below. In each, the error term of first-stage analysis provided ρ_i, the correction term,[12] which was used for second stage estimates (see Pindyck and Rubinfeld, 1976).

$$P_t = \alpha_i + \beta_i X_{it} + \epsilon_{it}$$

where P_t =probability of entry in time_t where 1 designates entry occurred, 0 otherwise.

x_{it} = where i = 1, 2, 3, . . ., 11 correspond to the variables in Table 1 which were developed above, and t = 1,2,3, . . . , 9.

Exhibit 5 presents the signs, coefficients, and standardized coefficients of the models tested, and compares these with the relationships hypothesized in Exhibit 1. The natural coefficients of a model using a binary dependent variable may be interpreted as contributions to the relative likelihood of entry by a fringe competitor in period_t (when multiplied by their respective variables). The coefficients of the standardized variables may be interpreted as relative contributions to the value of the coefficient of multiple determination (R^2). As is explained below, Exhibit 5 presents models which offer variables which have drawn from a number of sources and is richer in terms of variables germane to the entry decision model. Thus, this model obtained better results because some of the traditional variables do not have the explanatory power of those constructed for this study.

For example, the variables constructed to reflect the capital and investment implications for management are better explainers than the "crude" traditional economic measure of capital requirements. (Also it is scarcely surprising that the capital requirements variable should not be significant in the presence of stronger variables such as the labor-to-capital ratio, newness of physical plant, or excess capacity measure.)

The percentage change in relative age of physical plant variable has the expected sign in both models 2 and 3. The variable is statistically significant in model 2 and contributes substantially to the coefficient of multiple determination. It would appear from this analysis that increases in plant and equipment made by leading firms in some environments could act as entry barriers to firms seeking entry.

The labor-to-capital ratio variable has the expected sign in models 1 and 2 and is statistically significant in both models. This result would suggest that markets populated by firms with high capital-to-labor ratios discourage new entry. Mar-

Exhibit 5. Regressions on Entry Behavior

		Model 1		*Model 2*		*Model 3*		*Model 4*	
	Expected Effect	*Natural Coefficient*	*Standardized Coefficient*	*Natural Coefficient*	*Standardized Coefficient*	*Natural Coefficient*	*Standardized Coefficient*	*Natural Coefficient*	*Standardized Coefficient*
Capital requirements$_{t-1}$	–	–	–	.00549	.02964	−.00202	−.00547	–	–
Changes in average scale economies$_{t-1}$	–	–	–	.00148	.05276	.00109	.03884	–	–
% change in relative age of physical plant	–	–	–	−.35786***	−.13629	−.12741	−.04852	–	–
Labor to capital ratio$_{t-1}$	+	.17177**	.07017	.27475***	.11225	–	–	–	–
Variability of average R & D expenditures$_{t-1}$	–	–	–	–	–	–	–	−.04600	−.01868
Entries in previous periods$_{t-1}$	–	−.03409***	−.53784	–	–	−.03415***	−.53859	−.03679***	−.58033
Entries in previous periods$_{t-2}$								−.00879***	−.112133

Changes in dispersion of relative market $shares_{t-1}$	–	.19025	.02126	.26519	.02963	.21635	.02417	.30920	.03455
Average industry advertising $outlays_{t-1}$	–	–.00080***	–.25752	–.00085***	–.27475	–.00081***	–.26066	–	–
Excess $capacity_{t-1}$	–	–	–	–.00402***	–.14434	–	–	–.00539***	–.19353
Relative sales $growth_{t-1}$	+	–.00130	–.01625	–.00432	–.05402	–.17044	–.03262	–.00295	–.03690
Relative industry $attractiveness_{t-1}$	+	.01602	.05059	.00486	.01536	.01785**	.05638	–	–
Intercept		1.25329***	.00000	.38378***	.00000	1.28979***	.00000	.42207***	.00000
R^2 coefficient of multiple determination		.4151		.1727		.4142		.3989	
F-statistic test of significance		62.93***		12.27***		46.84***		58.83***	
Durbin-Watson D-statistic		2.2145		2.2629		2.6078		2.6467	

Notes: Average likelihood of entry = 50% (Standard deviation = 45.94%)
Mean = 0.000 (Standard deviation = 1) using standardized coefficients
**Significant at the 5% confidence interval.
***Significant at the 1% confidence interval.

kets where technologies are more highly labor intensive are more likely to be entered successfully.

The entries in previous periods variables have the expected signs and are statistically significant in models 1, 2, and 4. These variables also contribute relatively substantially to the explanatory power of these models. Recent entry reduces the likelihood of successful entry in mature industries.

The average industry advertising outlays variable has the expected sign and is statistically significant in models 1, 2, and 3. Its presence in these models contributes a large percentage of their explanatory power. It would appear from this analysis that markets where advertising expenditures are high are less likely to be entered successfully.

The excess capacity variable has the expected sign and is statistically significant in models 2 and 4. The presence of the excess capacity variable contributes substantially to the explanatory power of the equations, and the results obtained indicate that markets where high proportions of productive assets are idle are less likely to be entered successfully.

In summary, the capital requirements and changes in scale economies variables were not statistically significant when tested using a sample composed of mature industries. Measures of changes in the age of physical plant appear to indicate that newer plant and equipment could discourage entry, particularly, as the labor-to-capital ratio variable appears to indicate, if the change in the ratio of net to gross physical assets represents a change to a more capital-intensive technology. Findings regarding the R&D variable are inconclusive. Its sign was negative (indicating an entry barrier) but not statistically significant. Recent entries in a mature industry appear to discourage subsequent entries and act as an entry barrier. Evidence of market share instability does not appear to act as the entry barrier that was expected. The relative sales growth variable appears to act as an entry barrier (the opposite of what was expected). This result may be due to arithmetic effects associated with deflating the sales growth variable. (It could signify inflation is making entry too costly to contemplate.) Finally, excess capacity appears to act as a significant entry barrier in mature industries.

The four models presented suggest the relative importance of the variables tested in explaining the likelihood of entry. For example, the excess capacity and recent entry variables both have high standardized coefficients, as do the advertising, labor-to-capital, and changes in relative age of physical plant variables. These are the variables this analysis suggests might be employed to influence entry behavior.

C. Using Entry Barriers

If, as this analysis appears to suggest, capital requirements alone are not adequate entry barriers, firms wishing to defend their markets against potential entrants might aggressively shift their capital-to-labor ratios in favor of more efficient, technologically innovative assets. Frequent improvements in manufacturing technologies (new assets) also appear to be suggested.

Firms defending their markets against entry, this analysis suggests, must not allow their products to become commodity-like by being complacent. Continued expenditures for advertising and R&D, this analysis suggests, can act as entry barriers, as well.

Potential entrants appear to be less likely to attempt entry where they expect little chance for success. If a market is already suffering excess capacity, this analysis suggests, firms may be discouraged from entering. This finding suggests that defending firms might adopt a policy, as in Dixit (1980), of keeping some level of capacity idle by always building first and in the most appropriate locations to preempt would-be competitors (see Rao and Rutenberg, 1980).[13]

Finally, if, as this analysis suggests, the recent entry of a competitor will act as a significant deterrent to subsequent entry, defending firms should give some thought to the selection of the firm they might wish to permit to enter. Some competitors are preferable to others due to their different competitive styles (which can be observed by studying their behaviors in other industries). Firms which seek to control the profitability of their industries could take actions (such as those this analysis suggests) to make entry especially difficult for the types of firms they would prefer not to admit.

A policy of raising customers' expectations for service, variety, and quality may be appropriate to those relying upon admitting new (but selected) competitors or creating excess capacity. Increased investment levels for these types of assets, this analysis suggests, appear to be more effective in deterring entry than merely raising capital requirements with attending to improvements in product or process attributes. Also, patented process improvements (leading to cost leadership) where scale economies are substantial appear to increase entry barriers. These barriers are more controllable than those created by excess capacity. The latter is a malevolent type of barrier that could explode into price warfare (and create an unpleasant exit barrier later) if it is not controlled properly.

For aspiring entrants, the analysis suggests that firms which are determined to keep new firms out would be more effective in undertaking particular competitive responses, depending upon the traits of their particular industry. (Where industry marketing expenditures have been generally low, for example, firms which devoted substantial budgets to maintaining trade relations, improving delivery and customer service, or other forms of marketing may be more effective in shielding their niches from entry than others.) If ongoing competitors do *not* undertake the defensive actions this analysis suggests are best suited for discouraging entry, informed entrants which recognize this discrepancy and exploit it may ease into an industry without setting off price wars or incurring other significant forms of resistance.

In summary, this study suggests that the firm could use excess capacity (created internally or by admitting new competitors) to discourage potential entrants.

However, given the difficulties excess capacity might create, the discussion of the results of this study has suggested other factors the firm could influence instead, which also appear to act as deterrents to entry. The discussion of entry barriers should thus alert the firm in a mature manufacturing industry to the types of technological investments which might be used most advantageously to guard its market advantages.

Declining sales appear to be a major deterrent to new entry. Recent increases in the number of competitors appear also to discourage potential competitors lest production capacity outstrip the demand it was constructed to satisfy. Thus changes in the concentration of an industry or its sales volume could discourage new entry.

By contrast, changes in technology appear to indicate market opportunities. If firms cannot (or will not) upgrade their assets, an opportunity for competitors to enter with newer plant configurations appears to exist. If, however, existing competitors update their production facilities frequently and incorporate innovations, the opportunity for outsiders to invade successfully seems to be decreased. Thus, the results of this study suggest that fluctuations in scale economies, capital-to-labor intensities, and vintage capital should be monitored to assess whether the strategic window is opening or closing for new firms which possess the needed capital and can afford to make the appropriate investments to enter.

TECHNICAL APPENDIX: ENTRY BARRIERS IN MATURE MANUFACTURING INDUSTRIES—CONSTRUCTION OF THE DATABASE

Data Transformations

In time series specifications which are pooled with cross sections, the residual is assumed to be composed of a time-series error, a cross-section error, and an interaction effect. Transformations are required to correct for autocorrelation, and special interpretation of the error term is needed. Moreover, the pooling of data describing heterogeneous-sized firms required generalized differencing corrections using weighted least-squares estimates to obtain the appropriate error term (see Bass et al., 1978; Hatten, 1974).

Preliminary values of the residual were obtained from ordinary least-squares estimates. Corrections were made by multiplying the variables of the first-stage estimate by this term and using ordinary least squares after this procedure to obtain unbiased and consistent estimators (see Blair and Kraft, 1974; Chang and Lee, 1977; Hsaio, 1974; Johnson and Lyon, 1973; Mundlak, 1978; Pindyck and Rubinfeld, 1976). Heteroskedasticity in the cross section was reduced both by the generalized differencing corrections and by specifications employing variables which had been transformed into financial ratios, thus minimizing the range of values under analysis (see Nerlove, 1971).

After corrections, there was relatively little serial correlation in the models estimated (as indicated by the Durbin–Watson d-statistic), and the correlation coefficients of the absolute values of the observed residuals to the predicted values of the dependent variable were quite low, which suggests that the variance of the residuals generated by this process does not depend upon the values of the independent variables (see Balestra and Nerlove, 1966).

The data were not completely homogenized after corrections, of course, but the residuals seemed more uniformly distributed and there were fewer disparate clusters of residuals. There is also some risk that information regarding an industry's evolution could be reduced by suppressing information contained in the outliers when, in fact, it was the key to understanding an industry's dynamics. Error components models were not tested in the correction procedure due to the lagged structure imposed upon the models (see Maddala 1971).

Variable Lag Structures

A lagged structure was imposed upon the models tested to reflect the assumed reaction time necessary before firms could convert liquid assets to capital goods and production capacity following industry performance stimuli. As Exhibit 1 indicates, this adjustment period was assumed to be 1 year (in most cases). The lag structure is a fundamental element of this model because specifications which allowed entry to occur during the same period as the impetus encouraging entry violated the basic assumptions of a nonfrictionless environment where assets are not completely flexible nor immediately available. (Measurement difficulties in separating impetus from response would also be compounded without the assumption of lagged responses).

Different lag structures were tested for each industry in preliminary tests, but this structure was rejected because there were no statistically significant differences among industries with respect to the independent variables, with the exception of the advertising variables. Briefly, it would appear that differing delays in response rates, differing damped movements in the lags, and differing levels of significance in the values of the coefficients existed among industries where the effects of advertising upon ROI were tested. Advertising's effects were felt most strongly over a 3-year period, with most of the effect felt in the first two periods before entry occurred. In general, the estimates for advertising expenditures were significant at the 1% level for a 1- or 2-year lag and at the 5% level for a 3-year lag, using Almon lag variables. Furthermore, the value of the coefficient for a 2-year lagged advertising expenditure was less than that of a 1-year lag but almost double that estimated for a 3-year lag. It would appear that the deterrent effect of firms' advertising expenditures upon entry is stronger when campaigns are first launched (not surprisingly, profits are reduced by such outlays), but this effect is sustained for a few periods thereafter. The cigarette and aircraft industry tests indicated that nonlinear specifications provided a slightly better description of advertising's effects than linear ones, but the differences were not substantial. There were no other indications that individual industry lag structures were needed.

ACKNOWLEDGMENT

I am indebted to Ian C. MacMillan for helpful comments on previous drafts of this paper.

NOTES

1. This paper assumes that the controversy surrounding industry boundaries has been resolved in favor of the definition of an "industry" as the group of firms producing goods and services that are close substitutes for each other (Porter, 1980). It does not try to distinguish between customer groups, product classes, technologies, or other useful means of segmenting a *market* (Abell, 1980). Rather, it recognizes the potential existence of strategic groups which might be isolated or protected by internal entry barriers ("mobility barriers" in Caves and Porter, 1977), and distinguishes between *competitive postures*.

2. There may be several "niches within an industry" (i.e., differing market segments to serve) where a potential entrant might gain entry. The abilities of some industries to sustain different competitive profiles due to these niches provides the foundations of the concept of "strategic groups" (Caves and Porter, 1977; Hunt, 1972; Newman, 1978; Porter, 1979b). These various niches will not be equally desirable because they are not equally profitable. Some will, however, offer an initial entry point for firms which cannot afford to invade the "oligopolistic core" (i.e., the markets dominated by the top four firms).

Core competitors are generally believed to possess substantial market power due to their relatively large market shares. Acting collectively, core competitors can influence prices and conduct in their market. Frequently, their rate of return is higher than that of "fringe" competitors which do not serve specialized niches of demand. Because new entrants are less likely to enjoy scale economies or advantages of experience initially, they are most likely to hover on the "fringes" or periphery of industry influence until they penetrate the "core."

3. Both de novo and acquisition forms of entry are treated by Yip (1980). The definition of entry used by Biggadike (1976) is narrower but also encompasses acquisitions.

4. Superior profits, competitive position, and market share were determined to be attributable to luck (Manke, 1974). This line of argument, which was based upon Gilbrat's law of proportionate growth, was refuted by Manfield (1962) and Marcus (1969). Several important differences distinguish these types of studies from those germane to strategists and students of corporate strategy. These earlier simulations were undertaken to study corporate performance in terms of allocative efficiency, technical efficiency, and consumer welfare. Firms measure their performances in terms of market share and ROI goals. Findings regarding equilibrium numbers of competitors and their asset size distribution are useful for developing theories of economic survival (see Hymer and Pashigian 1962), but the "survivors technique" offers little guidance to business managers puzzling over the best strategic posture to assume when entering a new market (Shepherd, 1967; Weiss, 1964).

5. Interested readers may study other measures of entry using dependent variables such as, for example, market share, price–cost margins, return on invested capital, or "net residual entry" (numbers of firms within the industry in $time_t$) by reviewing Deutsch (1975), Hines (1957), McGuckin (1972), Mann (1966), Orr (1974), Qualls (1972), and Stonebreaker (1976).

6. An interesting observation by Menge (1962) concerning the ages of durable and specific assets notes that, although the cost of acquiring assets for manufacturing products which are subject to frequent style changes may be high, the most specialized, hence inflexible, forms of these assets

will quickly become vulnerable to obsolescence. This means some industries characterized by increases in the newness of physical plant (a seemingly attractive attribute) would also be subject to high exit barriers (Caves and Porter, 1977; Harrigan, 1981; Porter, 1976). Such industries would offer market opportunities for successful entry but volatile returns once entry were accomplished.

7. If other structural factors (not including R&D) tended to create either exceptionally high or low entry barriers, their presence tended to reduce firms' incentives for investing in R&D (Comanor, 1967). This finding suggests that, although scholars have generally held that the creation of technical barriers to entry would insulate the firm's respective submarket from would-be imitators, the firms which will be motivated to do so have relatively few other such protective advantages. Indeed, research concerning R&D outlays which framed the problem in terms of nonprice-competitive warfare concluded that, like advertising, accelerated R&D outlays tended to become necessary if other firms were also accelerating their expenditures (see Needham, 1976).

8. Measures of the absolute cost advantages of advertising could also be constructed using a similar methodology. A "variability of average advertising expenditures" variable was not included in the model due to its high collinearity with the "variability of average R&D expenditures" variable. Apparently, the proportion of firms' R&D expenditures to sales is similar to the proportion of firms' advertising to sales, and the relationship in general, aggregate terms is also similar for these two competitive tactics.

9. This argument parallels that in Menge (1962), which says that, although the high cost of frequent style changes should reduce the absolute number of competitors and deter entry, the existence of an opportunity to satisfy diverse consumers' preferences suggests that several firms could occupy modest but specialized niches of the market.

10. It is possible, of course, for firms to be listed as manufacturers within a particular industry when, in actuality, they subcontract many of their manufacturing tasks to the plants of existing firms, acting primarily as marketers of their branded product offerings. This variation in the nature of individual firms' activities is consistent with the theory of strategic groups although identification of the tasks performed by each competitor in each time period was beyond the scope of this study.

11. Special reports issued by the FTC which tracked the behavior and performance of the 12 largest firms in these industries were available for several years. (In the tobacco products industry, eight competitors were tracked.)

12. The error term is corrected for the three components of bias such that:

$$
\begin{aligned}
E(\epsilon^2_{it}) &= \sigma^2 \\
E(\epsilon_{it}\epsilon_{jt}) &= 0, \quad i \neq j \\
E(\epsilon_{i,_{t-1}}\, u_{jt}) &= 0, \quad i \neq j \\
u_{it} &\sim N(0,\sigma_u{}^2)
\end{aligned}
$$

and ρ_i is the correction used in generalized differencing.

13. The most appropriate location for new capacity will be half the distance between the firms' existing facilities, assuming the firm wishes to preempt a potential entrant in a particular geographic region; see Hotelling (1929).

REFERENCES

Abell, Derek F. (1980), *Defining the Business: The Starting Point of Strategic Planning,* Englewood Cliffs, Prentice-Hall.

Abell, Derek, F. (1978), "Strategic Windows," *Journal of Marketing,* (July), pp. 21–26.

Bain, Joe S. (1956), *Barriers to New Competition,* Cambridge: Harvard University Press.

Bain, Joe S. (1972), *Essays on Price Theory,* Cambridge: Little, Brown.

Balestra, Pietro and Marc Nerlove (1966), ''Pooling Cross Section and Time Series Data in the Estimation of a Dynamic Model: The Demand for Natural Gas,'' *Econometrica,* Vol. 34 (July), pp. 585–612.

Bass, Frank M., Phillippe Cattin, and Dick Wittink (1978), ''Firm Effects and Industry Effects in the Analysis of Market Structure and Profitability,'' *Journal of Marketing Research,* Vol. XV, (February), pp. 3–10.

Bass, Frank and Dick R. Wittink (1965), ''Pooling Issues and Methods in Regression Analysis with Examples in Marketing Research,'' *Journal of Marketing Research,* Vol. 12, (November), pp. 414–425.

Biggadike, Ralph (1976), ''Entry, Strategy and Performance,'' Unpublished doctoral dissertation, Harvard Business School.

Blair, Roger D., and John Kraft (1974), ''Estimation of Elasticity of Substitution in American Manufacturing Industry from Pooled Cross-Section and Time-Series Observations,'' *Review of Economics and Statistics,* Vol. 56, (August), pp. 343–347.

Boston Consulting Group, *Perspectives on Experience,* (1968), Boston Consulting Group.

Caves, Richard E., J. Khalizadeh-Shirazi (1975), and Michael E. Porter, ''Scale Economies in Statistical Analyses of Market Power,'' *Review of Economics and Statistics,* (May), pp. 133–140.

Caves, Richard E. and Porter, Michael E. (1976), ''Barriers to Exit,'' in Qualls, David P. and Masson, Robert T., eds., *Essays in Industrial Organization in Honor of Joe S. Bain,* Cambridge, Mass.: Ballinger Publishing Company.

Caves, Richard E. and Michael E. Porter (1977), ''From Entry Barriers to Mobility Barriers,'' *Quarterly Journal of Economics,* (May), pp. 241–262.

Chamberlain, E. M. (1962), *The Theory of Monopolistic Competition,* Eighth ed., Cambridge, Mass.: Harvard University Press.

Chang, Hui-shyong and Cheng F. Lee (1977), ''Using Pooled Time Series and Cross Section Data to Test the Firm and Time Effects in Financial Analysis,'' *Journal of Financial and Quantitative Analysis,* Vol. 12, (September), pp. 457–471.

Collins, N. and L. Preston (1969), ''Price-Cost Margins and Industry Structure,'' *Review of Economics and Statistics,* Vol. 51, (August), pp. 271–286.

Comanor, William S. (1967), ''Market Structure, Product Differentiation, and Industrial Research,'' *Quarterly Journal of Economics,* Vol, 81, (November), pp. 639–657.

Comanor, W. S. and T. Wilson (1974), *Advertising and Market Power,* Cambridge: Harvard University Press.

Comanor, William S. and Thomas A. Wilson (1967), ''Advertising Market Structure, and Performance,'' *Review of Economics and Statistics,* (November), pp. 423–440.

Demsetz, Harold (1979), ''Accounting for Advertising as a Barrier to Entry,'' *Journal of Business,* Vol. 52, No. 3, pp. 345–360.

Deutsch, Larry L. (1975), ''Structure, Performance and the Net Rate of Entry into Manufacturing Industries,'' *Southern Economic Journal,* (January), pp. 450–456.

Dixit, Avinash (1980), ''The Role of Investment in Entry-Deterrence,'' *The Economic Journal,* (March), pp. 95–106.

Esposito, L., and F. F. Esposito (1974), ''Excess Capacity and Market Structure,'' *Review of Economics and Statistics,* Vol. 56, (May), pp. 188–194.

Fellner, W. J. (1949), *Competition Among the Few: Oligopoly and Similar Market Structure,* New York: Knopf.

Gaskin, Darius W., Jr. (1971), ''Dynamic Limit Pricing: Optimal Pricing Under Threat of Entry,'' *Journal of Economic Theory,* (September), pp. 306–322.

Gorecki, Paul K. (1976), ''The Determinants of Entry by Domestic and Foreign Enterprises in Canadian Manufacturing Industries: Some Comments and Empirical Results,'' *Review of Economics and Statistics,* (November), pp. 485–488.

Harrigan, Kathryn Rudie (1980), ''Deterrents to Divestiture,'' *Academy of Management Journal,* Vol. 24, No. 2, pp. 306–323.

Hatten, Kenneth J. (1974), ''Strategic Models in the Brewing Industry,'' Unpublished doctoral dissertation, Purdue University.

Henderson, Bruce (1974), ''The Experience Curve . . . ,'' Boston Consulting Group.

Hines, Howard H. (1957), ''Effectiveness of Entry by Already Established Firms,'' *Quarterly Journal of Economics,* (February) pp. 132–150.

Hotelling, Harold (1929), ''Stability in Competition,'' *Economic Journal,* Vol. 39, (March), pp. 41–57.

Hsaio, Cheng (1974), ''Statistical Inference for a Model with Both Random Cross-Sectional and Time Effects,'' *International Economic Review,* Vol. 15, No. 1, (February), pp. 12–30.

Hunt, Michael S. (1972), ''Competition in the Home Appliance Industry, 1960–1970,'' Unpublished doctoral dissertation, Business Economics Committee, Harvard University, (May).

Hymer, Stephan and Peter Pashigian (1962), ''Firm Size and Rate of Growth,'' *Journal of Political Economy,* Vol. 70, (December), pp. 556–569.

Ijiri, Y. and H. A. Simon (1964), ''Business Growth and Firm Size,'' *American Economic Review,* Vol. 54, (March), pp. 77–89.

Johnston, K. H. and H. L. Lyon (1973), ''Experimental Evidence on Combining Cross-Section and Time Series Information,'' *Review of Economics and Statistics,* Vol. 55, (November), pp. 465–474.

Kamien, Morton J. and Nancy L. Schwartz (1975), ''Market Structure and Innovation: A Survey,'' *Journal of Economic Literature,* Vol. 13, (March), pp. 1–37.

McGuckin, Robert (1972), ''Entry, Concentration Change and Stability of Market Shares,'' *Southern Economic Journal,* (January), pp. 363–370.

MacMillan, Ian C. (1980), ''How Business Strategists Can Use Guerilla Tactics,'' *Journal of Business Strategy,* Vol. 1, No. 2, (Fall), pp. 63–65.

Maddala, G. S. (1971), ''The Use of Variance Components Models in Pooling Cross Section and Time Series Data,'' *Econometrica,* Vol. 39, (March), pp. 341–358.

Manke, Richard B. (1974), ''Causes of Interfirm Profitability Differences: A New Interpretation of the Findings,'' *Quarterly Journal of Economics,* Vol. LXXXVIII, No. 2, (May), pp. 181–193.

Mann, H. Michael (1966), ''Seller Concentration, Barriers to Entry, and Rates of Return in Thirty Industries, 1950–1960,'' *Review of Economics and Statistics,* Vol. 48, (August), pp. 296–307.

Mansfield, Edwin (1962), ''Entry, Gilbrat's Law, Innovation and Growth of Firms,'' *American Economic Review,* Vol. LII, (December), pp. 1031–1034.

Marcus, M. (1969), ''A Note on the Determinants of the Growth of Firms and Gilbrat's Law,'' *Canadian Journal of Economics,* Vol. 3, (November), pp. 580–589.

Menge, John A. (1962), ''Style Change Costs as a Market Weapon,'' *Quarterly Journal of Economics,* Vol. 76, (November), pp. 632–647.

Modigliani, Franco (1958), ''New Developments on the Oligopoly Front,'' *Journal of Political Economy,* (June), pp. 215–232.

Mueller, W. F. and Richard T. Rogers (1980), ''The Role of Advertising in Changing Concentration of Manufacturing Industries,'' *Review of Economics and Statistics,* (February), pp. 89–96.

Mueller, D. C. and J. E. Tilton (1968), ''Research and Development Costs as a Barrier to Entry,'' *Canadian Journal of Economics,* (November), pp. 570–579.

Mundlak, Yair (1978), ''On the Pooling of Time Series and Cross Section Data,'' *Econometrica,* Vol. 46, No. 1 (January), pp. 69–85.

Needham, Douglas (1976), ''Entry Barriers and Non-Price Aspects of Firms' Behavior,'' *The Journal of Industrial Economics,* Vol. XXV, No. 1, (September), pp. 29–43.

Needham, Douglas (1975), ''Market Structure and Firms' R & D Behavior,'' *Journal of Industrial Economics,* Vol. XXIII, No. 4, (June), pp. 241–255.

Nerlove, Marc (1971), ''Further Evidence on the Estimation of Dynamic Economic Relations From a Time Series of Cross Sections,'' *Econometrica,* Vol. 39, (March), pp. 359–382.

Newman, H. H. (1978), ''Strategic Groups and the Structure-Performance Relationship,'' *Review of Economics and Statistics,* (August), pp. 417–423.

Ornstein, S. I., J. F. Weston, and M. D. Intriligator (1973), ''Determinants of Market Structure,'' *Southern Economic Journal,* (April), pp. 612–625.

Orr, Dale (1974), ''The Determinants of Entry: A Study of the Canadian Manufacturing Industries,'' *Review of Economics and Statistics,* Vol. 56, (February), pp. 58–60.

Pindyck, Robert S. and Rubinfeld, Daniel L. (1976), *Econometric Models and Economic Forecasts,* New York: McGraw-Hill.

Porter, Michael E. (1976), ''Please Note Location of the Newest Exit: Exit Barriers and Strategic Planning,'' *California Management Review,* Vol. 19, No. 2, (Winter), pp. 21–33.

Porter, Michael E. (1979a), ''How Competitive Forces Shape Strategy,'' *Harvard Business Review,* (March–April), pp. 137–145.

Porter, Michael E. (1979b), ''The Structure Within Industries and Companies' Performance,'' *Review of Economics and Statistics,* Vol. 60, (May), pp. 214–227.

Porter, Michael E. (1980), *Competitive Strategy: Techniques for Analyzing Industries and Competitors,* New York: Free Press.

Qualls, David (1972), ''Concentration, Barriers to Entry, and Long Run Economic Profit Margins,'' *Journal of Industrial Economics,* (April), pp. 146–158.

Rao, Ram and David P. Rutenberg (1980), ''Preempting an Alert Rival: Strategic Timing of the First Plant by Analysis of Sophisticated Rivalry,'' *Bell Journal of Economics,* Vol. 11, No. 2, (Autumn), pp. 412–428.

Reddy, J. (1980), ''Incorporating Quality in Competitive Strategies,'' *Sloan Management Review,* (Spring), pp. 53–60.

Rosenbluth, G. (1957), *Concentration in Canadian Manufacturing Industries,* Princeton: Princeton University Press.

Rumelt, Richard P. and Robin Wensley (1980), ''In Search of the Market Share Effect,'' Working Paper MGL-61, Graduate School of Management, UCLA, November 7.

Scherer, Frederic M. (1973), ''The Determinants of Industrial Plant Sizes in Six Nations,'' *Review of Economics and Statistics,* (May), pp. 135–145.

Scherer, Frederic M. (1980), *Industrial Market Structure and Economic Performance,* Second ed., New York: Rand McNally.

Schmalensee, Richard (1976), ''Advertising and Profitability: Further Implications of the Null Hypothesis,'' *Journal of Industrial Economics,* Vol. XXV, No. 1, (September), pp. 45–53.

Schmalensee, Richard (1978), ''Entry Deterrence in the Ready-to-Eat Breakfast Cereal Industry,'' *Bell Journal of Economics,* Vol. 8, No. 2, (Autumn), pp. 305–327.

Shepherd, William G. (1972), ''The Elements of Market Structure,'' *Review of Economics and Statistics,* (February), pp. 25–37.

Shepherd, William G. (1967), ''What Does the Survivor Technique Show About Economies of Scale?'' *Southern Economic Journal,* (July), pp. 113–122.

Simon, H. A. and C. P. Bonini (1958), ''The Size Distribution of Business Firms,'' *American Economic Review,* (September), pp. 607–617.

Spence, A. Michael (1977), ''Entry, Investment, and Oligopolistic Pricing,'' *Bell Journal of Economics,* Vol. 8, No. 2 (Autumn), pp. 534–544.

Spence, A. Michael (1979), ''Investment Strategy and Growth in a New Market,'' *Bell Journal of Economics,* Vol. 10, No. 1, (Spring), pp. 1–19.

Stigler, George J. (1958), ''The Economies of Scale,'' *Journal of Law and Economics,* (October), pp. 54–71.

Stonebreaker, R. J. (1976), ''Corporate Profits and the Risk of Entry,'' *Review of Economics and Statistics,* (February), pp. 33–39.

U.S. Bureau of the Census, *Census of Manufactures, 1973, 1977,* Washington, D.C.: U.S. Government Printing Office.

Utterback, James M. and William J. Abernathy (1975), ''A Dynamic Model of Product and Process Innovation,'' *Omega,* Vol. 3, No. 2.

Vernon, John M. (1972), *Market Structure and Industrial Performance: A Review of Statistical Findings,* Boston: Allyn & Bacon.

Weiss, Leonard W. (1964), ''The Survival Technique and the Extent of Suboptimal Capacity,'' *Journal of Political Economy,* (June), pp. 246–261.

Wright, Neil R. (1978), ''Production Differentiation, Concentration and Changes in Concentration,'' *Review of Economics and Statistics,* Vol. 60, (November), pp. 628–631.

Yip, George S. (1980), ''Barriers to Entry: A Corporate Strategy Perspective,'' Unpublished dissertation, Harvard University.

ALTERNATIVE STRATEGIES FOR PRODUCT OPTIMIZATION

Howard Moskowitz and Samuel Rabino

I. INTRODUCTION

In the increasingly competitive marketplace, product marketers are forced to rely upon the combination of information, judgment, and experience. Information about the strengths and weakness of competitors, and about changing costs of goods, combined with judgment about what to launch and how to support the product, are very important inputs for marketers.

The complexity of products in this competitive environment requires a technology which can accomplish the following goals:

1. Rapidly provide a comparative profile of the different products on the market, in terms of strengths and weaknesses. From this comparative profile, the marketer can quickly determine which of the products in the

Advances in Strategic Management, Volume 2, pages 99–123.

ISBN: 0-89232-409-0

competitive frame are well accepted, which are not well accepted, and the reasons underlying acceptance.

2. Generate a variety of prototype products which are highly acceptable to the consumer. By using a technology which quickly spins off an array of highly acceptable products, the marketer can take advantage of the weaknesses of the competition, and can provide consumers with acceptable products.
3. Generate alternative products, which are optimized in acceptability and which simultaneously satisfy given profit objectives. By providing consumers with products at lower costs of goods than the products offered by the competition, the marketer can sell products at a lower cost and still maintain profitability and consumer acceptability.

This paper presents a technology for obtaining the necessary category information and for product optimization. By a combination of theory and a case history it illustrates how the marketer can use information about competitors to pinpoint targets for new products, and how marketers and R&D can develop products which fulfill these targets.

II. EVALUATION OF THE COMPETITIVE FRAME

A. Background

Every company that considers new product development as an important contributor to corporate growth must understand the dimensions of the risks involved. Beyond the financial risk of allocating developmental and testing funds that may never be recovered, there is the time commitment by various levels within the company, including management. That time commitment should be viewed as an opportunity cost, which is often substantial.

The high risk of failure emanates from numerous obstacles which stand between the new product idea and its eventual success in the marketplace. Some of these obstacles only recently have become important. Among the more "problematic" trends are the following:

1. *Inflation.* It now costs more to develop, test, and introduce those products which emerge from the screening process. Thus, writing off an unsuccessful venture has become a continually increasing drain of profits.

2. *Regulatory agencies.* The scope and depth of control exercised by the regulatory agencies has grown steadily. The Federal Trade Commission now rejects many types of claims that once were acceptable. The Food & Drug Administration has become much more demanding in its interpretation of "safe and effective." The Environmental Protection Agency regulates those products and services which threaten to contaminate the environment. The Consumer

Products Safety Commission protects the consumer against hazardous products and packaging. There are many other agencies which regulate individual industries.

3. *Product maturity.* Most markets have reached the stage of maturity where the consumer has a number of successful products from which to choose. Thus, a new product must convince its potential customers that it offers a better solution than the products they have been buying.

4. *Consumer movement.* Consumerism has become a major social and political force which must be accurately assessed by marketers of new products. It is imperative that a new product not be in conflict with areas of consumer interest such as personal health, safety, or energy conservation.[1]

B. Understanding the Competition

In order for the manager to make valid decisions regarding products, it is important to understand the dynamics of the marketplace. Of particular interest is the profile of the competitors. Many marketers content themselves with a continuing, comparative evaluation of their own product(s) against the single leading market competitor. The underlying assumption behind this approach is that the market leader must be doing "something right," and therefore an analysis of how leading brands perform can provide insights for bettering one's own performance in the market.

In some categories there are different types of competitors. Some competitors perform strongly and others weakly (in terms of total share, profitability, growth, etc.). It is often not clear why the market leader is in first place. Is it because of the product's unique characteristics or being earliest in the market? Or has the marketing group done an excellent sales job with an average or even below-average product? Or has the market leader outspent competitors in terms of advertising and/or promotion?

One of the most important areas of information needed for the development of a new product strategy is an assessment of the strength and weaknesses of the *entire* range of competition. It is important to perform this evaluation of the competitive frame on both a blind and a branded (or identified) basis, for the following reasons:

- Some products may be highly acceptable on a blind basis and yet achieve low share
- Other products may achieve high share, yet fare poorly on a blind basis
- Some products may do exceedingly well on a share basis, yet perform poorly on blind *and* branded tests

Only by evaluating a broad range of competitive products already in the marketplace does it become possible to identify trends, relating share (objectively measured by an auditing service, such as Nielsen) to product characteristics and product image.

C. Techniques for Measuring the Competitive Frame

In order to adequately measure consumer reactions to products in the competitive frame, it is important to obtain a "report card" of the products, on a series of attributes. By comparing products on this report card it becomes possible to diagnose quickly which products perform well on which specific attributes.

A recent article (see note 2) discusses four product testing procedures that currently dominate the product testing area. Although numerous other designs are possible and have been used occasionally, we briefly discuss these four procedures in order to provide a background for the approach.

1. *Monadic Test*

The simplest of all product testing procedures, this test is very popular with research departments of large packaged goods manufacturers. Typically, a sample of respondents is asked to examine a product in terms of attributes such as taste, smell, touch, use, etc., and then rate the product, purchase intent, degree of liking, and so on. Then scores (e.g., mean rating, proportion of individuals checking the most favorable response, the most favorable two responses, and so on) are evaluated. If significant differences emerge vs. a competitor then the candidate is selected for the further refinement or test marketing. It is of great importance to carefully control for sample differences within the evaluation groups when testing more than one product. This requirement generates one of the major problems in monadic testing. Furthermore quite often the sure monadic test often lacks requisite sensitivity to differentiate among products.

2. *Comparative Test*

In the comparative test the respondent is asked to examine attributes of two or more test products (or a prototype vs. an in-market control) and to choose the preferred one. Choice can be in terms of simple preference (the product most liked or likely to be bought), the rank order of preference, or a rating (as in the monadic test). A rating scale or constant sum procedure permits measurement of the intensity of rated difference from the monadic test, in that the frame of preference is explicitly controlled. In this case the products (usually a new product vs. an established one) are compared side by side.

3. *Staggered Test*

The staggered test (also known as sequential monadic) is a compromise between the monadic test and the comparative test. In the staggered test the respondent is instructed to use one product ("A") and then wait a prespecified period of time, then to use the second product ("B"), and then to make a judgment between A and B. Proponents of this procedure argue that it more closely resembles the way in which consumers actually compare products in the marketplace. This requirement of long-term use is especially critical in testing products which require some continued usage prior to making a choice, such as cosmetics and detergents.

Their first three methods are generally associated with situations in which management had two or more promising product prototypes and simply wished to know which version showed the greatest potential.

4. *Conjoint Analysis: Testing for Patterns*

Instead of simply testing whatever products are currently under consideration, a number of product prototypes are constructed which systematically vary in terms of product features. The objective is no longer simply to identify the singly most promising product (although that identification is one result of the process). The focus of conjoint and related analysis is shifted to developing a clear understanding of the relative importance of relevant product features, to provide guidance for the construction of new product formulations.[2]

D. Strategies for Field Testing

Selecting the proper test to measure a competitive frame requires an understanding of how the product is used and the specific characteristics on which consumers can rate the product. For some product categories, such as beverages and meats, it is possible to recruit panelists to participate in a central location test in a classroom setting. Respondents participate for a test lasting from 2 to 4 hours. They evaluate a wide variety of products by tasting them (or smelling them, in the case of fragrances). In other categories, such as medicines or health and beauty aids, the consumers must "live" with each product for an extended period of time. In those instances it is better to select a large sample of consumers and test each product with a subset of consumers from the sample. In either instance, however, it is imperative to develop a test design which allows the consumer to evaluate one or several products, with a sensitive scale, on a wide variety of attributes pertinent to the product.

The scaling technique employed in this study is magnitude estimation. Magnitude estimation refers to a class of psychophysical scaling procedures which were developed by S. S. Stevens at Harvard University in the 1950s. In its simplest form, the method allows respondents to assign numbers to sensory/attitudinal stimuli, without restriction, so that the ratios of the numerical assignments reflect ratios of sensory perceptions or of attitudinal levels. Using magnitude estimation, a product planner who finds that products are assigned ratings of 40 and 10 for sweetness can conclude that they are perceived to lie in a 4/1 sensory ratio.[3] Magnitude estimation is currently recognized as the simplest, most direct, and most widely used method of constructing sensory scales with ratio properties. This is the principal reason for applying it to the development process of packaged goods. It permits the rapid, cost-efficient assessment of many products using a sensitive scale. This benefit generates:

- The necessary "report card" of the category.
- The sensitivity to develop models that the marketer and R&D can use for product modification.

III. CASE HISTORY: THE FISH CAKE MARKET

The fishcake category is very competitive. There are five major manufacturers of national brands, along with a host of regional manufacturers. Most of the products in this market are targeted toward the convenience market and children. It is adults, however, who buy the majority of the product. Therefore, the analysis of the competitive frame must include both adult and child evaluations, because the purchase pattern demands acceptance by both groups.

A. Step 1—The Category Screen to Generate a Database

In order to evaluate the competitors it is important to test a selection of representative products, both blind and branded. These products typify the range of fish cakes available to the consuming public. In this particular study it was relevant to evaluate a total of six different fish cakes, representing a wide-spectrum of product types, flavors, and costs of goods and qualities.

The project required the evaluation of the products under well-controlled test conditions, summarized in Table 1, which provides the test protocol. The respondents were 100 adults (females) and 100 teens/children (half male, half female, ages 8–18), who participated in a 3½ hour tasting session. During this time each respondent had the chance to taste and rate the six fish cakes "blinded" and six fish cakes branded. Each product was tested by a total of 100 adults and 100 children. The respondents scaled their impressions of sensory characteristics, acceptance characteristics (e.g., taste acceptance, flavor acceptance), and image (e.g., value for the money, high quality, etc.).

Part of the data base of ratings (products A–F on selected attributes) appears in Table 2.

The following results emerge from the evaluation of the competitive frame:

- Consumers can and do perceive statistically significant differences among fish cake products on a blind basis. (This can be tested by comparing

Table 1. Sequence of Testing of Fish Cakes Products

Step	*Activity*	*Purpose/Benefit*
1.	Pre-recruit panel	Allow panelists to set aside time to participate Can tailor panel to precise requirements in terms of usage
2.	Panelist (N=25) report to central location for a 3½ hour test	Allows the test to be conducted in a cost-efficient way, with control on all phases of the evaluation.
3.	Panelist introduced to scaling	Insures understanding of rating system
4.	Panelist introduced to the proper method of evaluating a product	Insures understanding of what to do in actual tasting—and what the attributes mean
5.	Panelist tastes and rates first product on a variety of attributes	
6.	Interviewer checks ratings for comprehension	Insures panelist motivation, and generates quality control of data as it is being gathered
7.	Panelist waits 8 minutes and tries second product	Insures sensitivity of taste
8.	Step 6–7 repeated	
9.	Panelist rates the "ideal" product and on the same scale, with the same attributes	
10.	Respondent "calibrates rating"	Allows the researcher to coalesce ratings from different individuals, without forcing the individuals, a priori, to use an arbitrary scale.

differences between product ratings on an attribute vs. the standard error of the ratings.)

- The share of market (obtained separately for each brand) does not parallel overall product acceptance on a blind basis.
- Consumers report specific problems in flavor and texture, as well as problems in appearance. This means that consumers can and do notice intrinsic product differences, and can communicate their perceptions on the relevant attributes.
- On a branded basis, the ratings of purchase intent and product acceptability change, sometimes dramatically. The market leader (C), which is an average to poor product on a blind basis (rating = 20), becomes highly acceptable when it is presented under the brand name (rating = 55).
- Some of the brands in the category exert strong influences on product acceptance. This applies especially to the products which are heavily advertised and promoted (products C, A, E). Other products show little or no

Table 2. Database—Ratings of Fish Cakes on Attributes (Products A–F) (Numbers Are Magnitude Estimates)

	"A"		"B"		"C"		"D"		"E"		"F"		*Average Standard Error*
	BL	*BR*	*BL*	*BR*	*BL*	*BR*	*BL*	*BR*	*BL*	*BR*	*BL*	*BR*	
Liking													
Total	32	47	44	51	20	55	45	28	34	45	−30	02	6.5
Adults	22	60	50	61	−10	41	36	28	23	52	−35	20	8.4
Teens/Children	42	34	38	41	40	69	54	28	45	38	−25	−16	8.1
Purchase Intent (Adults)	35	61	55	63	12	47	45	39	37	55	10	08	5.6
Appearance (Adult)	26	35	38	60	42	39	50	55	45	51	25	15	7.5
Flavor (Adult)	29	40	57	65	−15	34	46	51	30	39	−45	15	7.9
Texture (Adult)	35	47	22	26	44	54	32	36	28	29	35	40	7.7
Sensory													
Spicy	26	29	34	37	15	18	40	46	31	33	27	24	5.6
Mildness	39	34	24	26	43	40	36	32	19	17	40	44	5.9
Smoky Flavor	30	26	49	57	33	37	41	40	27	20	39	36	5.3
Softness	45	42	40	47	38	43	36	40	30	27	33	39	5.7
Juiciness	39	48	28	46	51	40	38	29	25	29	65	61	5.5
Fishy Flavor	22	27	33	39	50	52	47	42	39	33	40	41	5.5
Image													
Quality	28	45	39	47	39	73	51	40	37	38	12	25	5.9
Value for Money	36	39	39	45	27	54	49	42	27	34	25	27	6.6
Share of Market	–	03	–	19	–	24	–	12	–	05	–	02	

100 = Extreme } All Attributes
0 = None } Except "liking"
BL = Blind
BR = Branded

Liking
−100 = Dislike extremely
0 = Neutral
+100 = Like extremely

brand effect, primarily because, by their own admission, consumers are not familiar with these brands (e.g., B).

- There is a suggestion that the leading in-market competitor (product C) is weak on a product basis but that its image as a brand leader is propping up acceptance. This weakness appears from the gap between product acceptance blind (which is quite low, −10 for adults) and product acceptance branded (which is quite high, +41 for adults).
- Adult ratings of product acceptance vs. children and teen ratings show different acceptance patterns. The children prefer the blander products on a blind basis (e.g., C) whereas the adults show higher liking of B. Where it is necessary to satisfy both groups, it might be necessary to deliver a bland product (to gain children's acceptance) but to position the product as relatively flavorful in order to attract adult interest. This could be accomplished by finding a unique spice/flavoring system which provides a point of difference to attract adults, but which is acceptable to children and teenagers.

B. Benefits of the Category Screening

Analysis of the competitive frame for fish cakes shows the opportunity to improve acceptance of a product for children and teenagers. It provides R&D with a target set of products which consumers like. The sensory profile of those products provides concrete guidance to R&D regarding the qualities or "sensory attributes" acceptable to the consumer.

To the marketer, the pattern of ratings demonstrates which particular products in the marketplace are strong, which are weak, and why. It is clear that the market leaders in these categories (brands B and C) are successful for different reasons. Both brands promote heavily to the consumer and to the trade. Product C, an intrinsically poor product, is a heavily discounted brand, and is heavily advertised. Therefore, success can be ensured by keeping cost of goods down and by maintaining the already heavy effort in marketing. Product B, an exceptionally good product, is not widely promoted in the stores, although it is heavily advertised. The contributory factors underlying the success of these two brands could not have emerged as easily, had the marketer only tested the market leader without discovering the acceptance pattern generated by the array of other competitors.

C. First Research Steps in Optimizing: Selecting Alternative Prototypes

The initial phase of research showed that it would be possible to penetrate the market with a product that appealed to both children and adults. Furthermore, competitor D, which scored well for both groups on a blind basis, did poorly on a branded basis. It is neither heavily advertised nor heavily promoted. In light of the appeal of product D to the target consumer groups, the marketing group decided to forge ahead and develop a test set of products representing variations of the flavor, texture, and appearance of competitor D.

In order to perform an efficient assessment of alternative prototypes, in order to ensure product acceptance by consumers, it is necessary to consider many qualitatively different prototypes in the initial test. For instance, in this project on fish cakes it is necessary to generate a gamut of products having different *spice types,* which produce a variety of flavor sensations, prior to varying the level of a single spice type in order to maximize acceptance. It is also necessary to vary the shape of the different fish cakes, in order to generate prototypes which are short and fat, long and fat, short and thin, or long and thin, respectively. Only by so doing the exploratory testing can the marketer gain empirical information on prototype acceptability.

For this particular project, R&D developed nine different spice types and two levels, all of one shape. The remaining three formulations were three different shapes, at one spice type (X) and one spice level (LOW). The spice variations were modifications of the spices which had previously showed greatest appeal to both adults and children/teenagers (e.g., variations of spices in products B and D, Table 2).

Table 3 shows the results of this research step. It reveals that some of the prototypes were definitely not acceptable to either group of consumers. Two spice types (X, Y) are acceptable to both adults and children, with spice type X more acceptable to adults and spice type Y more acceptable to children. Shape is important for acceptance, as well. It appears that a short and fat fish cake is acceptable to both adults and children.

The net results of these research steps are:

- A set of ratings on prototypes with a wide range of variations. By chance alone the marketer has increased the probability of generating a winning product. In contrast, many consumer product research programs do not take the time or effort to explore the many possible alternatives at this stage, using rigorous testing procedures. As a consequence, either the project is abandoned for lack of viable prototypes (which really did exist, had they been sought in a more systematic and disciplined fashion), or the marketing group settles for arbitrarily chosen prototypes because of lack of additional information.
- The product ratings for the prototypes augment the ratings obtained previously for the existing competitors, blind and branded. As a result, it becomes possible to discern trends in product acceptance as they emerge from a base of the different competitors' products and prototypes.
- It is possible to rank order the different prototypes in terms of acceptance to children, to adults, to both, and in terms of cost of goods. With this data base, the marketing manager can determine which of several options to

Table 3. Consumers Reactions to Qualitatively Different Prototypes of Fishcakes

	Spice			*Liking*			
Prototype	*Type*	*Level*	*Shape*	*(Total)*	*(Adults)*	*(Teen)*	*(Children)*
A	X	(Low)	ST	36	42	30	36
B	Y	(Low)	ST	40	37	30	53
C	Z	(Low)	ST	16	32	24	−8
D	X	(High)	ST	38	49	20	45
E	Y	(High)	ST	34	30	24	48
F	Z	(High)	ST	26	33	31	14
G	X	(Low)	SF	43	45	30	54
H	X	(Low)	SF	29	31	34	22
I	X	(Low)	LF	24	29	32	19

S = Short
L = Long
F = Fat
*Numbers are magnitude estimates
−100 = Dislike Extremely
0 = Neutral
−100 = Like Extremely
3 Spices: X,Y,Z
2 Levels: High, Low
2 Lengths: Short (S) and Long (L)
2 Widths: Thin (T) and (Fat) (F)

pursue early on in the project timetable, and can focus attention on that particular prototype which satisfies several goals simultaneously.

D. Product Modeling

The third stage of research uses product modeling. The modeling technology develops a set of quantitative relations between formula variations, sensory perceptions, cost of goods, and product acceptance. In contrast to the previous stages, which explored qualitative product variations, product modeling works with a limited set of ingredients, which vary on a continuum of levels.

1. *Experimental Designs*

In order to develop a product model, it is vital to constrain the number of feasible formula ingredients to a narrow set. In this project R&D recommended an investigation of five formulation variables which they thought would influence acceptance.

1. Spice level (of the winning spice type)
2. Amount of fish component 1 (whitefish)

3. Amount of fish component 2 (pollock)
4. Amount of filler
5. Weight of emulsion (viz, weight of the final fish cake)

Depending upon the formula variations, it is possible to produce many different types of products. One might produce a fish cake with low spice level, and a great deal of whitefish (to the exclusion of pollock and filler), with the fish cake being of moderate size. This prototype might be acceptable to adults but not to children. On the other hand, a rearrangement of the formula, using the same set of five variables, could generate a mild, nonspicy product, comprising half whitefish and half pollock, of a moderate size, which would appeal to children.

There are many thousands of formula combinations for fish cakes that one could produce for this particular project. Some prototypes will, by trial and error, achieve acceptance among children and adults. Most may not be acceptable at all. From a strategic standpoint, limiting the focus to these variables and varying them systematically helps to reduce the uncertainty. Furthermore, the product developer can further refine the test, to select the optimum combination.

Statisticians have developed procedures whereby they can consider the effect on acceptance of several variables simultaneously, with each variable (e.g., spice level) taking on one of several values. In this particular case, there are four independent variables: spice level, fish cake volume, and three of the three fish levels. (The total of white fish + ''filler'' + pollock must equal a constant, e.g., so that knowing any two of these automatically fixes the third.) The experimental design for this required that R&D formulate a total of 27 products, covering a wide range of different fish cakes, all of which however, are quantitative variations of the same set of ingredients. Table 4 presents this experimental design (called a ⅓ replicate, fractional factorial design).

2. *Test Procedures*

As in the previous tests, we allowed consumers to evaluate a range of different fish cakes. This time, the consumers evaluated a total of 8 of the 27, along with 3 control fish cakes (representing the B and D, the best two products tested among the competitors, and the market leader C). Consumers used the scaling method of magnitude estimation, and followed the same evaluation procedure. Adults previewed the fish cake in the uncooked state, cooked it, and then consumed as much as they wished. Children ate the cooked fish cakes, but did not view the uncooked product. In order to ensure comparability of ratings to the previous studies, two in-market ''controls'' were used to ''bridge'' the two studies. Thus, it was possible to adjust the ratings in either study by a constant multiplicative factor, in order to align the absolute sizes of numbers.

3. *Database*

The ratings for the 27 products, and the 2 controls, generate a database for the category. It appears (in part) in Table 5. A correlation table of attributes vs.

Table 4. Schematic of a ⅓ Replicate, Fractional Factorial Design for 4 Variables

	Variable			
	A *Whitefish*	*B* *Pollock*	*C* *Weight*	*D* *Spice*
1.	H	M	H	H
2.	H	H	M	H
3.	H	L	L	H
4.	H	L	H	M
5.	H	M	M	M
6.	H	H	L	M
7.	H	H	H	L
8.	H	L	M	L
9.	H	H	L	L
10.	M	H	H	H
11.	M	L	M	H
12.	M	H	M	M
13.	M	M	H	M
14.	M	L	L	M
15.	M	L	H	L
16.	M	H	M	L
17.	M	H	L	L
18.	L	L	H	H
19.	L	M	M	H
20.	L	H	L	H
21.	L	H	H	M
22.	L	M	L	M
23.	L	L	M	M
24.	L	M	H	L
25.	L	H	L	L
26.	L	L	L	L
27.	M	M	L	H

formula levels appears in Table 6. Quickly scanning the database and the correlation Table 6, we see the following trends:

- Consumers can and do see dramatic differences among the different fish cake prototypes.
- The balance of fish composition dramatically alters attributes of flavor and texture.
- The size of the fish cake (in terms of weight) changes the perception of flavor and texture. This effect occurs because the size of the fish cake influences the rate of cooking, and thus indirectly affects the texture and flavor.

Table 5. Ratings of Test Product (1–10) and Competitors B,C,D

Prod.	*Whitefish*	*Pollock*	*Spice*	*Weight*	*Liking Dislike Total*	*Liking Dislike Adult*	*Liking Dislike Teen*	*Liking Dislike Child*	*Mild*	*Soft*	*Juicy*	*Fatty*	*Fishy*	*Spicy*
1.	4.4	2.5	2.0	1.2	18	12	19	32	45	67	46	63	43	54
2.	4.4	5.0	2.0	1.1	24	16	31	47	48	46	46	65	46	59
3.	4.4	0.0	2.0	1.0	34	08	89	53	50	52	52	67	45	63
4.	4.4	0.0	1.8	1.2	35	14	65	72	62	54	54	79	46	57
5.	4.4	2.5	1.8	1.1	43	30	61	63	73	59	59	66	59	66
6.	4.4	5.0	1.8	1.0	18	13	−03	54	68	51	51	66	57	58
7.	4.4	5.0	1.6	1.2	25	27	14	28	65	57	57	60	56	63
8.	4.4	0.0	1.6	1.1	12	−04	19	49	74	50	50	56	62	58
9.	4.4	5.0	1.6	1.0	11	04	−09	59	70	51	51	59	63	58
10.	2.2	5.0	2.0	1.2	23	17	−01	58	52	44	44	62	49	58
				Competitors										
				B	42	54	28	44	25	42	29	51	29	34
				C	22	−02	25	43	40	34	47	35	49	12
				D	40	34	31	55	33	38	40	39	48	44

Whitefish = WF
Pollock = POLL

Table 6. Correlations* of Formula Levels of Fish Cake Prototypes with Consumer Attribute Rating

	Formula		*Variable*	
	Whitefish	*Pollock*	*Spice*	*Weight*
Liking—Total	0.66	−0.13	0.03	0.28
Liking—Adult	0.51	0.16	−0.21	0.24
Liking—Children	0.46	−0.14	0.36	−0.06
Liking—Teens	0.38	−0.40	0.10	0.04
Soft	0.70	0.23	−0.45	−0.22
Juicy	0.60	0.01	−0.23	0.16
Fatty	0.62	−0.11	0.20	−0.05
Fishy Flavor	0.42	−0.09	−0.50	−0.09
Spice	0.54	−0.08	−0.19	0.12
Mild	0.13	0.28	−0.71	−0.36

*Correlations are the Pearson "R" value, which indicates the degree to which ratings follow a straight line relation with a specific formula variable.

4. *Models*

Having developed the database, one can now develop a set of equations to relate formula variables to ratings of consumer attributes and to product costs. Product modeling follows these steps:

- Selection of attribute to be modeled.
- Selection of equation form to represent how changes in formula variables impact on consumer ratings. It is important to keep in mind that in any consumer product the ingredients often interact with one another in complex ways. Although it is usually impossible to determine the true, underlying nature of the interaction one can develop an ad hoc model which will allow significant interactions.
- Run a statistical curve fitting program, in order to estimate the coefficients or multiplicative factors of the model, and to determine the goodness-of-fit of the model to the actual data.

There are a variety of equations from which one can choose to develop product models. Some of the simpler models appear later:

- *Simple Linear Equation:* Response = $k_0 + k_1$ (Ingr. A) + K_2 (Ingr. B). The simple linear equation assumes panelist ratings to be a linear combination of the different formula variations. It allows no interaction. When interactions do exist, the linear model does not indicate them. Rather, the linear model adjusts the coefficients so that the model fits the data. Interactions among formula variable will lead to incorrect linear model.

- *Simple Parabolic Equation:* Response = $K_0 + k_1$ (Ingr. A) + k_2 (Ingr. A)^2 + K_3 (Ingr. B) + K_4 (Ingr. B)^2. This parabolic function assumes that the response changes in a continuous manner with the formula levels. In most instances the parabola will peak somewhere in the middle range of ingredient levels or in other cases peak at either extreme, and be lowest in the intermediate level. At the peak the consumer rating of the attribute reaches its maximum level. When we deal with two or more variables, however, we generate a surface rather than a simple curve. The surface may look like Figure 1 or Figure 2. In Figure 1 we see *tolerance* of a wide range of formulation levels. In Figure 2 we see *intolerance* of a wide range of formulation variables.
- *Parabolic Function with Interactions:* Response = $K_0 + k_1$ (Ingr. A) + k_2 (Ingr. A)^2 + k_3 (Ingr. B) + k_4 (Ingr. B)^2 + k_5 (Ingr. A) (Ingr. B). This parabolic function allows interactions. Some of the interactions may be simple multiplicative interactions, as shown in Figure 3. Other interactions,

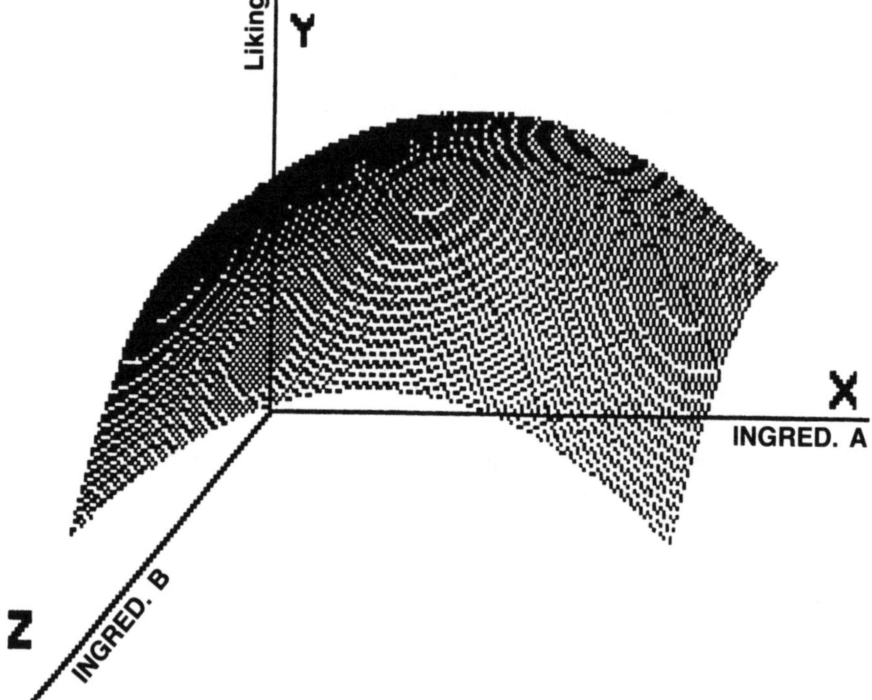

Figure 1. A typical situation in which the consumer's rating of acceptance (Y axis) is highly sensitive to levels of ingredients X and Z respectively.

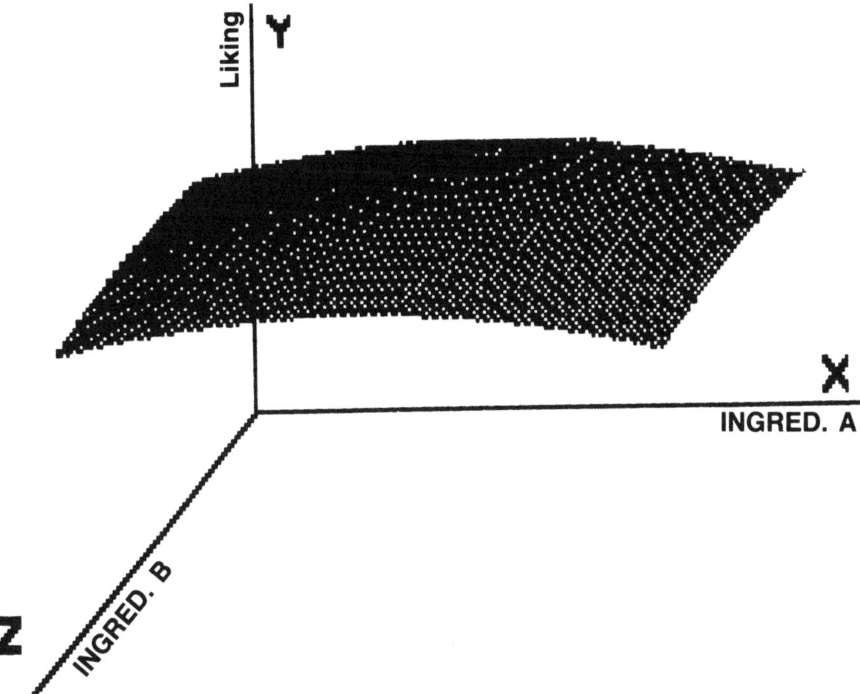

Figure 2. Example of surface relating product acceptance (liking ratings: Y axis) vs levels of two ingredients (X, Z). Note the relatively wide range of acceptable levels of ingredients X and Z.

may involve ratios of variables rather than products (or multiplicative interactions). They are represented in Figure 3.

4. *Product Models for Fish Cakes*

By carrying through the exercise of fitting different curves to the data, we arrive at a set of equations for the fish cake product. Tables 7A and 7B show the best-fitting equations for selected attributes. It provides data on overall liking for the total panel of consumers, as well as separate equations for the adult, teen, and children subgroups. It also provides equations for the cost of goods and for specific attributes (e.g., spiciness). The equations shown in Table 7B summarize the relation between the formula variables and the consumer reactions. The equations for the most part fit the data adequately. In some instances there is a clearly better fit of equations to data (e.g., softness vs. formula variables, with an R^2 of 0.81), whereas in other instances there is a poorer fit (e.g., juiciness as an attribute vs. formula variables, with an R^2 of 0.49).

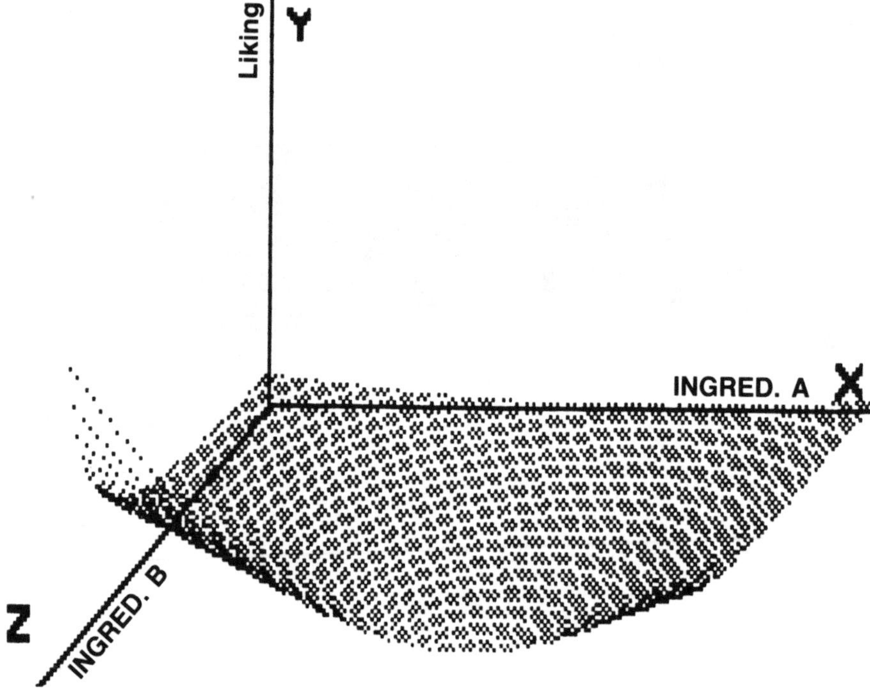

Figure 3. Example of a case in which acceptance (Y axis) is proportional to ingredient levels (X, Z) and to the ratio of ingredients (e.g., X/Z).

Table 7(A). Product Models for Fish Cakes

—Each Product Model is an equation
—The equations have different terms
  a) Additive constant (INCPT = intercept of k_0)
  b) Linear Term (e.g. A = Whitefish, B = Pollock, SP = Spice, WT = Weight)
  c) Square Terms (e.g., A^2, B^2, SP^2, WT^2) or cube terms (B^3)
  d) Cross Product Terms (e.g., A × SP; A × WT)
  e) Ratios (e.g., A/SP, Whitefish/Spice Ratio)
—Goodness of Fit is indexed by two measures
  a) Multiple R^2 (× 100 = percentage of variability in the ratings accounted for by the equation)
  b) F Ratio = Ratio of explained variance to unexplained variance in the ratings

*All terms in the equation were statistically significant according to a ''T'' test
A = Whitefish
B = Pollock
SP = Spice
WT = Weight

Table 7(B). Product Models for Fish Cakes*

*Term in Model***	*L/D Total*	*L/D Adult*	*L/D Children*	*L/D Teens*	*Mild-ness*	*Spicy*	*Soft-ness*	*Fishy Flavor*	*Juicy*
INCPT	−641.65	−1349.51	1989.45	−3129.71	−179.26	70.17	236.85	125.6	72.95
A	−8.88	−437.18	32.48	75.55				23.38	
A^2	−1.03	−2.15		2.65		−0.41	.33	−2.15	
A^3									0.06
B			10.62	−62.95	0.77	−2.88			
B^2	−0.16	−0.14	−2.45	2.01		0.37		−0.91	
B^3							−0.02		
WT				1942.61					
WT^2	23.27		711.43	−845.96	−11.36		−6.25		
SP	721.35	1484.72	−1256.08	2249.93	300.40	−8.01	−85.13		100.44
SP^2	−208.80	−420.32	366.87	−624.12	−89.22		−4.52		
SP^3									10.66
AB		0.76		−2.11		0.30	1.42		
A/SP	13.82	132.81	−14.60		−4.13	1.44			
B/WT	−5.59								
B/WT									
SP/WT		−444.26							
A/SP		374.50		−128.87	14.56		1.9278	−24.00	5.26
A/SP				92.34			1.7534		
WT/SP		75.35	−1439.95					−47.03	
Multiple R^2	0.70	0.71	0.52	0.73	0.70		0.81	0.68	0.49
F	5.228	4.81	2.04	3.61	7.81		15.16	5.72	5.27
Degree/Freedom	7.27	10.27	10	12	7.27		7.27	8.27	5.27

INCEPT = Additive Constant (k_0)
**A = Whitefish, B = Pollock, WT = Weight, SP = Spice
L/D = Liking/Disliking
*NOTE: Not all terms were inserted into the product model.

5. *Optimizing the Product for Consumer Acceptance*

Since the product model provides a summary of the relations between formulations and perceptions, one can use the model to determine the particular formulation at which acceptance by consumers is highest. To optimize acceptance, we first consider the model for liking, and determine the maximum point. This maximum is reached by a "hill-climbing procedure."

Table 8 shows the best product, for the total panel (Column A), for the adult panel alone (Column B), and for the child panel alone (Column C). Since we have the equations, we can predict the likely acceptance rating that the product would obtain from each consumer segment. These predictions appear in Table 8. Furthermore, since we have comparable data on competitor products B, C, and D, we can estimate the likelihood that the acceptability rating of the optimized product will equal or exceed the acceptability rating of other competitor products. Table 9 compares the expected ratings of the optimum vs. the ratings that three competitors (B, C, D) achieve. The adult product generated by the optimization procedure (rating by adults = 32) can successfully compete against competitors C and D, but will probably lose, on average, to competitor B. On the other hand, the optimum child product (rating by children = 71) will compete successfully against all three competitors, B, C, and D, respectively.

Table 8. Optimal Formulations for Various Consumer Segments

Formulation	*(A)* *Total*	*(B)* *Adult*	*(C)* *Child*	*(D)* *Teen*
Whitefish	4.4	4.4	4.4	4.4
Pollock	3.89	5.0	2.12	0.0
Filler	1.71	0.6	3.48	5.6
Weight	1.2	1.2	1.0	1.15
Spice	2.0	1.87	1.61	1.93
Expected Liking				
L/D Total	**32.**	27.0	15.	31.0
Adults	11.	**32.**	4.	11.0
Teens	87.	45.	0.	**93.0**
Child	53.	42.	**71.**	47.0
*Cost of Goods**	46.8	41.	37.0	45.0
Expected Sensory Profile				
Mild	44.	58.	74.	51.
Spicy	59.	61.	58.	58.
Fishy	58.	29.	39.	56.
Soft	36.	70.	84.	44.
Liking of Competitor Products				
Products				
B	42.	54.	44.	28.
C	22.	−2.	43.	25.
D	20.	34.	55.	31.

*Estimated from known ingredient

Table 9. Optimal Formulations for Fish Cakes Subject to Acceptance Constraints

	Adult Oriented			*Child Oriented*		
Formulation	*Optimal Adults (A)*	*Optimal Adult* — *Child L/D >50 (B)*	*Optimal Adult* — *Child L/D >45 (C)*	*Optimal Child* — *Adult L/D >20 (D)*	*Optimal Child* — *Adult L/D >25 (E)*	*Optimal Child (F)*
Whitefish	4.4	3.85	3.49	4.39	3.77	4.4
Pollock	5.0	3.75	4.19	2.8	3.12	2.12
Filler/F	0.6	2.4	2.32	2.81	3.18	3.48
Weight	1.2	1.2	1.19	1.18	1.19	1.0
Spice	1.87	1.87	1.83	1.76	1.87	1.61
Liking						
L/D Total	27	33	31	32	33	15
Adults	32	26	28	20	25	4
Teens	25	20	13	34	14	0
Child	42	52	45	58	55	71
Cost of Goods	41	41	40	43	41	37
Sensory Profile						
Mild	58	57	59	64	57	74
Spicy	61	58	59	58	58	58
Fishy	29	43	41	40	48	39
Soft	70	73	76	80	68	84

6. *The Sensory Profile of the Optimum Products*

The equations that were developed to relate formula variables to ratings can be used to predict the cost of the optimum as well as the likely profile of attribute ratings. One needs to insert the formula levels into each equation, respectively, in order to estimate the likely attribute ratings. Table 9 shows the expected sensory profile of the "optimum formulations." It demonstrates that the adult "optimum" product will have a clearly different sensory profile than will the child "optimum" product. The adult product will be harder and less mild than the child product. Furthermore, the adult product will cost substantially more (41.0 cost units) than will the child product (37.0 cost units).

7. *The Optimal Product for Two Consumer Segments Simultaneously*

The previous exercise with the product model revealed that the formulation of the adult and the child products differ from each other. Optimizing a product for children may not produce an acceptable adult product, and vice versa. It may be necessary to develop a product which simultaneously satisfies both consumer segments (namely, adult and child), recognizing at the same time that this single product will not be the overall optimum for either segment alone.

In order to simultaneously optimize the acceptance of fish cakes for the two consumer segments, it is necessary to select one of the segments as the target for optimization and then to optimize the produce formulations for that group, subject to a constraint. The constraint is that the acceptance (or liking rating) of the product by the segment must exceed a specific cutoff level. For instance, we might wish to optimize the acceptance rating of fish cakes for adults, subject to the constraint that the children's liking rating of the optimum must exceed a predetermined value. We can look at the ratings of the competition, to get an idea of the best cutoff value, above which the children's liking must lie. For instance, we find that the majority of fish cakes products are rated between 30 and 45 by teens and children (see Table 2). If we want a highly acceptable adult product, and yet a product which is acceptable to children (vs. competitors), we would opt to produce a product whose acceptance to children should equal or exceed 45.

Table 9 presents a formulation which is highly acceptable to adults and which satisfies constraints on child acceptance. The most acceptable products are shown, one for child acceptance constrained to lie above 50, and one for child acceptance lying above 45 (Formulas B and C). They differ in formulation and in cost of goods.

The right hand side of Table 9 shows optimal formulations for child acceptance, subject to constraints in adult acceptance (while most exceed either 20, or 25, respectively). Below the formulations are the attribute profiles of the products.

8. *The Optimal Products for Specific Cost Constraints*

Another problem which often arises is to generate an acceptable product, at a specific cost of goods. The cost of spice, whitefish, pollock and filler fluctuates. Furthermore, bigger fish cakes are often more acceptable to the consumer than are smaller fish cakes (especially to adults, who look for a high quality-to-price relation). The bigger fish cakes are proportionally more expensive to the manufacturer. In a competitive market, therefore, one advantage to the marketer is the ability to offer higher-quality products at a competitive or lower price.

A product model, such as the one we have constructed here, can facilitate the discovery of those particular formulations which generate high-quality products at current prices of goods. (Quality is measured either by overall acceptability, or even by direct ratings of "perceived quality".)

In order to determine the particular formulations of products which are most acceptable, we can optimize product liking, subject to a cost constraint. Table 10 shows four different formulations that are obtained when we subject the product

Table 10. Optimal Formulations for Total Panel under Cost Constraints

Formulation	*No Cost Constraint*	*Cost 37.5*	*Less Than 35.0*	*This Amount 32.5*
Whitefish	4.4	4.4	4.4	1.68
Pollock	0.0	5.0	4.44	1.03
Filler	5.6	.6	1.16	7.29
Weight	1.2	1.1	1.0	1.0
Spice	2.0	1.87	1.87	1.63
Liking				
L/D Total	32	29	27	13
Adults	11	23	18	10
Teens	87	25	11	−31
Child	54	38	55	44
Cost of Goods	47	37.5	35	32.5
Sensory Profile				
Mild	44	61	63	66
Spicy	59	61	59	58
Fishy	58	32	38	57
Soft	36	83	81	83

to the different cost constraints. Each constraint lowers the total allowable cost of goods (thus increasing the profit margin). We see from Table 10 that when we do not impose cost constraints we still have a product which costs less than the most expensive product we could make. The costliest product is not necessarily the most acceptable product. It may be too spicy, be too large, etc. The cost of goods of the optimal product without constraints equals 47. Suppose, now, we wish to lower the cost of goods. What combination of formula variables generates the most acceptable product, subject to the particular cost constraint. Table 10 shows the formulations and the sensory and attribute profiles that we would obtain. We can continue this exercise, continuing to lower the allowable cost of goods. By using the product model, we can ascertain precisely what formulation at specified cost of goods generates the best product.

9. *Sensory Characteristics As Constraints: Marketing Two Products*

One of the more interesting areas of marketing concerns the selection of the optimal set of products to produce for specific manufacturing capabilities. Let us assume, for a moment, that we have only these five ingredients to vary. Is it possible to generate two very highly acceptable products for adults, one product with a flavor that is bland and one that is very sharp or spicy (not bland)? This strategy should appeal to two different "taste" segments simultaneously in the adult segment.

In order to address this issue, let us up the product model to generate two

Table 11. Optimal Formulations of Two Adult-Oriented Products—"Mild" Fish Cake and a Sharper-Tasting Fish Cake

Formulation	*Sharper (Not Mild)*	*(Mild)*
Whitefish	4.4	4.4
Pollock	5.0	5.0
Filler	0.6	0.6
Weight	1.2	1.2
Spice	1.90	1.76
Liking		
L/D Total	29	29
Adult	23	25
Teens	12	23
Child	52	41
Cost of Goods	41	41
Sensory Profiles		
Mild	47.5	65
Spicy	59	60
Fish Flavor	40	23
Soft	65	94

products. One product will be very bland or mild. Its perceived mildness (of flavor) should lie at the high end of the scale. The scores achieved by the competitors on mildness range between a low of 15 and a high of 46 (see Table 2). We can set our constraint for mildness to lie lower than 50 (spicy, not mild) or higher than 65 (very mild, bland). The first product will be a spicier, more flavorful product.

Continuing this approach, consider the two products generated by the model, in Table 11. The profile of the mild product (mild = 65) differs from the profile of the less mild, more flavorful product (mildness = 47.5); this allows the marketer to introduce two different products.

10. *Comparison of Product Modeling to Traditional Methods*

Product modeling procedures answer many of the same questions as does traditional product testing. The primary difference lies in the approach. Traditional market researchers concentrate on the reactions of many consumers to a limited set of product alternatives. Generally, researchers prefer to deal with two to four different products when they perform their consumer tests. With this limited scope it takes several tests to generate the database needed to properly guide R&D in the formulation of consumer-acceptable products which meet manufacturing and marketing specifications.

In contrast to the traditional approach, product modeling requires the development of a large number of product prototypes early in the marketing process.

Although many researchers and product manufacturers feel that this is an expensive investment, it may be a very effective way by which the marketer can truly guide the product development process toward a specific marketing or business target. The discovery and proper utilization of patterns in the consumer data facilitate a quick determination of the path a product developer should take to meet the needs of the marketing and manufacturing objective. It has been shown how the same integrated database can generate these benefits:

- Develop the product overall
- Develop the product within constrained costs of goods
- Develop the product to satisfy two groups simultaneously, each of which has a unique preference spectrum

IV. SUMMARY AND CONCLUSIONS

Since the early 1960s many methodologies have been introduced to deal with the problem of product development. The consensus is that product development is a time-consuming, costly, and risky endeavor. In this paper we have addressed all these issues. It has been shown how laboratory testing can reduce the lead time for product introductions. To the extent that laboratory testing complements test marketing, both time and financial savings take place. Since this methodology facilitates the simultaneous testing of a wide array of alternative products (and the selecting of the most acceptable one), the risk of missing a superior product is reduced. In addition to these product planning aspects, this strategy also carries with it implications for advertising and pricing. By identifying the levels of attributes that characterize the winning product, the product planner provides the advertising agency with the components for the creative strategy and a unique advertising message. Similarly, the ability to develop a less costly product (as in the case of constrained optimization) facilitates a flexible pricing strategy. Thus, for example, a company can price its product at the lower end for any given product category or not raise its price at the same rate as the competition.

Either way, guidelines for product, advertising, and pricing strategies become clearer at an earlier stage of the development process, thus increasing the likelihood of favorable market performance.

NOTES

1. Section II is based on *Management of the New Product Function,* New York: Association of National Advertisers, Inc. 1981, pp. 1–9.
2. Subsection C is based on Richard R. Batsell and Yoram Wind, "Product Testing: Current Methods and Needed Developments," *Journal of Market Research Society,* Vol. 22, No. 2, 1980, pp. 115–39.
3. Moskowitz, Howard R., "Magnitude Estimation: Notes on What, How, When, and Why to Use It," *Journal of Food Quality,* Vol. 3, 1977, pp. 195–227.

STRATEGIES OF COLLECTIVE ACTION:
THE CASE OF THE FINANCIAL SERVICES INDUSTRY

Charles Fombrun and W. Graham Astley

I. INTRODUCTION

During the course of 1981:

- The BankAmerica Corp., parent company of Bank of America, the largest U.S. commerical bank, offered $53 million in common stock for the nation's largest discount brokerage firm, Charles Schwab and Company.
- The Security Pacific National Bank announced that its 600 branches throughout California would execute securities transactions for the bank's customers through an agreement with Fidelity Brokerage Services, one of the largest discount brokerage firms in the United States.

Advances in Strategic Management, Volume 2, pages 125–139.

ISBN: 0-89232-409-0

- Key executives from a dozen U.S. and Canadian banks, including Manufacturer's Hanover, First Chicago, Bank of Montreal, and First Interstate Bancorp, flew to a secret meeting in Chicago to form a joint venture that would create the first national retail banking network.
- The Prudential Insurance Company of America jumped into the brokerage business with its $385-million acquisition of Bache Group, Inc.
- Over 200 savings and loan associations across the United States joined forces in creating a firm which would provide nationwide marketing and technical assistance in a jointly owned nationwide brokerage business.

These seemingly isolated events are symptomatic of an era of turmoil for the financial services industry. A long tradition of conservatism and protectionism is being cast aside as banks and nonbanks scramble for position in the new and continually emerging financial services industry, where such unlikely institutions as Citibank, American Express, Sears, Roebuck, and the Prudential Insurance Company are brought into competitive disarray. At the same time, government is forced to reassess its role as the powerful overseer of the banking industry. The ensuing debates over the Glass–Steagall Act that separates commercial banking from investment banking and the McFadden Act restricting interstate banking, polarize groups of banks and institutions, which in turn creates significant opportunities for collaborative lobbying and other forms of interorganizational relations between banks and nonbanks. Thus, the current backdrop of the emergent financial services industry is provoking both competitive and collaborative relations among a host of firms vying for strategic position.

The purposes of this paper are to:

- Present some conceptual frameworks for understanding the trends facing the financial services industry and the kinds of interorganizational relationships they are provoking;
- Discuss the role of collective action in producing these interfirm structures;
- Develop a model of collective planning as a strategic activity at the interorganizational level of analysis that goes beyond business strategy and corporate strategy.

II. ENVIRONMENTAL TRENDS AND STRATEGIC RESPONSES

The traditional financial services industry includes a wide range of firms ranging from commercial banks and savings and loan associations to brokerage houses and insurance companies. Into this familiar set of firms has penetrated a wide range of competitive raiders that includes a department store chain and a steel company. These nonregulated competitors, through far-flung retail empires and credit services, offer a feasible and desirable alternative to traditional consumer banking services and threaten the survival of institutions subject to Regulation Q and other "safeguards" of the U.S. financial system.

The current pressures on the financial services industry are multifaceted. They stem from a complex combination of government policy, Federal Reserve action, global disinflation, corporate activity, and consumer reaction, which have created an environmental context characterized by recession and lofty interest rates (*Business Week,* April 12, 1982).

Exhibit 1 summarizes some of the current environmental trends and their impact on the delivery of financial services. The persistence of high real interest rates has created an environmental context that favors innovation in the efficient delivery of financial services while driving some of the institutions constrained by Regulation Q (such as thrift associations) into bankruptcy. Threatened with basic survival, the responses of firms within the industry have varied. Thrift institutions have sought mergers with larger institutions possessing more balanced portfolios. Competitive regional banks like Texas Commerce Bancshares

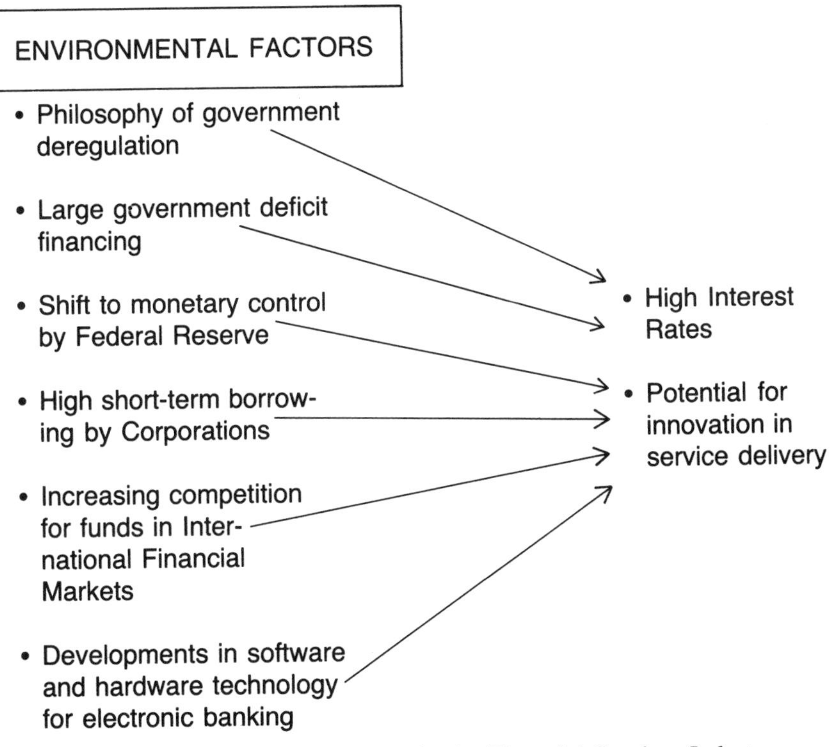

Exhibit 1. Environmental Trends in the Financial Services Industry.

and First City Bancorporation of Texas are emphasizing different markets, one retail, the other wholesale. At the same time, national banks like Bank of America look forward to becoming financial supermarkets (Osborn, 1981). First Interstate Bancorp, on the other hand, plans to franchise its name and services nationwide in a move that challenges the continued viability of the McFadden Act restricting interstate banking (Edwards, 1981).

These responses are taking place amid a general governmental stance favoring deregulation and increased competition, promised by the Depository Institutions Deregulation and Monetary Control Act of 1980, and scheduled for progressive implementation over the decade. As a consequence it raises the possibility of influence over legislative proceedings, and lobbying activity abounds. The American Bankers Association is a visible group in Washington, as is the U.S. League of Savings Associations. Possibly collusive agreements between institutions to influence the repeal of the McFadden Act can be surmised through the emergence of numerous national Automatic Teller Machine networks.

These pressure groups and interfirm arrangements represent a distinct level of strategizing that has been slow to infiltrate the theory and practice of planning. As the degree of interorganizational activity increases, and as formal and informal agreements, acquisitions, and mergers bind organizations in the industry closer together, the entire industry takes on a degree of integration and unity which goes beyond current conceptions of industrial competition. As an interorganizational network, single firms are related through their vested interests in an interlocked set possessing a high degree of internal cohesion and coordination (Astley and Fombrun, 1982). Consequently, the emergent situation increasingly calls for a strategic awareness of the dynamics of wider integrating networks of organizations and action appropriate for influencing the environmental context itself.

The role of government in this situation is to design legislation that acknowledges the existence of a high degree of interfirm organization and that channels the multiple sources of feedback generated by such collective action into socially preferred directions. The rest of this paper focuses on developing frameworks for relating organizational strategies at the business and corporate levels to what we term "collective strategy" and its attendant structural manifestations (Astley and Fombrun, 1982), and lays the groundwork for government's role as institutional manager of collective networks of interorganizational action.

III. COLLECTIVE STRATEGY: THE MISSING LINK

Strategic planning is typically described in terms of two levels: business strategy and corporate strategy. At the business level, strategy focuses on competition within a particular industry or product/market segment, whereas corporate-level strategy is primarily concerned with defining the set of businesses the organization should be in (Hofer and Schendel, 1978). Whether at the business level or at the corporate level, however, strategy is formulated from the point of view of a focal organization forced to deal with its external environment.

For organizations, strategy is a mechanism for voluntaristic adaptation to either the "task environment" or the "general environment" (Dill, 1958).

The task environment consists of particular customers, suppliers, competitors, regulatory agencies, and anyone with whom a focal organization has direct links during the normal course of its operations. The general environment, on the other hand, lies beyond the task environment and refers to domains which are not currently occupied by the focal organization but which have the potential for being so occupied.

As Bourgeois (1980) points out, these characterizations of the environment are tied to the perspective of a focal organization and directly correspond to business-level and corporate-level strategy. The task environment approximates the organization's industry or product/market sector and hence is relevant to business strategy, while the general environment, since it lies beyond present domains, is only relevant when corporate strategy attempts to reorient the organization toward new product/market niches. The notion of "turbulence" advanced by Emery and Trist (1965), however, goes well beyond these definitions. Turbulent environments exist when organizations are unable to select a viable course of action because the environment is richly interconnected and interdependent. Interdependence, per se, is not a problem if it can be grasped. However, turbulence results from the fact that environmental interdependencies arise which are obscured from the focal organization. Parts of the environment itself, beyond the purview of the focal organization, become interrelated, and since the focal organization is unaware of the existence of such interrelations it cannot plan to cope with their ramifications.

These linkages constitute an environmental "system" exhibiting properties that are independent of the action of any particular organization within the system. If this is so, then strategic planning is missing an important link in defining the relationship between firms and their environment. It has failed to adequately conceptualize collective strategies for coping with the system dynamics of interorganizational environments. As Exhibit 2 suggests, a collective strategy is a systemic response by a set of organizations which collaborate in order to absorb the variation presented by the interorganizational environment.

Following Alfred Chandler's (1962) familiar argument, each level of strategy is implemented through a set of structural mechanisms. Business strategy is largely effected through a set of organizational systems and processes that channel resources to relevant areas of the organization and give it its distinctive competence in the competitive product/market sector (Lawrence and Lorsch, 1967; Galbraith and Nathanson, 1978).

Corporate strategy, on the other hand, is implemented through a multidivisio-

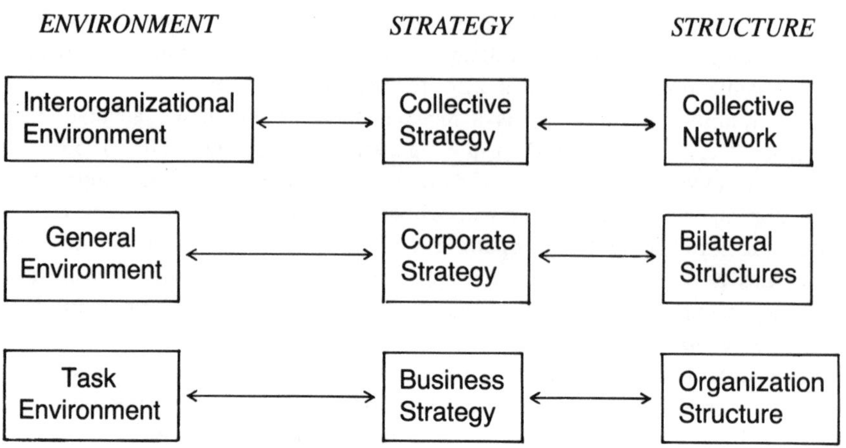

Exhibit 2. Environment, Strategy, and Structure.

nal structure driven by product, market, or functional interdependencies in the portfolio of businesses (Williamson, 1975; Thompson, 1967).

A collective strategy formulated to respond to environmental turbulence and designed to influence, through the interorganizational network, the nature of the environment itself is implemented through various interfirm linkages. Exhibit 3 distinguishes the different kinds of interorganizational linkages that emerge as firms struggle to implement the collective strategy they formulate for the network as a whole. Multilateral structures in and of themselves are designed to reflect a commitment by a subset of firms in the network to a joint position vis-à-vis an environmental circumstance. They are therefore tools for directly implementing

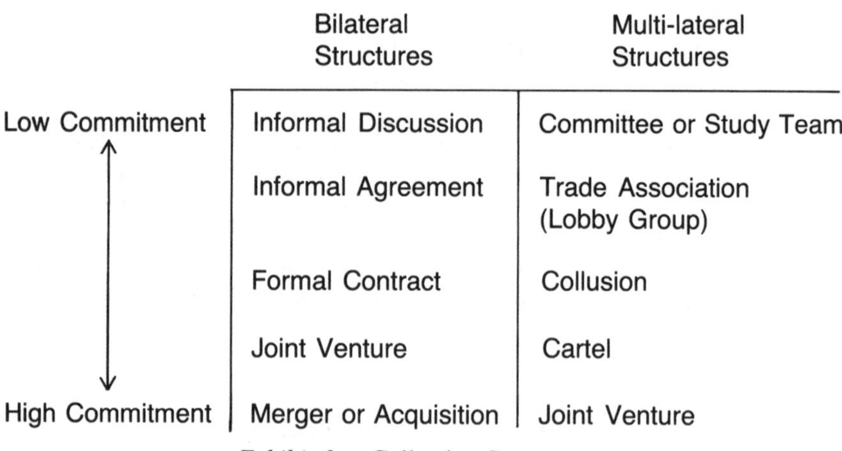

	Bilateral Structures	Multi-lateral Structures
Low Commitment	Informal Discussion	Committee or Study Team
	Informal Agreement	Trade Association (Lobby Group)
	Formal Contract	Collusion
	Joint Venture	Cartel
High Commitment	Merger or Acquisition	Joint Venture

Exhibit 3. Collective Structures.

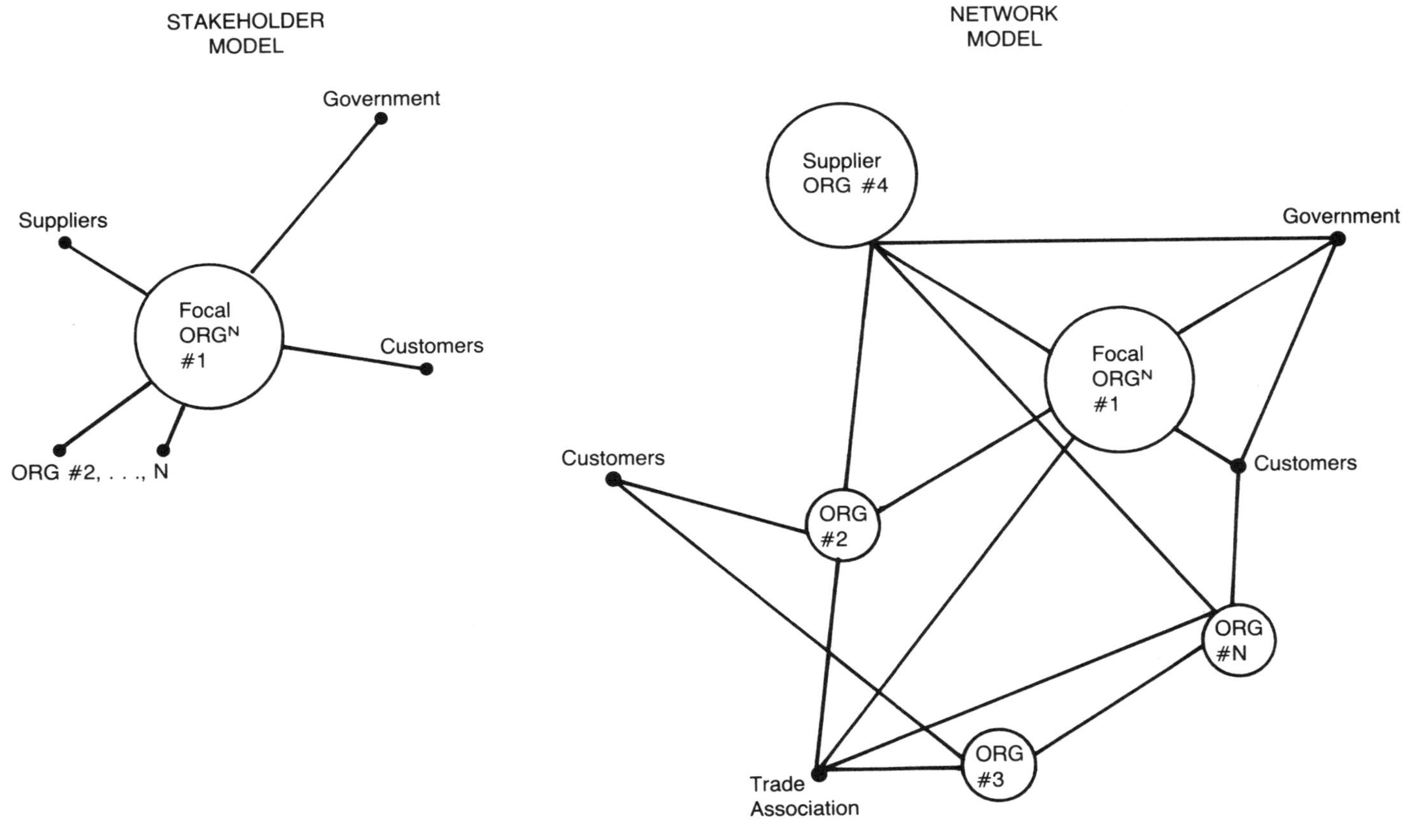

STAKEHOLDER
MODEL

Government
Suppliers
Focal
ORG^{N}
#1
Customers
ORG #2, . . ., N

NETWORK
MODEL

Supplier
ORG #4
Government
Focal
ORG^{N}
#1
Customers
Customers
ORG
#2
ORG
#N
ORG
#3
Trade
Association

Exhibit 4. Stakeholders and Networks.

collective strategy. Pairwise linkages, however, emerge in the process of implementing a corporate-level strategy to respond to the environment. These bilateral structures are largely developed by differentiated organizations in the industry. However, at an aggregate level, they have a synergistic effect and bind together into an interorganizational network the entire set of organizations in the industry. Thus single organizations are also unconscious actors in the coordination of the activities of all organizations in the network and in their net impact on the social system, government, and the consumer (Fombrun and Astley, 1981).

This point is illustrated in Exhibit 4. Single organizations pursuing a corporate strategy designed to respond to threats and opportunities in the external environment will negotiate with their stakeholders to resolve uncertainties in their operating domain (Emshoff and Freeman, 1978). The bilateral structures they create are manifestations of the organization's corporate strategy.

Beyond these bilateral structures, however, lies an intricate patterning of relationships that effectively binds the organizations in the network into a collectivity. It is this aggregated effect of multiple organizational interlocks that differentiates a "collective" approach from traditional stakeholder analysis (Astley and Fombrun, 1982).

The mutual interdependence among a varied set of organizations that are not directly interacting calls for strategizing at a different level of analysis, an understanding of the network pattern. The emergence of multilateral structures for coordination (e.g., study teams, cartels) is an explicit recognition of the interlocking interests of a group of organizations. It is reinforced by an aggregate pattern of relationships that is the bedrock of the collectivity.

IV. STRATEGIC PLANNING AND STAGE OF GROWTH

In his historical study of American industry, Chandler (1962) described the emergence of a formal strategy and its accompanying structure as a function of organizational growth. Exhibit 5 diagrams the development of the three levels of strategy as a function of growth stage.

Small firms are typically concerned with business-level activity, and their primary external linkages involve negotiation and resolution of input–output dependencies (Pfeffer and Salancik, 1978). Increasing volume and geographical expansion lead organizations toward involvement in the external domain. More linkages are built with relevant actors in the environment, though these may be primarily responsive or defensive linkages. Reciprocal personnel flows, informal contracts, and interfirm agreements which create a "negotiated environment" (Cyert and March, 1963) are characteristic of this stage, and the emergent structures of coordination are largely bilateral.

As new products or markets are added, a corporate strategy is formulated to

Organizational Growth (Time, Size, Complexity)	COLLECTIVE STRATEGY	CORPORATE STRATEGY	BUSINESS STRATEGY
CREATION OF BUSINESS	Negotiate input/output dependencies	Informal	Design operational Systems
INCREASED VOLUME GEOGRAPHIC EXPANSION	Personnel exchanges Bilateral Agreements	Product/Market Expansion Innovation	Formalize Departmental Structure
NEW PRODUCTS DIVERSIFICATION	Lobbying Pressure Groups	Formalized Portfolio Mgt.	Multi-Divisional Structure
MULTINATIONAL CONGLOMERATE	Political Statesmanship Institutional Management	Stakeholder Management	Global Structure

Exhibit 5. Strategy and Organizational Growth.

manage the diversified portfolio of businesses. Key organizational personnel are assigned public relations duties, and their role takes on a quality of organizational representation. They are involved in community activities and frequently are active and influential members of civic associations. Informally, multilateral relations begin to emerge and the organization is visible in trade associations and other pressure groups, and frequently called upon to exert influence on key legislators in matters of public policy.

As the organization continues to grow across geographical regions and product domains, the opportunity for collective influences increases rapidly. Multilateral structures for lobbying, through membership in formal and informal associations or pressure groups, become obvious tools for strategic influence across the interorganizational network. Key organizational representatives take on an institutional function, the representation of the interests of all participants in the interorganizational network. Through membership and leadership in such influential groups as the Business Roundtable, the American Bankers Association, or on multilateral study teams, they advise and influence governmental bodies and the legislative apparatus (Weidenbaum, 1980).

While growth favors the emergence of a collective awareness, it is important to recognize that all organizations are under pressure to generate more and more elaborate collective strategies if they are to effectively respond to their environments. Adjusting corporate strategy is a far less effective response than controlling the contextual preconditions that create favorable operating environments. As organizations attain central positions in the interorganizational network, they emerge as managers of the collectivity. Their activities must therefore fulfill a statesmanship role involving the negotiation of preferences, the resolution of conflict, the control of collective outcomes, and a host of other political functions.

V. STRATEGIC RESPONSES IN THE FINANCIAL SERVICES INDUSTRY

The frameworks of Exhibits 2–5 provide an underlying rationale for understanding some of the dynamics currently taking place among firms involved in the delivery of financial services. As we suggested earlier, a wide range of traditionally noncompetitive firms have entered the protected terrain of banks and thrift institutions to offer broad-based financial services. Merrill-Lynch's famous Cash Management Account, in offering checking services through Banc One of Ohio, largely threatens the operating domain of mainline retail banks. In infringing the intent of the Glass–Steagall Act, it calls for a strategic response that goes beyond a business strategy concern for maintaining competitiveness.

Simultaneously, in Sears, Roebuck's purchase of Dean Witter Reynolds, the giant retailer sidesteps the provisions of the McFadden Act and the Douglas

Amendment designed to restrict interstate banking. A nationwide market for financial services is available to it through its Sears outlets and credit card. This also calls for an institutional response from banks and thrift associations that goes beyond a reformulation of corporate strategy.

Exhibit 6 diagrams the strategies banks and other financial intermediaries are pursuing as a result of increased competition in their primary domain. As the exhibit suggests, a threat in the basic "task" environment of banks and thrifts is provoking realignments at the business, corporate, and collective levels.

A. Business Strategy

At the business level, commercial banks are considering response strategies that involve capitalizing on their strengths as short-term investors for organizations and operational agents for consumers. For them the business-level decision is whether to specialize in the delivery of a single service to a specific client group (consumers or business) or to move to universal banking and the provision of an entire range of services on a national level. The larger commercial banks seem to be choosing the generalist route, while smaller regional banks stress specialization and market segmentation. For thrift institutions weighted down by the cost of capital in relation to their loan portfolio, bankruptcy has been a frequent solution. To stem the outflow of funds and reduce the competitive pressure for both banks and thrifts, government allowed the creation of NOW accounts and all-savers certificates (Blount, 1982).

B. Corporate Strategy

At the corporate level, all firms in the traditional segment of the industry have been pursuing mergers and acquisitions as ways of coping with competitive pressures from mutual funds, money funds, and cash management accounts, and strengthening their operations across a range of financial services. Thus INA's merger with Connecticut General places it in second position behind Aetna Life and Casualty as a publicly held insurance company. INA also holds a controlling interest in Paine Webber, the brokerage firm, which gives the merged firm considerable potential for consolidating its financial service offerings across both risk and investment management. Chemical Bank's struggle to acquire the Florida National Banks of Florida chain is an attempt to strategically diversify across markets and should position the bank better for interstate banking when the McFadden Act is rescinded.

A number of firms outside the traditional boundaries of the financial services industry are diversifying into it. Such well-publicized mergers as American Express with Shearson, Sears, Roebuck with Dean Witter, and Prudential Insurance with the Bache Group are significant delineations by nonbanks of a corporate strategy that puts them in direct competition with regulated banks.

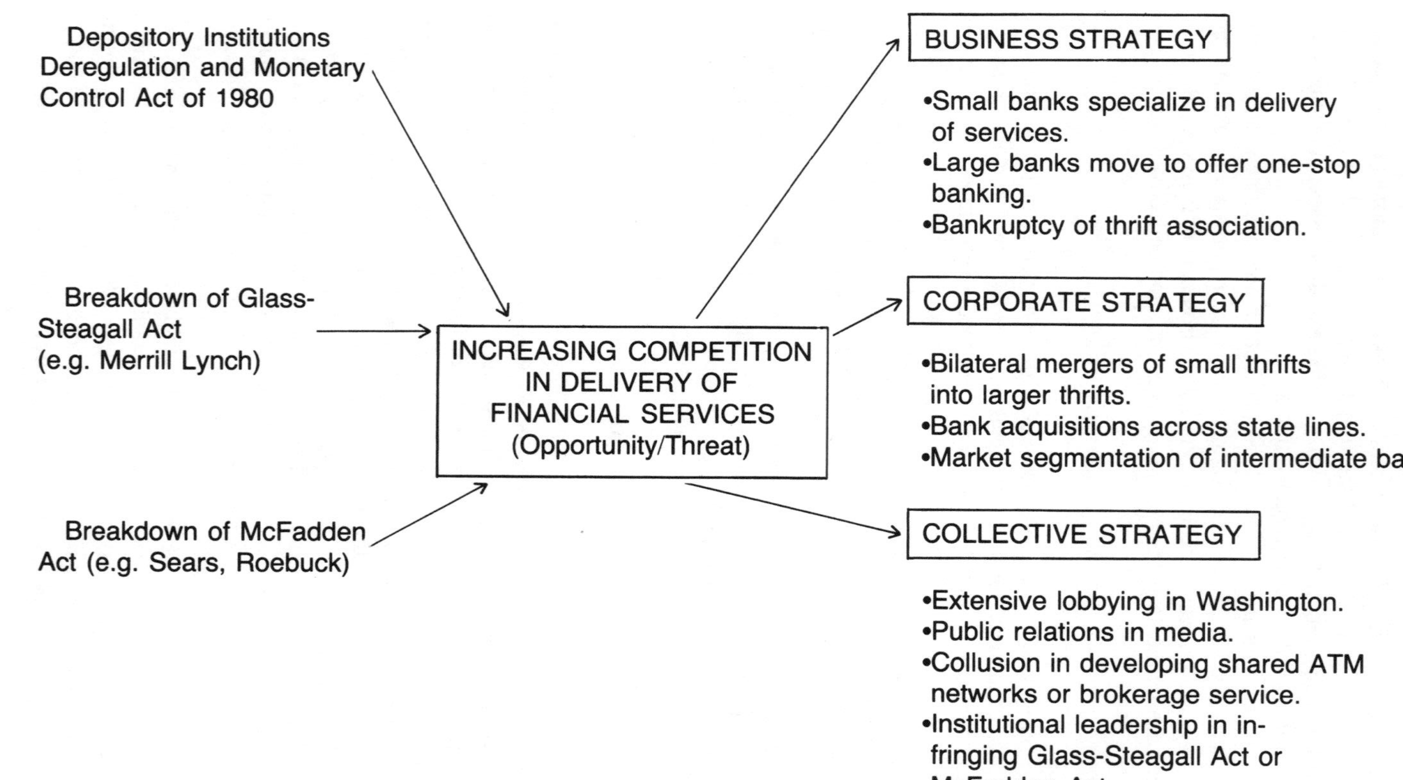

Exhibit 6. Strategic Responses in Financial Service Delivery.

C. Collective Strategy

Finally, at the collective level, an awareness of joint interests among different segments of the industry is manifest in the widespread emergence of shared Automatic Teller Machine networks. As banks and thrifts hook into electronic networks, interstate banking becomes a reality limited only in terms of the kinds of transactions regulators are allowing.

The Savings Association Financial Corporation announced in November 1981 brings together savings and loan associations from across the U.S. for a nationwide brokerage service that will provide joint marketing and technical assistance for a wholly owned brokerage subsidiary, the Savings Association Investment Securities.

At the same time, numerous bilateral agreements and acquisitions are linking firms both within traditional industrial sectors and across sectors. Exhibit 7 lists some of the more significant acquisitions that have taken place or are under negotiation. Clearly these bilateral linkages are promoting a high degree of interconnectedness across a broad range of traditionally unrelated firms and industrial sectors. They act to bind them into an emergent collectivity.

D. The Role of Government

In this collective environment of banks and nonbanks, government has an important role to play, one that involves carefully considering the impact of

INTRA-INDUSTRY ACQUISITION/MERGER	• Marine Midland and Industrial Valley • INA and Connecticut General • Chemical Bank and Florida National Banks • Chase Manhattan and Equimark • Girard and Farmers Bank of Delaware • NCNB and First National Bank of Lake City, Florida • First National Boston and Casco-Northern
INTER-INDUSTRY ACQUISITION/MERGER	• Sears, Roebuck and Dean Witter • Prudential and Bache Group • BankAmerica and Charles Schwab • INA and Paine Webber • Phibro and Salomon Brothers • National Steel and United Financial

Exhibit 7. Strategic Acquisitions/Mergers.

de-regulation and the repeal of the Glass–Steagall and McFadden Acts in terms of two key criteria:

1. *Equity:* The net effect of these collective strategies is to favor some sectors at the expense of other sectors. Thus, small regional banks may be absorbed by large national banks crossing state lines. To what extent does that mean a loss of service and responsiveness to local banking needs? Who loses? Who gains?
2. *Efficiency:* How much more efficient is the financial system in delivering banking services and facilitating transactions under increased competition? How much more fragile and susceptible to failure is the financial system as a whole?

These issues are largely complicated by the involvement of government at three levels: local, state, and federal. It is also compounded by the incursion into the United States of foreign banks which, under current regulation, are far less restricted in terms of interstate operations and investment banking. To resolve these regulatory strains, it is vital that both distributive justice and efficiency be carefully assessed.

As this article has stressed, these enormously pragmatic considerations cannot be discussed without an appreciation for the interorganizational embeddedness and complex pattern of interfirm linkages that has emerged over time as banks and nonbanks have attempted to resolve the problem raised by technological progress in the processing of transactions and the high potential for cooperation between traditionally unrelated organizational sectors.

IV. CONCLUSION

Collective action looms as the challenge of contemporary strategic management. The importance of formulating strategies that recognize the interorganizational network of organizations in which the focal firm is embedded cannot be denied. As interdependence among different industrial sectors continues to amplify, strategic planning will increasingly require, as an explicit part of its activities, the formulation and channeling of influence across an interorganizational network. As the financial services industry demonstrates a lingering query is government's awareness of the broad landscape of interrelationships it is trying to control. Are governmental control systems capable of apprehending the complexity of the industry? Are its data-gathering systems geared to a mapping of collective aggregated effects? Can government effectively guide the system toward both efficient and equitable ends? These are challenges that require a collective response.

REFERENCES

Astley, W. G. and Fombrun, C. (1983), "Collective Strategy: The Social Ecology of the Interorganizational Environment," The Academy of Management Review, Vol. 8, forthcoming.

Blount, E. (1982), "New Directions in the Financial Services Industry," *Journal of Business Strategy,* Vol. 2, No. 4, (Spring), 21–29.

Bourgeois, L. J. (1980), "Strategy and Environment: A Conceptual Integration." *The Academy of Management Review,* Vol. 5, No. 1, (January).

Business Week (1982), "Banking's Squeeze", (April 12), pp. 67–86.

______ (1982), "Electronic Banking", (January 18), pp. 70–80.

Chandler, A. D. (1962), *Strategy and Structure,* Cambridge, Mass.: The M.I.T. Press.

Cyert, Richard M. and J. G. March (1963), *A Behavioral Theory of the Firm. Englewood Cliffs, N.J.: Prentice-Hall.*

Dill, William R. (1958), "Environment as an Influence on Managerial Autonomy" Administrative *Science Quarterly,* 2, (March), pp. 409–443.

Edwards, R. D. (1981), "Commercial Banking Review: Geographic Expansion", *United States Banker,* (March), pp. 18–30.

Emery, F. E. and E. L. Trist (1965), "The Causal Texture of Organizational Environments" *Human Relations,* 18, (February), pp. 21–32.

Emshoff, J. R. and R. E. Freeman (1978), "Stakeholder Management," Wharton Applied Research Center, Working Paper No. 3-78.

Fombrun, C. and W. G. Astley (1983), Beyond "Beyond Corporate Strategy: The Role of Collective Action", Journal of Business Strategy, Vol. 4, No. 1.

Galbraith, J. R. and D. Nathanson (1978), *Strategy Implementation: The Role of Structure and Process* New York: West Publishing Co.

Hofer, Charles W. and D. Schendel (1978), *Strategy Formulation: Analytical Concepts,* New York: West Publishing.

Lawrence, Paul R. and J. W. Lorsch (1967), *Organization and Environment: Managing Differentiation and Integration,* Boston: Graduate School of Business Administration, Harvard University.

Osborn, N. (1981), "Will America Embrace Universal Banking?", *Institutional Investor,* (December), 91–103.

Parker, G. C. (1981), "Now Management Will Make or Break the Bank," *Harvard Business Review,* (November–December).

Pfeffer, J. and G. R. Salancik (1978), *The External Control of Organizations,* New York: Harper and Row.

Thompson, J. D. (1967), *Organization in Action.* New York: McGraw-Hill.

Weidenbaum, M. L. (1980), "Public Policy: No Longer a Spectator Sport for Business," *Journal of Business Strategy, 1,* 46–53.

Williamson, O. (1975), *Markets and Hierarchies: Analysis and Antitrust Implications* New York: The Free Press.

AN INVENTORY OF SELECTED ACADEMIC RESEARCH ON STRATEGIC MANAGEMENT

Lawrence R. Jauch

ABSTRACT

The paper provides a description of a variety of pieces of research conducted by a sample of leading scholars from North American universities. Current work is categorized as dealing with process, content, integrated efforts, methodology, and pedagogy. No attempt is made at evaluative commentary. Rather, the intent is to array the various current efforts to illustrate the type of work going on in the domain of strategy.

I. INTRODUCTION

The publication of Schendel and Hofer's book (1979) summarizing the state of the art of strategic management research has spurred heightened interest in the

Advances in Strategic Management, Volume 2, pages 141–175.

ISBN: 0-89232-409-0

field. A variety of "branches" of inquiry have been developing. At this juncture it is useful to identify some of the various kinds of work in progress or recently completed by leading researchers to get a sense of the directions in which the field may be moving and its scope.

To accomplish this objective, the author conducted a survey of selected academics in North America to discern the types of research topics currently under investigation. A list of over 80 potential respondents was identified from recent (1980/81) authors compiled from three sources: (1) strategic management papers in 1980 *Proceedings* of American Institute for Decision Sciences and the Academy of Management; (2) strategic management articles in 1980 issues of the Academy of Management *Review, Journal,* and *Strategic Management Journal;* and/or (3) a recent book related to strategic management. A request was made for abstracts and/or working papers describing recent research projects these authors had conducted. Fifty-five respondents provided the requested information.

Before proceeding to describe the areas of research, several limitations should be recognized. First, the sample does not include researchers or practitioners outside North America. Second, this is not a comprehensive literature review of current published research. Third, some of the "categories" of research may be over- or underrepresented, given the original compilation of respondents and the response pattern. Fourth, some of the descriptions of research are more thorough than others since some respondents provided only brief abstracts of their research while others provided more detailed working papers or summaries of their work. Thus, the bibliography provides references for those interested in more details of the work going on.[1]

Despite these limitations, it is believed that this overview of selected recent and "not-yet-published" literature provides some indication of the general directions in which many strategic management researchers are moving. To get a quick glance at this overview, a framework of research areas was developed inductively, as shown in Tables 1, 2, and 3.

Similar to Hofer's (1975) literature review, research by this sample focuses on strategy process and content. Those working on "process" emphasize behavioral and decision structure variables affecting strategy formulation and implementation in the organization. Those emphasizing "content" examine various conditions under which different types of strategies (decision outcomes) are (or should be) used. There were some efforts in this sample which do not fit neatly into these two categories—works trying to integrate process and content, methodological prescriptions, and research on pedagogy. The writing is further categorized by whether it is empirical or conceptual in nature. In each case, however, putting anyone's work in one cell or another may ignore some overlaps which exist. Thus, the entries in the framework are not necessarily indicative of the amount of attention devoted to any given area.

In the remainder of the chapter, brief descriptions of the general category in the framework will be followed by summations of the work being done in each area. Finally, brief conclusions are offered.

II. RESEARCH EMPHASIZING STRATEGIC PROCESSES

Three major topics of study which relate to the formulation and implementation of strategy are (1) behavioral decision processes, (2) strategy formulators, and (3) planning and implementation processes (see Table 1).

A. Behavioral Decision Processes

Studies of behavioral factors influencing the strategy decision-making process include political factors, managerial values, management ideology, and strategic change. A common theme is the question of whether strategic decision making can, or ought to be, "rational."

1. *Politics, Power, and Coalition Development*

Research here explores conceptual models of how politics and power are used to influence strategic decisions.

Bower and Doz (1979) argue that the principal difficulty in formulating strategy is based on the problem for the manager of combining "positional and managerial aspects of the management task". They point out that "the management of power is an explicit CEO function." Mintzberg (WIP) is completing a book on *Power In and Around Organizations,* and Pennings (WIP) is working on sociopsychological and political aspects of strategic decision making in public- and private-sector organizations.

Narayanan and Fahey (1981) have developed a conceptual framework centering on the evaluation of coalitions and their behaviors in the context of individual strategic issues or decisions. Fahey (1981) has also done some empirical work indicating that rational *and* political behaviors are interwoven at every phase of the decision process. Other theoretical papers by Fahey (1981), Dutton and Fahey (1981), and Mazzolini (1980b, 1981b) outline the linkages and interactions among rational/analytical, organizational/bureaucratic, and political/rational modes of strategic decision making.

Huff (1980c) also outlines five ways in which organizational politics might be viewed:

1. A structural model in which power derives primarily from subunit jurisdiction.
2. A group model in which power comes from organized special interests.
3. An elite model in which power is the result of the informal influence of key individuals.

Table 1. Research Emphasizing Strategic Processes

Subjects of Study	*Primarily Conceptual*	*Primarily Empirical*
A. Decision Processes		
1. Power, Politics and Coalitions	Bower & Doz, 1979; Dutton & Fahey, 1981; Fahey, 1982; Huff, 1980c; Mazzolini, 1980b, 1981b; Mintzberg, WIP; Narayanan & Fahey, 1981; Pennings, WIP;	Bourgeois, 1981b; Fahey, 1981;
2. Managerial Values	Mitroff, 1981;	Jenson, O'Neill & Saunders, 1981a,b,c; Jenson & Saunders, 1981;
3. Management Ideology and Philosophy	Camillus, 1981a; Mitroff & Mason, 1980, 1981; Quinn, 1980a,b; 1981; Ramaprasad & Bourgeois, 1981; Wu, 1981;	Anderson, WIPa; Huff, WIP; Huff & Pondy, WIP; Miller, DeVries & Toulouse, 1980;
4. Strategic Change	Jauch & Wilson, 1979; Miller, 1980; Mintzberg & Waters, 1980; Ramaprasad, 1981;	Bourgeois, 1980a; Huff, 1980b, 1981; Lyles, 1981; Lyles and Mitroff, 1981a,b; Miller & Friesen, 1980a;
B. Strategy Formulators		
1. Roles and Activities		Hambrick, 1981a,b,c; Jemison, 1981a,c; Lenz, WIPa,b; Pennings, WIPa; Tichy, WIP; Tichy, Devanna & Warren, WIP;
2. Turnover		Jauch, Martin & Osborn, 1981; Osborn, Jauch, Martin & Glueck, 1981;
3. Entrepreneurs and Venture Strategy	Brockhaus, 1980; Vesper, 1980a, 1982; Vesper, Sexton & Kent, 1981;	Cooper, WIPa; Pennings, WIPb; Vesper, WIPa,b,c; Vicars, Jauch & Wilson, 1980;
C. Planning and Implementation		
1. Planning: Value, Models	Klein & Newman, 1980; Lachenmeyer, 1980; Leontiades, 1981b; Montanari, 1981a; Montanari & Wetherbe, 1980;	Farley, Capon & Hulbert, WIP; Henry, 1980, 1981; Leontiades & Tezel, 1980; Ramaprasad & Knod, 1981;

continued

Table 1—Continued

Subjects of Study	*Primarily Conceptual*	*Primarily Empirical*
2. Implementation	Camillus, 1980a,b, 1981b,c,d; Camillus & Grant, 1980; Camillus & Birnberg, WIP; Grant & Snodgrass, WIP; Iyer & Ramaprasad, 1980; Lenz & Lyles, 1981a; Lorange, 1980, 1982a, 1982b; MacMillan, 1980; Tavel, 1980; Tushman, WIP; Vancil, 1979, 1980; Yavitz & Newman, WIP;	Lenz & Lyles, 1981b;

WIP—Work in progress

4. An incremental/bureaucratic model in which the influence on policy comes primarily from past commitments and current crises.
5. A systems/resource model in which power depends upon control over resources.

Huff's paper suggests that each approach to organization politics leads to different views of how policy level decisions are generated, and each model suggests different ways in which policy decisions can be changed over time.

Finally, Bourgeois (1981b) describes a pilot study to test the implications of more or less "rational" policymaking methods for economic performance of firms in varying environments.

2. *Managerial Values.*

Values can, of course, influence how power is viewed or used and alter the way in which strategic issues are recognized and dealt with.

In a series of papers drawing on the National Opinion Research Council General Social Survey data, Jensen, O'Neill and Saunders (1981a,b,c) and Jensen and Saunders (1981) have explored opinion differences among managers, technical personnel, "support personnel," and the more general population. As a group, managers hold quite different opinions from those outside the firm and from technical personnel. While the data are cross-sectional, various gaps are found to exist between external groups and those internal to the firm. "The process of absorbing these value gaps is a strategic problem." In fact, value clusters may be a variable used to predict the formation or existence of coalitions whose objective may be to exercise influence over strategy formulation and implementation.

Mitroff's (1981) paper begins an exploration of how two personality theories (Jung and Transactional Analysis) might be integrated to explain strategic behavior. To the extent that this can be done, a richer understanding of personality-based value orientations of strategists may result.

3. *Management Ideology and Philosophy*

The analysis of general ideology or philosophical orientation of managers is another important attempt to explain and predict strategic decision behavior.

A major line of work here is based on the assumption that an incremental process is the inevitable mode used for strategy setting. Such a philosophy is best represented by the work of Quinn (1980a,b, 1981). In his book Quinn (1980a) describes how 10 large companies arrived at their most important strategic changes. Parts of the incremental process logic used include: broad, tentative goals and iterative commitments; subordinate participation and flexible option modes; interactive learning and innovative posturing; and proactive consensus building among different management styles. He argues that incremental processes should be consciously used to integrate the psychological, political, and informational needs of organizations in setting strategy.

Anderson (WIPa) has examined cognitive decision styles of executives which are most closely related to high strategic performance. Contrary to what an incrementalist philosophy might hypothesize, his preliminary results suggest that systematic, logical thinking is more closely tied to high performance in strategic tasks than intuitive thinking.

In a different but related vein, Miller, de Vries, and Toulouse (1980) suggest that "locus of control" was closely related to strategy, structure, and environment in 33 different types of firms. "Internals" (those who believe they exert control over their environment) are more activity oriented and are more likely than externals (those who attribute life events to fate) to possess entrepreneurial tendencies such as greater innovation and risk taking.

Some work on the logic of strategic management is also going on. Since policy and planning treat issues which are open-ended, fuzzy, and ill structured, Mitroff and Mason (1981) argue that the subject is essentially philosophical. In another paper they point out how various philosophical approaches might be used (Mitroff and Mason, 1980). There they note that:

> organizations are bodies of knowledge which are the accumulation of past debates with regard to goals, purposes and beliefs. Policies, plans and strategies are current dialogues intended to change that corpus of knowledge. Through processes of assumptions, claims in arguments, support for claims, etc., the resultant inconsistencies and changes can be studied to lead to an understanding of how strategies emerge.

Huff contends that content analysis of speeches allows her to empirically identify shifts in strategic thinking of key decision makers. Using Mitroff and Mason's paradigm, her methods reveal that shifts in claims, data to back up claims, and causal beliefs can be linked to a "mental map" held by the CEO. One recent paper (Huff, WIP) does a rhetorical analysis of documents in a school of business over a 6-year period to show that the choice and success of a new strategy was affected by the previous development of an "enabling" symbolic language. Huff and Pondy (WIP) are conducting a 2-year field study to further refine the methodology for analyzing the language used by decision makers.

One other piece of theoretical work also reflects the interest in exploring the philosophical underpinnings of strategic processes. Ramaprasad and Bourgeois (1981) posit a preliminary model of a logical theory of strategy based on deductive reasoning rather than the more traditional inductive approach. Using symbolic logic, they propose a model to explain a strategist's concerns about gaps between anticipated, actual, and desired states of a system, and present logically deduced algorithms for action which a strategist might consider to achieve congruence among these states.

4. *Strategic Change*

Work in this area attempts to elucidate the processes involved in changing strategy.

Bourgeois (1980a) studied top management consensus on objectives and competitive weapons to attain them in 12 nondiversified corporations. He found that agreement on means and ends were both important for performance; but agreement on goals without agreement on means correlated with poor performance. According to Huff (1980b), the metaphor-and-analogy method may provide a way to reach such consensus. She outlines three exercises which use metaphor to find or develop overlap among policymakers who are unclear or do not agree about the nature of a situation. "Of course, given the highly uncertain situations usually confronted in strategic situations, this process of consensus may be an important way to structure or frame the novel data presenting itself" (Huff, 1981).

A related issue is whether strategies arrive full-blown or result from an emerging process different from what might be intended strategy (Mintzberg and Waters, 1980). While this is related to implementation, the issue is raised here to suggest that overall consensus at the top may be inadequate to explain the impact of lower-level operative decisions on emerging strategy. For example, Jauch and Wilson (1979) suggest that make-or-buy decisions can have substantial strategic impact, and unintended vertical integration decisions may be made by purchasing agents based on price factors alone. Unless strategic consensus is pushed to lower levels, then, consensus at the top could be rendered meaningless.

Papers by Lyles (1981) and Lyles and Mitroff (1981a,b) explore other dimensions of the strategic change process. The basic questions addressed are:

1. How do executives become aware of the existence of problems?
2. What processes are used to formulate definitions of problems?

3. What impact do individual differences of managers have on problem formation?
4. What information is gathered and how does it affect problem formation?

Case histories and surveys of upper-level executives are used to answer these questions, and several patterns of problem formation emerge along with certain behavioral processes.

Another set of papers involves the question about whether strategic changes are (or ought to be) evolutionary or revolutionary. Miller (1980) argues that there may be hidden costs in incremental changes to cope with new environments. In particular, "piecemeal alternatives in strategy and structure may result in disharmonies which destroy an existing integral configuration. Thus, delays in these changes might better be made until such time that a quantum or revolutionary change is justified by reconfiguring the entire system." Empirical work by Miller and Friesen (1980a) supports such a contention. They studied changes over time in 24 structure and strategy variables in 26 companies. They found periods of momentum where little or no trend was altered, and they observed dramatic periods of revolution where a very great many trends were reversed. Ramaprasad (1981), however, takes issue with some of these contentions. Using deductive logic and biological analogies, he suggests that revolutions may not be the stereotypical cataclysm often conjured up. For example, a revolutionary change is seen as extremely rare (contrary to Miller's work). The biological equivalent is that of mutation. A revolutionary change is found if one or more characteristics of the system changes, not in the effects of the change. Thus, very revolutionary changes may not have dramatic effects (particularly in the short run), even while dramatic effects may be due to nonrevolutionary changes.

B. Strategy Formulators

Some of the respondents have examined the roles of key managers, the potential personal outcomes of their decisions, and the role of entrepreneurs.

1. *Roles and Activities*

There are several research efforts where primary attention is paid to the roles of actors in the strategic management process.

Much of the work here is going on at Columbia University. Some examples include: (1) a study of the antecedents and consequences of linkages among corporate boards of directors (Pennings, WIPa); (2) studies of environmental scanning and communications patterns and power of various functional areas within top management groups (Hambrick, 1981,a,b,c); and (3) the interaction between key executives and strategic action (Tichy, Devanna, and Warren, WIP). Tichy (WIP) is also involved in a 3-year observation of executive behavior related to strategy in a single large strategic business unit (SBU).

Aside from the Columbia efforts, Lenz (WIPa) is studying the sources of managerial discretion and its use in strategic management; he also plans to conduct a field study on issues confronting corporate boards (Lenz, WIPb). Jemison (1981c) is also examining the roles and activities of managers. In a study of sources of influence on strategic decision making, internal vs. external sources were explored in a field study of 15 organizations (Jemison, 1981a). "Results indicate that environmental interaction has a greater absolute association with a department's ability to influence strategic decisions than do internal activities. In addition, regarding internal sources of influence, position power and expert power were seen to be more significant than political or resource power."

2. *Turnover*

Strategic decisions can have an impact on the careers of top executives and may be a prime determinant in their tenure.

Based on some prior work the author was intrigued by the lack of statistical significance in expected relationships between strategy, environment, and performance. However, when the criterion was changed from performance of the organization to top-management change, significant findings began to emerge (Osborn, Jauch, Martin, and Glueck, 1981). It appears that some strategic actions may be made for very personal reasons (preventing turnover). A series of recommendations are made for CEOs who wish to remain in their job, based on these findings (Jauch, Martin, and Osborn, 1981). For instance, the CEO should self-monitor and personally make decisions about divestitures, mergers, and sources of supply, but can delegate issues such as changes in labor, competitors, or technology if CEO tenure is the major criterion.

3. *Entrepreneurs and Venture Strategy*

While much of the work already discussed could have relevance for smaller firms and owner–managers in small businesses, they represent a significant subset of units which command research attention in their own right.

Vesper (1980a, 1982) and Vesper, Sexton, and Kent (1981) have books forthcoming on aspects of entrepreneurship. Vesper (WIP) also has three empirical research projects in process exploring: (1) obstacles impeding would-be entrepreneurs; (2) systematic strategies for finding and implementing business start-up ideas; and (3) the degree to which new enterprises are spawned directly by schools, and how.

Pennings (WIPb) is exploring urban–environmental determinants of entrepreneurship. Some work based on psychological characteristics of entrepreneurs and their implications has been reviewed by Brockhaus (1980); and Vicars, Jauch, and Wilson (1980) have begun development of an instrument to tap general entrepreneurial tendency. Cooper (WIPa) and some of his current and former students also have a continuing stream of related projects on influences upon entrepreneurship. One example of a current project involves responses from 1800 small business owners, focusing on their personal backgrounds, their "incubator" organizations, and the processes by which they start.

C. Planning and Implementation

The final set of efforts emphasizing strategy processes revolve around more formal systematic decision structure systems for planning and implementing strategy.

1. *Models, Techniques, and the Value of Planning*

The planning literature suggests that formal planning models and techniques will lead to better performance. Various models and techniques are explored here.

A study by Leontiades and Tezel (1980) suggests no relationship between firm performance and various aspects of planning. Interestingly Lachenmeyer (1980) suggests some 15 categories of reasons why planning is bounded in its potential effectiveness. Nevertheless, writers and researchers continue to prescribe improved models and techniques of planning. For example, Leontiades (1981b) proposes use of a multidimensional model of planning that takes into consideration different corporate circumstances—i.e., corporate vs. business level, steady state vs. evolutionary, and planning for different stages of development. Similarly, Montanari (1981a) develops "an open systems nine-stage model incorporating a four-stage environmental scanning procedure, audits of firm resources, duration of the planning cycle and budget generation as well as several other more familiar stages of strategic planning." Montanari and Wetherbe (1981) also suggest how zero-based budgeting might be related to the planning process.

While these prescriptive efforts are going on, several researchers update the state of corporate use of strategic planning. Farley, Capon, and Hulbert (WIP) have conducted a comprehensive study of what leading companies are doing. Detailed interviews were made in large companies known to have corporate planning staffs to examine the procedures and techniques used, the role and influence of the staff, and the impact of planning on company action. Henry (1980, 1981) has tracked the evolution of strategic planning systems in major corporations based on three separate field study interviews (in 1963, 1973, and 1979) with planners and executives in about 50 large companies. Major findings suggest there is now more effort to formulate, implement, and evaluate explicit strategies; greater evaluation of managers on strategic factors; more flexible corporate guidelines for business unit plans; continued stress on portfolio analysis; greater involvement of top executives; and the development of planning cultures.

Finally, respondents in this sample offer two new techniques which could aid in various stages of planning. One technique is A Systematic Procedure for Identifying Relevant Environments for Strategic Planning (Klein and Newman, 1980). These researchers are extending this "SPIRE" technique to answer the basic question: "What environmental factors should company X monitor?" The second technique (Ramaprasad and Knod, 1981) is used to establish a hierarchy of activity–constituent–mission linkages to create a conceptual map of strategy. Users prioritize activities and constituents to create a hierarchy of linkages reflecting their relative importance to mission attainment. On the basis of the data gathered, a series of analyses can be made. The resulting conceptual map can be used to make planning decisions, form new hierarchies, or redefine criteria for another iteration. Some other techniques of industry and competitor analyses are elaborated by Porter (1980a).

2. *Implementation*

This section explores work which emphasizes integration of strategy planning and implementation processes.

The importance of these efforts cannot be ignored since field studies by Yavitz and Newman (WIP) indicate that obstacles encountered by companies in implementing strategy are leading to executive disenchantment with strategic planning because "nothing happens, or what happens is not a consequence of planning."

The translation of strategic plans into executive actions has been analyzed in policy, planning, and control literature. Camillus (1981b,c) seeks to integrate these perspectives into a framework that defines the stages in the transition from strategy to action. One article focuses on how to ensure that action plans are congruent with and reinforce the corporate strategic plan, and the other identifies the dimensions of linkages between the stages of transition.

Work by Lenz and Lyles (1981a,b) sheds some light on what some of the behavioral problems are which may be frustrating the translation of strategic planning into operational terms. Some of the basic problems identified by chief planning officers were: achieving goal consensus, communication breakdowns, ambiguity of subunit roles, obtaining commitment to a plan, lack of strategic thinking, line–staff conflicts, etc. (1981a). In a follow-up empirical field study of six regional commercial banks with about 70 managers, they found that many problems basically stem from: (1) imposition of planning onto an existing organization; (2) cognitive capabilities of persons expected to plan; and (3) the quality of top-level administration of the planning process (1981b).

Management control is another area of strategy implementation which has attracted some attention. If control systems can be integrated with planning systems, the assumption is that implementation will be enhanced (Camillus, 1980a; Camillus and Birnberg, WIP). An integral part of this is the design of a capital budgeting and expenditure system which is strategic in nature (Camillus,

1980b, 1981d). Camillus and Grant (1980) have proposed a method to integrate programming and budgeting for improved operational planning. Grant and Snodgrass (WIP) intend to present "a framework which fits within the requirements of external cultural systems and formal organizational systems to take advantage of external conditions and reduce dysfunctional consequences of elaborate formal planning and control systems." Lorange (1980) has also developed an integrated conceptual model for the strategic planning and control process. This emphasizes interactive, participative aspects for achieving broad commitment to strategic direction and change. Strategic process implementation issues are further elaborated in Lorange (1982a). An empirical, clinical study of strategic process in 12 European-based corporations is under way; the preliminary findings are generally in accord with the conceptual scheme (Lorange, 1982b).

Another set of implementation issues revolves around promoting innovation and linking R&D efforts to company strategy. Tushman (WIP) is beginning an exploratory study of interactions between company strategy and the management of technical research departments. A second paper here suggests that innovation has three phases—generation, acceptance, and implementation—which, though separately identifiable, may be overlapped if the organization chooses to do so (Iyer and Ramaprasad, 1980). The paper describes strategic postures for innovation in some detail, and an effort is made to link strategy and implementation for innovation. Tavel (1980) argues that managing innovation in product strategies will be the key for business survival in the 1980s. To do this, however, he calls for less formal planning procedures but more "reliance on the genius of an individual who combines creative imagination with good judgement."

Of course, implementation may not deal just with internal problems treated to this point. External boundary spanning can be critical. MacMillan (1980) has some preliminary thoughts on this in terms of identifying major intervention points in the regulatory process and identifying what tactical trade-offs need be made in selecting strategic access to the regulatory process.

The overall process of implementation has been treated by only one respondent in this sample. Vancil's (1979) book on *Decentralization: Managerial Ambiguity by Design* explored data on 291 large manufacturing firms to see how each corporation deals with its domestic divisions which are "profit centers," and how 317 profit center managers receive their relative autonomy. The managerial climate created by philosophy and style of corporate managers seems to be the most important determinant of a profit center manager's perceived autonomy. Functional authority is the second most important factor. Finally, the book and a second article (Vancil, 1980) point out that the profit center manager's job is ambiguous by design because his responsibility exceeds authority.

III. RESEARCH EMPHASIZING STRATEGY CONTENT

There are a number of people working on factors which influence choice of a strategic posture (see Table 2). Work here includes defining strategic perfor-

Table 2. Research Emphasizing Strategy Content

Subjects of Study	*Primarily Conceptual*	*Primarily Empirical*
A. Strategy Performance		Grant, WIP; Kirchhoff & Kirchhoff, 1980;
B. Environment, Strategy, and Structure	Bourgeois, 1980b; Bourgeois & Astley, 1979; Jauch & Osborn, 1981; Lenz, 1981; Miller & Mintzberg, 1980; Montanari, 1979;	Doz, 1980; 1981; Doz, Bartlett & Prahalad, 1981; Egelhoff & Newman, WIP; Grinyer, Al-Bazzaz, & Ardanaki, 1980; Jauch, Osborn & Glueck, 1980; Lenz, 1980; Pitts, WIPa; Prahalad & Doz, 1981;
C. Strategic Taxonomies		
1. Strategic Groups and Industry Structure	Hout, Porter, Rudden & Vogt, 1980; Porter, 1980c,d;	Hand, 1981a,b,c,d; Harrigan, 1980c; Huff, 1980a; Porter, 1980a,b; Porter & Caves, 1981; Porter, Caves & Spence, 1980;
2. Stage of Development/Product Life Cycle		Anderson, WIPb; Cooper, WIPc; Harrigan, 1981f; Harrigan, WIPa,b; Schendel, WIPa; Vozikis, 1979, 1980;
3. Strategy Archetypes and Definitions	Leontiades, 1981a; Pitts, WIPb;	Hambrick & MacMillan, WIP; Miller & Friesen, 1980b; Schendel, WIPb;
4. Mission or Scope Changes	Leontiades, 1980, WIP;	Cooper, WIPb; Duhaime, 1981a,b; Harrigan, 1980a,b; 1981a,b,c,d,e; Harrigan and Porter, 1981; MacMillan, Hambrick & Pennings, WIP; Mazzolini, 1980a, 1981a; Porter & Spence, 1981; Schendel, WIPc;

WIP—Work in Progress

mance criteria, searches for configurations of environmental, strategic, and structural variables, and defining frameworks for analyzing conditions under which various strategies might be effective. These writers are trying to prescribe what strategies are likely to lead to success for given firms in given environments.

A. Strategic Performance

Two papers illustrate that measuring performance in a strategic context is difficult. Grant (WIP) has designed some research to identify performance indicators which should attract management attention at different time intervals depending on the current portfolio position and direction of a particular SBU being examined. Given past criticisms of these approaches (such as problems with the Boston Consulting Group's "Directional Policy Matrix"), the objective of the research is to reduce distortion in resource allocation which could result, particularly for SBUs early or late in their product life cycles.

A second effort is reflected in the work of Kirchhoff, who has assembled a detailed data base on 37 measures of performance among 31 profit centers of a large conglomerate corporation. These measures extend over a 5-year period, providing a longitudinal and cross-sectional data base for analysis of profit center performance. This data base is unique in that it includes not only financial but economic, sociological, and psychological variables. A paper by Kirchhoff and Kirchhoff (1980) describes the use of this data base to demonstrate that "optimization of short run ROI requires actions different than those dictated by long run considerations." Hence, the time horizon for measuring performance is a key issue for strategy research.

B. Environment, Strategy, and Structure

Aside from performance per se, which is a criterion in a number of studies, several writers have been examining configurations of environment, strategy, and structure variables.

There is a fair amount of theoretical work being done here, and remarkable consistency in thrust. That is, the perspective is moving away from "analysis of linear relationships among few variables in search of causation towards synthesis or a focus on clusters among many attributes in search of gestalt" (Miller and Mintzberg, 1980). Jauch and Osborn (1981) offer several propositions suggesting that strategy itself is a resulting profile of factors which need to "fit" one another in particular ways. Lenz (1981) refers to this as "co-alignment" among interdependent factors which evolve over time.

Some empirical work has been done which supports this theoretical approach. Jauch, Osborn, and Glueck (1980) examined the connection between environment and strategy in an attempt to predict performance. Few significant relationships were found, suggesting a break from "causative" relationships among variables. Lenz (1980) reports that combinations of environment, strategy, and structure in high-performing savings and loan associations differ from those combinations associated with lower performers. Such combinations differ statistically and in their basic character. For instance, higher performers were in less developed socioeconomic areas, had greater domain consensus and wider spans of control.

Of course, complete agreement in the literature should not be expected. Grinyer, Al-Bazzaz, and Ardenaki (1980) do find stable strategy/structure fits, but these were found unrelated to financial performance and linked negatively with perceived hostile environments. Montanari (1979) suggests that the choice of strategy/structure relationships is a function of managerial discretion. Bourgeois and Astley (1979) also note that there are some differences in approach in the literature. Yet they conclude that "simultaneous reciprocal causation" operates with "strategy" in a central position. This is quite similar to the "configuration" approach noted before. Bourgeois (1980b) goes further to show how environment and strategy can be subdivided into components which are integrated with one another.

In a different but related vein, some work is reported on how multinationals fit strategy and structure. Pitts (WIPa) is updating the 1972 Stopford and Wells study on how diversified U.S. multinationals (MNCs) organize their foreign activities. Variables such as diversity, percentage of foreign sales, R&D intensity, etc., are assessed in terms of relationships with organization design. And Egelhoff and Newman (WIP) have interviewed executives in 50 MNCs (half U.S., half European) regarding strategy and relationships between headquarters and foreign subsidiaries. Their model, based on information processing theory, posits that "structure" includes a number of behavioral processes.

Finally, some work by Doz (1980, 1981) and several colleagues (e.g., Prahalad and Doz, 1981) shows how some process issues and implementation are involved here as well. This work focuses on the use of various types of administrative systems and managerial mechanisms to increase the capability of large complex firms to manage strategic change. Recently this has involved a detailed study of strategic reorientations within multinational companies. In a related project Doz, Bartlett and Prahalad (1981) have analyzed how the configuration of administrative systems in multinational corporations reflects different possible trade-offs between the desires for global efficiency and the need to remain flexible and responsive at the national level. The strategies and administrative systems of selected American and European companies in three industries (automobile, telecommunication equipment and computers/microelectronics) have been analyzed in detail. Doz is extending this research to a sample of Japanese companies to test the extent to which the current framework may be culturally bound.

C. Strategic Taxonomies

A variety of approaches are being used to classify strategic actions taken by organizations—defining strategic groups and industry structures, stages of development viewpoints, and strategic archetypes, or examining mission and scope changes. While the approaches vary, the underlying thrust is to identify conditions under which various strategies are appropriate.

1. *Strategic Groups and Industry Structure*

Much of this work is grounded in the industrial organization (I/O) area of economics and seeks to identify homogeneous groups of firms and strategic behavior.

The major use of I/O theory integrated with strategic concerns is the work of Porter (1980b,c,d) and Caves (e.g., Porter, Caves, and Spence, 1980; Porter and Caves, 1981). Illustrative of this work is Porter's book *Competitive Strategy* (1980a). This effort:

> provides a framework for analyzing industry structure and evolution, firm position within an industry, and competitive interaction and strategic moves of firms. The approach is aimed at providing a comprehensive and rigorous body of analytical techniques for the purpose of determining environmental threats and opportunities and internal strengths and weaknesses.

Factors Porter finds most important for the level of industry competition include: (1) barriers to entry; (2) bargaining power of suppliers; (3) bargaining power of customers; (4) threats of substitute products; and (5) jockeying for position among competitors. Porter suggests approaches whereby a firm can find a position in the industry presenting the best defense against these external forces. "In contrast to more traditional I/O theory, the unit of analysis has been expanded to include *both* the firm and the industry such that "strategic groups" can be identified (those which cluster based on relatively homogeneous strategies within an industry), and feedback of firm activities is recognized as an impact on market structure."

Harrigan (1980c) has extended the clustering analysis technique to provide a tool for strategists to gauge the relative power of various potential competitors. Using historical financial data, patterns in responses of various strategic groups can be isolated to predict which groups to avoid when entering a new industry or shifting strategic postures.

Hout, Porter, Rudden, and Vogt (1980) also extend the thrust of these contributions. They suggest that world competition is predictable, manageable, and economically rational in the long term. "While the competitive problem is more complex, the economic variables more subtle, the required time horizon longer, and the stakes larger," they suggest that recognizing global implications for firm strategy is taking on more significance; equally important, they argue the I/O framework can be fruitfully used to help strategists compete more successfully.

The importance of studying industry practices and competitor behavior has been recognized by others as well. Huff (1980a) suggests that industry members help identify niche-related problems (and solutions) for one another. This paper suggests that we need to know more about the pool of strategic concepts a competitive group holds in common.

Finally, Hand (1981a,b,c,d) is conducting a series of studies in various segments of the retailing industry replicating the Hatten/Schendel/Patten/Cooper work on the beer industry. He examined cross sections of 20 different classes of retailers, using 250 companies in one study and 110 retail gasoline service stations in another. "Using a variation of profit as the dependent variable, up to 90% of variance in profit can be explained when data are partitioned." His preliminary results suggest that the beer study will be replicated (identifying strategic groups clustering), but the strategy variables are very different for retailers.

2. *Stages of Development/Product Life Cycle*

Several individuals are investigating the dynamics of business strategy across the product–market life cycle—what strategies are followed at different stages of development.

Schendel (WIPa) and Cooper (WIPc) both have projects under way to examine performance and prospects for businesses in different positions on the growth/market share matrix. Cooper reports that several projects with doctoral students include empirical studies of effective low-market-share businesses, ineffective high-market-share firms, and so-called dogs.

Anderson (WIPb) is modifying PIMs data to include environmental uncertainty and additional performance measures. In addition to looking for contingency relationships, he is examining strategy and performance by stage of the product life cycle. For each stage, a regression relates 27 strategic variables to performance. Results suggest generic strategies common to each stage: growth—product development; maturity—productivity and standardization; decline—productivity and technological change.

Harrigan has several projects related to industry evolution, again drawing from an I/O framework. Two of these (Harrigan, WIPa,b) focus on companies whose products are subject to rapid obsolescence in industries characterized by short life cycles requiring high innovation, particularly in the face of foreign competition. A third study (Harrigan, 1981f) tracks the evolution of make-or-buy decisions in parts of the petrochemical industry. She is attempting to isolate the determinants of this decision and how it affects industry structure. Another piece of work here parallels the small business studies of Hand noted in the last section. Vozikis (1979, 1980) has investigated the relationships between small business problems and stages of development. He finds that:

> there are substages of transitional development the small firm goes through before reaching the functional stage (stage 2 in most theories), and these do not conform to the typical descriptions regarding stage 1 of most development theories. Similarly, small exporting firms experience significantly different problems among different exporting stages. (1980)

3. *Strategy Definitions and Archetypes*

Some writers are trying to define terms and categorize strategies using various typologies.

Leontiades (1981a) notes that the current jumbled and conflicting vocabulary and definitions of terms like "policy" and "strategy" impede progress on substantive issues; he proposes a solution for the confusion. "Diversity" is another such term which has been used in a variety of ways. Pitts (WIPb) reviews how economists and business policy researchers define and measure diversity, and makes suggestions for a common approach.

Aside from definitions of terms, a number of existing typologies of strategy have been proposed. Miller and Friesen (1980b):

> offer nine archetypes of organizational transition representing prevalent modes of adaption characterized by evolution of, and interaction among, environment, strategy, and structure variables. Using questionnaire and case history samples, 24 variables were examined to collectively define regions among score ranges loading the nine archetypes of organizational transition.

In parallel with the theory noted earlier they argue for multivariate and simultaneous consideration of patterns among variables.

Other examples of archetypes being examined include the BCG four-cell matrix as well as a typology developed by Miles and Snow (their work is addressed later in the chapter). Hambrick and MacMillan (WIP) are systematically exploring typologies such as this using the PIMS data base, with the intent of deriving a typology of business-level strategies. The thrust is to work from the theory to see if the PIMS data fits rather than analyzing the data and then searching for explanation. They are analyzing prescriptions in the BCG matrix using relationships between strategic attributes and performance criteria in each of the four quadrants.

Recall that similar work by Schendel and Cooper was noted earlier using a stages-of-development application. Schendel (WIPb) is also applying modern portfolio theory to the strategic question of what businesses to add, hold, or divest. Thus, strategy typologies are being empirically examined at both corporate- and business-level units of analysis.

4. *Mission or Scope Changes*

Related to the foregoing are a number of studies exploring particular types of strategies which alter the basic business definition. Major strategy choices being examined here include: to enter; to diversify; to widen scope to a global context; to commit to the basic business; to exit.

Examples of perspectives from the foregoing strategic taxonomies are also represented here. For instance, MacMillan, Hambrick, and Pennings (WIP) are using the PIMS data to study vertical integration using a strategic interdependency approach. And Porter and Spence (1981) have studied vertical integration from their I/O perspective.

In the area of decisions to enter new businesses, Harrigan (1981d,e) measures entry barriers to examine the structural and competitive factors which might constitute an attractive industry environment. Schendel (WIPc) is evaluating acquisition performance as measured by executive perception, internal accounting measures, and capital market assessments.

Leontiades (1980) examines corporate restructuring through acquisitions and divestments. His book suggests taking an historical perspective of corporate development and evolution; and he notes that the role of unrelated acquisitions is in need of more study. His work (WIP) on this is extending to consider the current emphasis by large companies on "rationalized diversity."

Mazzolini (1980a, 1981a) is working on strategy in government-controlled enterprises; based on field work in Europe, this study analyzes the international behavior of state enterprises. It explains why such companies do or do not have international activities. In addition, it explains the international operations of such enterprises, i.e., which of their major operating policy decisions are distinctive in any way and why.

Another perspective on factors affecting mission change is the work of Cooper (WIPb) on strategic responses to technological threats. This continuing stream of research now includes 53 firms in 11 industries faced with technological invasions which threaten to displace firms dependent on an older technology. Firms respond differently such that entry into the new technology, stability, growth of the old business, or retrenchment are all considered in this research.

Finally, divestment of whole business units or divisions has increased recently, but research has lagged; further, existing literature emphasizes elimination of *assets* from an economic rather than strategic viewpoint. Two recent dissertations and extensions focus on exit decisions or strategies pursued when an industry is in decline.

Duhaime's (1981a) thesis focused on the influences which various factors (financial strength, general economic growth, business units' interdependency, etc.) had on firms' decisions to divest business units. Personal interviews with corporate executives provided data on 60 recent divestment instances. General objectives of her post-thesis research (1981b) are "to confirm the existence of hypothesized *patterns* of divestment activity *in firms over time* and to determine the effects of those patterns on firms' subsequent divestment decisions."

Harrigan's thesis published in book form (1980a) was based on eight field studies of 61 firms in declining industries. The paradigm developed and tested suggests that:

> even where levels of demand in a declining industry are unlikely to return to their previous volume, there are some industries inherently more favorable than others. A firm in such a "favorable declining industry" may find market opportunity if it is positioned to serve attractive niches. A firm in a weak position might hurdle the advantages of its competitors or maneuver customers to make the firm better positioned to serve them.

While these approaches seek to protect survival and/or enhance position, extensions discuss appropriate conditions for exit as well as barriers to the exit decision. Spinoffs and extensions of this work are being published in various forms (Harrigan, 1980b, 1981a,b,c; Harrigan and Porter, 1981).

IV. INTEGRATED RESEARCH, METHODOLOGY AND PEDAGOGY

Works of a broader nature are outlined in this section (see Table 3). Here, writers are trying to integrate process and content efforts and are exploring various methodologies for research in the area. Finally, there is a brief section of a few pieces of research exploring pedagogical concerns.

A. Integrated Process and Content Efforts

Several works have appeared recently describing integrated models of strategic processes and content (Abell, 1980; Miles and Snow, 1978; Summer, 1980; Tavel, 1980). The following descriptions are examples of these efforts and extensions.

Drawing on field-force theory and 78 case histories of business and government, Summer (1980) presents a model of strategic behavior. His summary follows:

> Behavior in a strategic system is a function of the interrelated behavior of three actors: society, organization, and strategists. *Society* is seen as: (1) networks of constituencies in the

Table 3. Integrated Research, Methodology, and Pedagogy

Subjects of Study	*Primarily Conceptual*	*Primarily Empirical*
A. Integrated Process and Content Efforts	Abell, 1980; Melcher, 1980; Melcher, Melcher, Jones & Baliga, WIP; Miles & Snow, 1978, 1981, WIP; Mintzberg, WIP; Mintzberg & Waters, 1980; Summer, 1980; Tavel, 1980;	Harrigan, WIP;
B. Methodologies for Studying Strategic Management	Bourgeois, 1981a; Datta, 1980; Grant, 1980; Jauch et al., 1980; Mintzberg & Waters, 1980; Montanari, Moorehead & Montanari, 1980; Newman, WIP; Summer, 1980;	Harrigan, WIP; Wortman, 1979;
C. Pedagogy	Vesper, 1980b;	Henry, WIP; Jauch et al., WIP; Montanari, 1981b;

WIP—Work in Progress

> task environment and the cultural environment; (2) networks of constituencies in the zones of support, acceptance, opposition and indifference; and (3) formal and informal interest groups on whom the organization is resource-dependent and legitimacy-dependent. From a strategic view, the most significant characteristics of an *organization* are: (1) following Toynbee, it evolves through a five stage life cycle; (2) its evolution is determined by how well its distinctive competencies are continuously aligned with the demands of diverse constituencies. It is these competencies which determine: (a) resource support, and (b) legitimacy support in a society. *Strategists* are defined as key influentials who formulate competency alignments. Strategists are seen as performing three functions: (1) formulating strategies, (2) formulating policies, and (3) exercising strategic leadership.

Miles and Snow (1981) are building on their earlier book (1978) to develop a descriptive model of the required "fit" among key organization and environmental characteristics. The earlier work described the implications of alternative market strategies for organization structure and management processes. They argue that several general organizational "types" (defenders, prospectors, analyzers, and reactors) are identifiable by their particular strategy–structure–process patterns. Their current extension attempts to suggest predictable refinements imposed on these types by their industry setting and the managerial philosophies of their top executives. They see three variables—industry, strategy, and managerial philosophy—as the key factors shaping organization structure and process.

Miles and Snow (WIP) are also at work on two related fronts: (1) developing a diagnostic approach which will assist organizations in determining the fit between their present structure–process configuration and their current and desired market strategies and (2) exploring processes to simultaneously plan for market and human resources development.

Melcher and Melcher (1980) and Melcher, Melcher, Jones, and Baliga (WIP) have several efforts published or in progress which develop a comprehensive approach to formulating strategy. One of the efforts focuses on the analysis of interdependent relations and the implications for evaluation and formulation of strategy. A model is outlined, research on the variables is being codified, and empirical studies based on the model have resulted in an approach to analyze general management decision processes.

Harrigan (WIP) has done some preliminary research on how the strategic planning process differs within different types of industries. This, of course, follows up and superimposes process findings on her content research described earlier; she hopes to be able to "draw some relationships between industry context, strategic planning time horizons and how various types of firms within those contexts grapple with the problem of effective strategic planning."

Finally, Mintzberg (WIP) is conducting a series of studies to track strategies over long periods of time (25–60 years), and relate strategies to each other, to processes used, structure, effectiveness, etc. The basic assumption is that strategy is "a pattern in a stream of decisions regarding activities, outputs, structure, environment and performance.'' He reports that about 10 studies are in progress or near completion in various organizations. One example (Mintzberg and Waters, 1980) tracks strategies of a retail chain over 60 years from entrepreneurial creation to emergence as a billion-dollar corporation. In all, about 50 different strategies were pursued by the company in 10 distinct areas of activity. In describing a classic case of the growth and formalization of an entrepreneurial firm, the paper also seeks to draw conclusions about strategy formulation under such conditions. Among their conclusions are:

> the utility of growing in a sequence of sprints and pauses as opposed to a steady progression, the infrequency and irregularity of major strategic reorientation and the problems that poses for the notion of strategic management, the essence of entrepreneurship as rooted in knowledge of the business and in a controlled form of boldness, and the concept of planning not as the conceiving of a strategy but as the programming of a strategy already conceived.

B. Methodologies for Studying Strategic Management

Several papers are of interest for those wishing to explore the advantages and disadvantages of various methodologies useful for research and strategy.

Bourgeois (1981a) discusses various ways in which organizational slack is an important construct and how it has been approached heretofore. The article proposes several operational measures and an unobtrusive approach using secondary financial data yielding a combined index of slack.

Montanari, Moorhead, and Montanari (1980) discuss the utility and ''superiority'' of a laboratory method to investigate the strategic decision making process. They noted, however, that preliminary results showed no effectiveness of the model used in the training laboratory.

Jauch, Osborn, & Martin (1980) propose the use of content analysis of cases as a complementary method to other types of research. Published cases can be used as data sources; but they propose that a preestablished content analysis schedule should be prepared to guide the researcher.

Several other papers of a more general nature are also of interest. Grant (1980) provides a useful bibliography and summary of strengths and weaknesses of various quantitative and qualitative techniques used in strategic management research. Wortman (1979) seems to suggest that, at the current stage of development of knowledge in the field, qualitative approaches are to be favored (e.g., deductive reasoning, observation, historical case analysis, content analysis, interviews, and expert opinion). Summer (1980) goes further in a methodological appendix to his book. He argues that ''(1) case histories are the most appropriate data base for policy research (since only they can include the richness of variables in the policy system); and (2) methods from history, anthropology, law and medicine are most appropriate for ordering data.''

Mintzberg and Waters (1980) support such a contention, arguing that only intensive longitudinal research can do justice to complex processes involved in strategy. Datta (1980) partially agrees, preferring a focus on various parts of strategic planning through intensive descriptive studies of individual industries.

On a more philosophical basis, Newman (WIP) questions the suitability of any prevailing methods for dealing with *integration*. He argues that scientific *analysis* has led us away from adequate ways of dealing with effective synthesis. He suggests Eastern civilization thinking is ahead of Western, but the process is not explicit.

However, Harrigan (WIP) expects to see a new hybrid of methodology bringing together theory building, hypothesis testing, financial data bases, and field studies and statistical analysis of industries and competitors. Multiple site studies with different industries reflecting different contexts will allow inferences to be made about effective strategies for various types of environments.

C. Pedagogical Research

A small amount of work is being done in the area of transferring knowledge about strategy to students or executives and consultants. One effort in this direction is compendia of course and curriculum activity in the area. Vesper (1980b) has compiled experiments in teaching entrepreneurship and program and course descriptions from 98 schools in the U.S. and Canada.

Henry (WIP) is designing a study to determine the role of consultants in introducing strategic planning in business. Montanari (1981b) presents a lecture–simulation teaching methodology which combines the strengths of several traditional methods of teaching business policy. The paper describes a preliminary laboratory study designed to assess the effectiveness of this methodology for transference of course material to a setting other than the classroom.

In the classroom itself Jauch (WIP) is working with several colleagues in an experiment to examine whether "whole vs. part" learning is superior for student performance and satisfaction. They are manipulating the timing of coverage of text material, cases, exercises, and, simulations across nine different small sections of the basic policy course. They can then test whether an entire integrative model should be covered before students apply knowledge, or whether components of the model should be worked on before requiring a more macro integration by the student.

V. SUMMARY AND CONCLUSIONS

Several authors attempt to tie together some of the areas discussed earlier and provide viewpoints for directions the field should follow in the future. These efforts propose methodological integration and perspectives of what the strategic management field should focus on theoretically.

Jemison (1981b) suggests that richer findings in strategic management research will come through integrating concepts and theories from I/O Economics, Marketing, and Administrative Behavior. He compares prior research based on types of problems, research methods, causal inference patterns, and usefulness for strategy formulation and implementation. He suggests that areas where an integrated approach among these paradigms would be fruitful are: (1) evolution of industries, markets, and organizations; (2) process and content research; and (3) interorganizational relations.

Bower's (1980) address to the National Academy's Business Policy and Planning Division suggests that researchers have preoccupied themselves with topics of narrow focus and that too much attention has been given to individual firms' economic problems. He espouses field research examining large-scale problems with socioeconomic consequences far beyond the concerns of individual firms. In effect, he calls for research on global environmental impacts and their relationships to firms' strategies (particularly multinational corporations). He advocates that description based on historical or clinical observation in areas of specialized expertise should be undertaken at various schools around the country.

Weir (1979, 1981a,b) takes a bit different view. Based on the work of Dubin (1969), he argues for building an empirically based midrange theory of strategy and policymaking. He points out that current concepts tend to be unanalyzable or too abstract; thus, policy/strategy theorists are urged to imitate organizational theorists. To quote from Weir's abstract:

> The business policy field must be systematically defined in terms of its theoretical domain. The social science literature indicates that a field of knowledge is defined in terms of four interrelated dimensions: the central research questions currently under examination by scholars; the conceptual units of analysis; the laws of interaction or general propositions used to theoretically link these conceptual units; the focal system level or levels of analysis encompassing the scope of empirical reality under consideration. The desire of strategy theorists to accumulate an empirical base of research findings in the business policy field will not effectively evolve until researchers address all four interrelated domain dimensions.

Conclusion

Based on this sample survey of work on strategic management by representative North American scholars, it can be concluded that multiple viewpoints about the nature of strategy exist. Some research questions currently under investigation have been identified here, but there's little agreement about the domain of the field.

It is clear that complex decision processes are affected by a myriad of influences. Different perspectives about how organizational change is brought about leads us to question whether a commonly accepted theory is even possible at this point. Clearly, the roles, activities, and philosophy and style of key managers are critical areas to study as to their impact on formulation and implementation. Just as important is how variables of environment and structure result in choices about strategy and the performance implications of these outcomes. But given the complexity and large number of variables involved, it may be premature to attempt an integrated view of content and process perspectives.

In the papers cited previously a number of approaches for studying the subject have been referred to. These include deductive and inductive theory building, case studies, interview and questionnaire techniques, field studies, content analysis of speeches and documents, and use of financial data bases. While there are contrasting viewpoints about appropriate methodologies, this author would agree with Datta (1980) that "enthusiasm for method at the expense of substance is a danger to be avoided, and that appropriate methods should be selected and grounded on the basis of an adequate underlying theoretical structure." There remains room for eclectic approaches to the study of this field.

STRATEGIC MANAGEMENT THEORY: FUTURE CHALLENGES

Several issues and problems seem to emerge from the areas of research which have been outlined.

A. Issues in Process Research

Some of the literature in the other areas (e.g., content, methodology) raises some problems for those focusing on the process factors in strategic management. Perhaps one major challenge is to answer the question "How large a role *does* each component have, and how large a role *should* each component play, in strategic decision making?" The components addressed here include: analytical/rational (A/R), political/behavioral (P/B), intuitive/visceral (I/V). Figure 1 expresses these questions in a Venn diagram.

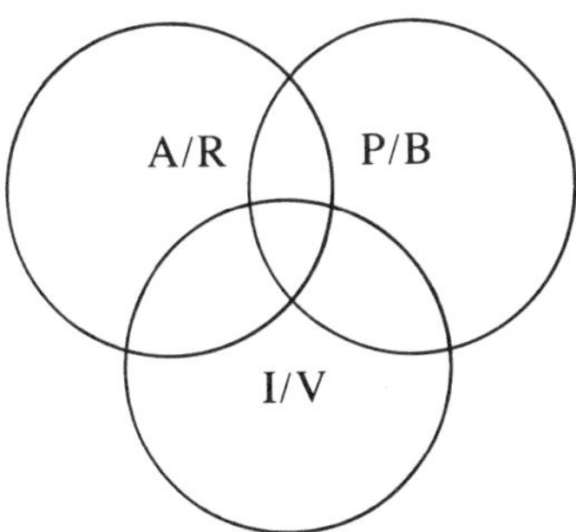

Figure 1. Components of Strategic Decision Processes

That is, how large is each component, and how large should each be for successful strategic decision making? Descriptive empirical work is needed for the first question; but the philosophical orientation is also needed to address the prescriptive question, followed by empirical work to test this out.

A concern here is the use of intensive interviews based on small sample case studies. Those arguing for this approach consistently emphasize the "richness" potential and tend to emphasize the political intrigues and discuss the mystique surrounding the intuitive decision maker. While this makes entertaining reading and can provide useful insights, vague comments about "successful executives" (without defining success) are often made and prescriptions urged for pursuing such styles. More rigorous research designs are needed here. Before accepting prescriptions based on small samples, it would be useful to examine whether those using the prescribed styles are more successful than those which do not in different types of firms and settings. Moreover, even if the descriptive reality turns out to reflect the state of affairs as described by these writers, is that what should be prescribed, or should a blending of rational and "extrarational" be prescribed? How much of our "knowledge" is a result of our methods and our own biases and theories based on our own systems? Do we expect more politics because we see it in academe and expect to find it in other systems as well?

A second challenge is to define change and when it takes place. Is it an event or a process? Several perspectives emerge here. Some see "emerging patterns in streams of decisions." Are these intended or not? Porter and others describe factors creating industry evolution, Miller and Friesen and others discuss evolution vs. revolution in firms, and Ramaprasad describes revolutions in systems as mutations. How much of what we call change is really revolutionary? What is the definition of a revolutionary change? Does it come about randomly? Once again, good theoretical and empirical work is needed to address some of these issues. They can indicate to the strategist some important processes to be considered and whether they can be influenced proactively or reactively; and they are related to some content issues regarding effective strategies during various stages of development of industries, firms, and products/markets.

A third challenge raised by those seeking integration and a focus for the scope of the field is to incorporate the range of macro variables and implementation issues into the emphasis on "problem and strategic formulation" processes. Some of this is being done; but it appears that the artificial distinction between formulation and implementation (resulting largely from pedagogical convenience) is still invoked by many researchers in the field. Interactions and joint influences of various aspects of strategy formulation and implementation, however, are both a boon and a bain. Too much detail at any one stage may hide the importance of an overall fit. This is a parsimony problem facing the field as a whole.

B. Issues In Content Research

Earlier it was noted that there appeared to be some agreement that a fit among configurations of variables was needed for coherent strategy. Yet, some of the challenges issued earlier apply here as well. How do these "fits" come about? When do changes occur? What creates these changes? If alterations are made in any of the components, what are the dysfunctions? Should a balance be sought, or are misfits needed to bring about change? What processes should be integrated into these frameworks to make them more complete?

A challenge to content researchers comes from the process orientation. That is, the generic problem statement from a contingency perspective is: given X environmental conditions and Y internal conditions, what strategy (Z) is prescribed for success? Several problems quickly arise: the process research suggests multiple success measures, managers are urged to "optimize" a "utility function" which is constrained by a host of factors, and actors in the process are presumably somewhat less than rational. Since there are no right answers for what organizational goals *should* be, and so many influences, can the generic question be answered other than through exploring the processes by which decisions are generated? Furthermore, the process approach alerts us to problems of *timing* and *intent*. Can we prescribe strategy Z given these forces?

A challenge to those focusing on identifying "strategic groups" within industries is raised by some process concerns and methodology problems. For instance, if past success leads to the prescription that "the example of the strategic group leader" should be followed, then creative strategies and innovation might be stifled. Perhaps we ought to prescribe uniqueness rather than the homogeneity which seems to implicitly result from this approach. Yet, therein lies a methodological problem; as strategic groups begin to emerge out of a set of data, how far will clustering techniques allow us to go before the large numbers of variables yield individual unique firms? And once unique strategies are identified, have we lost our ability to generalize about patterns which lead to success?

C. Issues for Integrators and Methodologists

There are some challenges here which, of course, overlap the previous concerns. All of those apply plus a few others.

One problem is that it is difficult to examine global strategy, structure, environment, and process issues across industries and across time given the large number of variables involved. The complexity is illustrated by considering that characterizations of each element of success, structure, environment, strategy, and administrative process could at best be limited to three variables each. Assuming this, a minimum of 81 cells of independent combinations would be constructed for any sort of rigorous research design. It is unlikely that samples fewer than 500 firms or so would even begin to fill in all these cells, in a cross-sectional study, to say nothing of considering a longitudinal design.

Further, few would be satisfied with a three-level success measure, or even three separate dependent variables. Moreover, questions about how to define or measure terms such as efficiency or effectiveness change as each new paradigm comes along.

Yet, given these difficulties and challenges, it is not time to call for cessation of any line or work, or urge all toward a particular area of focus, a particular methodological bent, or a paradigm which will be all-encompassing. Many areas still need good theory building and empirical work of both a qualitative and quantitative nature. The scope of the field should not be narrowed prematurely. The stage of development of strategic management still requires eclecticism in approach and ecumenical acceptance of multiple paradigms. Only after much more work has been done with a variety of approaches and some convergence of findings can we begin to feel more comfortable with the beginnings of a meta-theory of organizational strategy.

ACKNOWLEDGMENTS

The author acknowledges the helpful comments of two anonymous reviewers in the revision of this manuscript.

NOTE

1. The references indicate a number of papers as forthcoming or work in progress (WIP) as of the date of original compilation of this survey (1981). Some of this work has been published since then, but it serves little purpose to update references since the intent of this chapter is not to provide a complete literature review or bibliography. The survey respondents may be contacted by those interested in the status of this work.

REFERENCES

Abell, D. F. (1980), *Defining the Business: The Starting Point of Strategic Planning*, Englewood Cliffs, N.J.: Prentice Hall.

Anderson, C. R. (WIPa), "Executive Decision Styles," School of Business Administration, University of North Carolina.

Anderson, C. R. (WIPb), "Contingency Relationships in the PIMS Data," School of Business, University of North Carolina.

Bourgeois, L. J. (1980), "Performance and Consensus," *Strategic Management Journal, 1*, 227248, (a).

Bourgeois, L. J. (1980), "Strategy and Environment: A Conceptual Integration," *Academy of Management Review, 5*, 2539, (b).

Bourgeois, L. J. (1981), ''On the Measurement of Organizational Slack,'' *Academy of Management Review, 6,* pp. 29–40(a).
Bourgeois, L. J. (1981b) ''Political Behavior in Policy Making: An Empirical Investigation,'' Working Paper, University of Pittsburgh.
Bourgeois, L. J. and Astley, W. G. (1979), ''A Strategic Model of Organizational Conduct and Performance,'' *International Studies of Management and Organization, 9,* 4066.
Bower, J. L. (1980), ''Business Policy in the 1980s: Content and Method,'' Speech delivered at Academy of Management Meeting, Detroit, August 11.
Bower, J. L. and Doz, Y. (1979), ''Strategy Formulation: A Social and Political Process,'' in Schendel, D. E. and Hofer, C. W. (Eds.), *Strategic Management: A New View of Business Policy and Planning,* Boston: Little, Brown.
Brockhaus, R. H. (1980), ''Psychology of the Entrepreneur,'' paper presented at the Conference on Research and Education in Entrepreneurship, March 24, 25.
Camillus, J. C. (1980), ''Six Approaches to Preventive Management Control,'' *Financial Executive, 48* (December), 28–31 (a).
Camillus, J. C. (1980), ''Strategic Management of Capital Expenditure: A Systematic Contingent Framework,'' *Academy of Management Proceedings,* 26–30, b.
Camillus, J. C. (1981a), ''Reconciling Logical Incrementalism and Synoptic Formalism—An Integrated Approach to Designing Strategic Planning Processes,'' working paper, University of Pittsburgh.
Camillus, J. C. (1981b). ''Strategic Plans and Action Programs: Strengthening the Content Linkage,'' working paper, University of Pittsburgh.
Camillus, J. C. (1981), ''Corporate Strategy and Executive Action: Transition Stages and Linkage Dimensions,'' *Academy of Management Review, 6* (April), 253–260, (c).
Camillus, J. C. (1981d) ''Designing a Capital Budgeting System that Works,'' *Long Range Planning.* forthcoming,
Camillus, J. C. & Birnberg, J. G. (WIP), ''Behavioral Considerations in Designing Management Control Systems,'' University of Pittsburgh.
Camillus, J. C & Grant, J. H. (1980), ''Operational Planning: The Integration of Programming & Budgeting,'' *Academy of Management Review, 5,* (July), 369–379.
Cooper, A. C. (WIPa), ''Influences Upon Entrepreneurship,'' Krannert Graduate School, Purdue University.
Cooper, A. C. (WIPb), ''Strategic Responses to Technological Threats,'' Krannert Graduate School, Purdue University.
Cooper, A. C. (WIPc), ''Performance and Prospects Along the Growth/Market Share Matrix,'' Krannert Graduate School, Purdue University.
Datta, Y. (1980), ''New Directions for Research in Business Strategy,'' *Proceedings,* Midwest Academy of Management, 71–88.
Doz, Y. L. (1980), ''Strategic Management in Multinational Corporations,'' *Sloan Management Review* 21/2 (Winter), 27–46.
Doz, Y. L. (1980), *Multinational Strategic Management: Economic and Political Imperatives* (forthcoming).
Doz, Y. L., Bartlett, C. A. & Prahalad, C. K. (1981) ''Global Competitive Pressures vs. Host Country Demands: Managing Tensions in MNCs,'' *California Management Review* (forthcoming).
Dubin, R. (1969), *Theory Building* New York: Free Press.
Duhaime, I. M. (1981a), ''Corporate Divestment, unpublished doctoral dissertation, University of Pittsburgh.
Duhaime, I. M. (1981b) Corporate Divestment,'' University of Illinois WIP.
Dutton, J. E. and Fahey, L. (1981), ''Strategic Decision Diagnosis: Four perspectives,'' Working paper Evanston: Northwestern University.

Egelhoff, W. and Newman, W. H. (WIP), "Strategy-Structure in 50 MNCs," Strategy Research Center, Columbia University, WIP.

Fahey, L. (1981), "Rational and Political Behaviors in Organizational Decision Making An Empirical Study," Working paper, Evanston: Graduate School of Management, Northwestern.

Fahey, L. (1981), "On Strategic Management Decision Processes," *Strategic Management Journal,* 2/1, (Jan.–March), 43–60.

Farley, J. U., Capon, N. and Hulbert, J. M. (WIP), "Survey of Corporate Planning Practice," Strategy Research Center, Columbia University.

Grant, J. H. (1980), "Utilization of Quantitative and Qualitative Techniques in Strategic Management Research," Working paper address to Midwest Academy of Management, April.

Grant, J. H. (WIP), "Indicators of Strategic Performance," Graduate School of Business, University of Pittsburgh.

Grant, J. H., & Snodgrass, C. (WIP), "Cultural Influences on Planning and Control System Design," Graduate School of Business, University of Pittsburgh, WIP.

Grinyer, P., Al-Bazzaz, S. & Ardenaki, M. Y. (1980), "Strategy, Structure, the Environment, and Financial Performance in 48 United Kingdom Companies," *Academy of Management Journal,* (June), 193–220.

Hambrick, D. C. (1981a), "Environment, Strategy, and Power Within Top Management Teams," *Administrative Science Quarterly,* forthcoming.

Hambrick, D. C. (1981b), "Strategic Awareness Within Top Management Teams," *Strategic Management Journal,* 2/3 (July–Sept.)

Hambrick, D. C. (1981c), "Specialization of Environmental Scanning Activities Within Top Management Teams," *Journal of Management Studies,* forthcoming.

Hambrick, D. C. and MacMillan, I. C. (WIP), "Theory Testing With PIMS Data," Strategy Research Center, Columbia University.

Hand, H. H. (1981a), "Strategic Criteria in Retailing," Working paper, University of South Carolina.

Hand, H. H. (1981b) "Strategy Perspectives for Developers of Shopping Centers," Working paper, University of South Carolina.

Hand, H. H. (1981c), "Location Analysis as a Primary Determinant of Strategy in Retailing," Working paper, University of South Carolina.

Hand, H. H. (1981d), "Business-Level Strategies in the Service Station Sector," Working paper, University of South Carolina.

Harrigan, K. R. (1980a), *Strategies for Declining Businesses* D. C. Heath.

Harrigan, K. R. (1980b), "The Effect of Exit Barriers Upon Strategic Flexibility," *Strategic Management Journal, 1* (April–June), 165–176.

Harrigan, K. R. (1980c), "Clustering Competitors by Strategic Groups," *Proceedings,* Southwest Academy of Management, 46–50.

Harrigan, K. R. (1980a), "Deterrents to Divestiture," *Academy of Management Journal,* forthcoming.

Harrigan, J. R. (1981b), "Strategic Panning for Endgame," *Long Range Planning,* forthcoming.

Harrigan, K. R. (1981c), "Strategies for Declining Businesses," *Journal of Business Strategy,* forthcoming.

Harrigan, K. R. (1981d), "Barriers to Entry and Competitive Strategies," *Strategic Management Journal,* forthcoming.

Harrigan, K. R. (1981e), "Entry Strategies and InterIndustry Differences in Entry Barriers," Working paper, University of Texas at Dallas.

Harrigan, K. R. (1981f), "Competitive Dynamics and Evolution in the Energy Industry," Working paper, University of Texas at Dallas.

Harrigan, K. R. (WIPa), "The Influence of Business Unit Strategies Upon Industry Evolution," University of Texas at Dallas.

Harrigan, K. R. (WIPb) ''Analyzing the Influence of Industry Structural Context Upon Competitive Interactions,'' University of Texas at Dallas.

Harrigan, K. R. and Porter, M. E. (1981), ''Competitive Strategies in Declining Industries,'' *Harvard Business Review,* forthcoming.

Henry, H. W., (1980), ''Evolution of Strategic Planning in Major Corporations,'' paper presented at AIDS, Las Vegas: (November).

Henry, H. W. (1981), ''Then and Now: A Look at Strategic Planning Systems,'' *Journal of Business Strategy, 1* (Winter), 64–69.

Henry, H. W. (WIP), ''The Role of Consultants in Strategic Planning,'' Knoxville, Tenn.: University of Tennessee.

Hofer, C. W. (1975), ''Toward A Contingency Theory of Business Strategy,'' *Academy of Management Journal,* 18/4, 784–810.

Hout, T. M., Porter, M. E., Rudden, E., and Vogt, E. (1980), ''Global Industries: New Rules for the Competitive Game,'' Working paper, Graduate School of Business Administration, Boston, Mass: Harvard University, (August).

Huff, A. S. (1980a), ''Industry Sense Making,'' Paper presented at Academy of Management Meeting.

Huff, A. S. (1980b), ''Evocative Metaphors,'' *Human Systems Management, 1* (November), 219–228.

Huff, A. S. (1980c), ''Organizations as Political Systems: Implications for Diagnosis, Change and Stability,'' in Cummings, T. G. (Ed.), *Systems Theory for Organization Development,* Wiley.

Huff, A. S. (1981), ''Extraordinary Uncertainty,'' working paper, College of Commerce, Urbana: University of Illinois.

Huff, A. S. (WIP), ''A Rhetorical Examination of Strategic Change,'' in L. R. Pondy, P. Frost, G. Morgan and T. Dandridge (Eds.), *Organizational Symbolism.*

Huff, A. S. & Pondy, L. (WIP), ''Analyzing Decision Makers' Language,'' NIE Grant, College of Commerce, Urbana: University of Illinois.

Iyer, E. S. and Ramaprasad, A. (1980), ''Strategic Postures for Innovation,'' Working paper, Graduate School of Business, University of Pittsburgh.

Jauch, L. R., Martin, T. N. and Osborn, R. N. (1981), ''Succession in the Executive Suite,'' *Journal of Business Strategy,* forthcoming.

Jauch, L. R. and Osborn, R. N. (1981), ''Toward an Integrated Theory of Strategy,'' *Academy of Management Review,* forthcoming.

Jauch, L. R., Osborn, R. N. and Glueck, W. F. (1980), ''Short Term Financial Success in Large Business Organizations: The Environment-Strategy Connection,'' *Strategic Management Journal, 1* (Jan.–Mar.), 49–64.

Jauch, L. R., Osborn, R. N. and Martin, T. N. (1980), ''Structured Content Analysis of Cases: A Complementary Method for Organizational Research,'' *Academy of Management Review,* 517–525.

Jauch, L. R. and Wilson, H. (1979), ''A Strategic Perspective for Make or Buy Decisions,'' *Long Range Planning, 12,* (December), 56–61.

Jauch, L. R., et al. (WIP), ''Comparative Outcomes of Two Policy Course Structures,'' Carbondale: Southern Illinois University.

Jemison, D. B. (1981a) ''Organizational vs. Environmental Sources of Influence in Strategic Decision Making,'' *Strategic Management Journal,* 2/1 (January–March), 77–90.

Jemison, D. B. (1981b), ''Strategic Management Research—The Importance of An Integrative Approach,'' working paper, Indiana University.

Jemison, D. B. (1981c), ''Common Interorganizational Boundary Spanning Roles: An Empirical Analysis,'' working paper, Indiana University.

Jensen, O. W., O'Neill, H. M., and Saunders, C. B. (1981a) ''Opinion Differences Between Men and Women as Found in the NORC General Surveys: With Implications for Management,''

Working paper, Business Environment and Policy Department, Storrs, Ct.: University of Connecticut.

Jensen, O. W., O'Neill, H. M., and Saunders, C. B. (1981b), "Interest Group and Work Group Value Clusters: Interactions With Strategic Implications," Working paper, Business Environment and Policy Department, Storrs, Ct.: University of Connecticut.

Jensen, O. W., O'Neill, H. M. and Saunders, C. B. (1981c), "Value Clusters in American Business Firms: With Implications for Strategic Management," Working paper, Business Environment and Policy Department, Storrs, Ct.: University of Connecticut.

Jensen, O. W. and Saunders, C. B. (1981), "Some Fundamental Attitudes of American Business Managers: With Implications for Strategic Management," Working paper, Business Environment and Policy Department, Storrs, Ct.: University of Connecticut.

Kirchhoff, B. A. & Kirchhoff, J. J. (1980), "Empirical Assessment of the Strategy Tactics Dilemma," *Academy of Management Proceedings*, 7–11.

Klein, H. and Newman, W. H. (1980), "How to Use Spire: A Systematic Procedure for Identifying Relevant Environments for Strategic Planning," *Journal of Business Strategy, 1*, 32–45.

Lachenmeyer, C. W. (1980), *The Limits of Planning* Institute for the Analysis, Evaluation and Design of Human Action.

Lenz, R. T. (1980), "Environment, Strategy, Organization Structure and Performance: Patterns in One Industry," *Strategic Management Journal*, 1/3 (July–Sept.), 209–226.

Lenz, R. T. (1981), "Determinants of Organizational Performance: An Interdisciplinary Review," *Strategic Management Journal*, 2/2 (April–June), 131–154.

Lenz, R. T. (WIPa), "Sources of Managerial Discretion," School of Business, Indiana University.

Lenz, R. T. (WIPb), "Governance by Corporate Boards," School of Business, Indiana University.

Lenz, R. T. and Lyles, M. A. (1981a), "Behavioral Problems in Planning Systems: A Study in the Commercial Banking Industry," Working paper, Graduate School of Business, Indianapolis.

Lenz, R. T. and Lyles, M. A., (1981b), "Tackling the Human Problems in Planning," *Long Range Planning*, forthcoming, (Summer).

Leontiades, M. (1980), *Strategies for Diversification and Change* Boston: Little Brown.

Leontiades, M. (1981a), "The Confusing Words of Business Policy," *Academy of Management Review*, forthcoming.

Leontiades, M. (1981b) "A Multidimensional Model of Planning," Working paper, Camden College of Arts and Sciences, Camden, N.J.: Rutgers.

Leontiades, M. and Tezel, A. (1980), "Planning Perceptions and Planning Results," *Strategic Management Journal, 1* (January–March), 65–75.

Lorange, P. (1980), *Corporate Planning: An Executive Viewpoint*, Englewood Cliffs: Prentice-Hall.

Lorange, P., (ed). (1982a), *Implementation of Strategic Planning*, Englewood Cliffs, N.J.: Prentice-Hall.

Lorange, P. (1982b), *A Comparative Study of Strategic Processes in European Corporations*, forthcoming.

Lyles, M. A. (1981), "Formulating Strategic Problems: Empirical Analysis and Model Development," *Strategic Management Journal, 2* (January–March), 61–76.

Lyles, M. A., and Mitroff, I. I. (1981a), "Organizational Problem Formulation: An Empirical Study," working paper, Indiana University.

Lyles, M. A., and Mitroff, I. I. (1981b), "Information Gathering Processes and Strategic Problem Formulation," working paper, Indiana University.

MacMillan, I. C. (1980), "Strategy and Government Regulations," *Journal of Business Strategy, 1* (Summer), 70–73.

MacMillan, I. C., Hambrick, D., and Pennings, J. (WIP) "Vertical Integration in the PIMS data," Strategic Research Center, Columbia University.

Mazzolini, R. (1980a), "The International Strategy of State-Owned Firms: An Organizational Process and Politics Perspective," *Strategic Management Journal*, 1/2, (April–June), 101–118.

Mazzolini, R. (1980b), "Real World Decision-Making: The Limits of Top Management Power," *The Journal of Business Strategy,* 1/2, (Fall), 3–8.
Mazzolini, R. (1981a), "Strategic Decisions in Government-Controlled Enterprises," *Administration and Society,* 13/1 (May), 7–32.
Mazzolini, R. (1981b), Strategic Decisions as the Result of Management Processes and Routines," *Long Range Planning,* 14/3 (June), 85–96.
Melcher, A. J. and Melcher, B. (1980), "Toward a Systems Theory of Policy Analysis: Static Versus Dynamic Analysis," *Academy of Management Review,* 5/2 (April), 235–247.
Melcher, A. J., Melcher, B., Jones, R., and Baliga (WIP), R. *Strategy Formulation and Decision Making: Toward A Systems Framework.* Administrative Science, Kent State University.
Miles, R. and Snow, C. (1978), *Organization Strategy, Structure and Process* McGraw Hill.
Miles, R. E. and Snow, C. (1981) "Toward a Synthesis in Organization Theory," in Jelinek, Litterer and Miles, *Organization by Design,* Dallas: Business Publications. (in press).
Miles, R. E. and Snow, C. C. (WIP), "Diagnosing Strategic Fits and Planning for Human Resources Management," University of California, Berkeley.
Miller, D. (1980), "Evolution and Revolution: A Quantum View of Structural Change in Organizations," Working paper, Faculty of Management, Montreal, Canada: McGill University, (July).
Miller, D. and Friesen, P. H. (1980a), "Momentum and Revolution in Organizational Adaptation," *Academy of Management Journal,* pp. 591–614.
Miller, D. and Friesen, P. (1980b), "Archetypes of Organizational Transition," *Administrative Science Quarterly, 25* (June), pp. 268–299.
Miller, D., deVries, M. F. R., and Toulouse, J. (1980), "Top Executive Locus of Control and the Relationship to Strategy Making, Structure, and Environment," Working Paper, Montreal, Canada: McGill University, (December).
Miller, D. and Mintzberg, H. (1980), "The Case for Configuration," Working paper, Montreal, Canada: McGill University, Faculty of Management, (November).
Mintzberg, H. (1982), *Power In and Around Organizations,* forthcoming.
Mintzberg, H. and Waters, J. A. (1980), "Tracking Strategy in an Entrepreneurial Firm," Working paper, Montreal, Canada: McGill University, Faculty of Management.
Mitroff, I. I. (1981), "Is a Periodic Table of Elements for Organization Behavior Possible?" Working paper, Graduate School of Business, Los Angeles: University of Southern California.
Mitroff, I. I. and Mason, R. O. (1980), "A Logic for Strategic Management," *Human Systems Management, 1,* 115–126.
Mitroff, I. I. and Mason, R. O. (1981), "Bringing in Metaphysics: On the Philosophical Foundations of Policy," Working paper, Graduate School of Business, Los Angeles: University of Southern California.
Montanari, J. R. (1979), "Strategic Choice: A Theoretical Analysis," *Journal of Management Studies, 16* (May), 202–221.
Montanari, J. R. (1981a), "The Strategic Management Process," Working paper, Arizona State University.
Montanari, J. R. (1981b), "Combining Lecture and Simulation Teaching Methods: How Well Does It Work?" Working paper, Arizona State University.
Montanari, J. R. and Wetherbe, J. C. (1981), "Zero Based Budgeting in the Planning Process," *Strategic Management Journal,* 2/1 (Jan.–March), 1–4.
Montanari, J. R., Moorhead, G., and Montanari, E. O. (1980), "A Laboratory Study of a Strategic Decision Making Methodology," *AIDS Proceedings,* 472–474.
Narayanan, V. K. and Fahey, L. (1981), "The MicroPolitics of Strategy Formulation," *Academy of Management Review,* forthcoming.
Newman, W. H. (WIP), "Research Methodology for the Design of Integrated Systems," Working paper, Strategy Research Center, Columbia University.
Osborn, R. N., Jauch, L. R., Martin, T. N., and Glueck, W. F. (1981), "The Event of CEO

Succession, Performance, and Environmental Conditions,'' *Academy of Management Journal*, forthcoming.

Pennings, J. N. (WIPa), ''Antecedents and Consequences of Linkages Among Boards of Directors,'' Graduate School of Business, Columbia University.

Pennings, J. N. (WIPb) ''Urban-Environmental Determinants of Entrepreneurship,'' Graduate School of Business, Columbia University.

Pitts, B. (WIPa), ''Organizing Diversified U.S.M.N.C. Foreign Operations,'' College of Business, Penn State University.

Pitts, B. (WIPb) ''Defining Diversity,'' College of Business, Penn State University.

Porter, M. E. (1980a), *Competitive Strategy: Techniques for Analyzing Industries and Competitors.* New York: Free Press.

Porter, M. E. (1980b) ''Industry Structure and Competitive Strategy: Keys to Profitability,'' *Financial Analysts Journal,* (July–August), 30–42.

Porter, M. E. (1980c), ''The Contributions of Industrial Organization to Strategy Formulation: A Promise Beginning to be Realized,'' Working paper, Graduate School of Business Administration, Boston, Mass.: Harvard University, (August).

Porter, M. E. (1980d), ''Strategic Interaction: Some Lessons from Industry Histories for Theory and Antitrust Policy,'' Working paper, Harvard Graduate School of Business, Boston, Mass.: Harvard University.

Porter, M. E. and Caves, R. E. (1981), ''The Dynamics of Changing Seller Concentration,'' *Journal of Industrial Economics,* forthcoming.

Porter, M. E., Caves, R. E. and Spence, A. M. (1980), *Competition in the Open Economy.* Harvard Economic Studies, Cambridge, Mass.: Harvard University Press.

Porter, M. E. and Spence, A. M. (1981), ''Vertical Integration and Differentiated Impacts,'' *Journal of Industrial Economics,* forthcoming.

Prahalad, C. K. and Doz, Y. L. (1981), ''Strategic Control—the Dilemma in Headquarter Subsidiary Relationships,'' in L. Otterbeck (ed.), *Headquarter/Subsidiary Relationships in Transnational Corporations* London: Gower, forthcoming.

Quinn, J. B. (1980a) *Strategies for Change: Logical Incrementalism.* Homewood, Ill: Irwin.

Quinn, J. B. (1980b), ''Managing Strategic Change,'' *Sloan Management Review,* 21/4 (Summer), 3–20.

Quinn, J. B. (1981), ''Formulating Strategy One Step at a Time,'' *Journal of Business Strategy, 1* (Winter), 42–63.

Ramaprasad, A. (1981), ''Revolutionary Change and Strategic Management,'' Working paper, Department of Administrative Sciences, Southern Illinois University.

Ramaprasad, A. and Bourgeois, L. J. (1981), ''Toward a Logical Theory of Strategy: A Preliminary Model,'' Administrative Sciences Department, Southern Illinois University.

Ramaprasad, A. and Knod, E. M. ''Strategic Planning in an Academic Unit: Hierarchical Analysis with Eigenvector Weighting,'' Working paper, Administrative Sciences Department, Carbondale, Ill.: Southern Illinois University.

Schendel, D. (WIPa), ''Business Strategy Along the Product-Market Life Cycle,'' Krannert Graduate School, Purdue University.

Schendel, D. (WIPb), ''Portfolio Theory and Strategic Decisions,'' Krannert Graduate School, Purdue University, WIPb.

Schendel, D. (WIPc), ''Executive Perception of Acquisition Performance,'' Krannert Graduate School, Purdue University.

Schendel, D. E. and Hofer, C. W. (1979), *Strategic Management: A New View of Business Policy and Planning* Boston: Little Brown.

Summer, C. E. (1980), *Strategic Behavior in Business and Government* Boston: Little Brown.

Tavel, C. (1980), *The Third Industrial Age: Strategy for Business Survival* 2nd ed., Oxford: Pergamon Press.

Tichy, N. M. (WIP), "A Study of Executive Behavior," Strategy Research Center, New York: Columbia University.

Tichy, N. M. (WIP), Devanna, M. A. and Warren, E. K., "Strategic Management and Management Personnel," Strategy Research Center, New York: Columbia University.

Tushman, M. L. (WIP), "Company Strategy and R&D Management," Strategy Research Center, New York: Columbia University.

Vancil, R. F. (1979), *Decentralization: Managerial Ambiguity by Design*. Financial Executives Research Foundation.

Vancil, R. F. (1980), "Managing the Decentralized Firm," *Financial Executive*, 68/3 (March), 34–43.

Vesper, K. H. (1980a), *New Venture Strategies* New York: Prentice Hall.

Vesper, K. H. (1980b), *Entrepreneurship Education* Wellesley, Mass.: Babson Center for Entrepreneurship Studies.

Vesper, K. H. (1982), *Mechanics of Entrepreneurship* New York: Prentice Hall, forthcoming.

Vesper, K. H. (WIPa) "Obstacles Impeding Would-be Entrepreneurs," School of Business, University of Washington.

Vesper, K. H. (WIPb), "Systematic Strategies for Business Startup," School of Business, University of Washington.

Vesper, K. H. (WIPc), "How Schools Spawn New Enterprises," School of Business, University of Washington.

Vesper, K. H., Sexton, and Kent (1981), *Mini-encyclopedia of Entrepreneurship* New York: Prentice-Hall, forthcoming.

Vicars, W. H., Jauch, L. R., and Wilson H. (1980), "A Scale to Measure General Entrepreneurship Tendency," paper presented at National Academy of Management meeting.

Vozikis, G. H. (1979), "A Strategic Disadvantage Profile of the Stages of Development of Small Business: The Experience of Retail and Service Small Business in Georgia," unpublished dissertation, University of Georgia.

Vozikis, G. S. (1980), "A Strategic Disadvantage Profile of the Stages of Development and the Stages of the Exporting Process," SBA Grant 79-2716, Small Business Development Center, University of Georgia.

Weir, J. E. (1979), "Towards the Theoretical Foundations of a Contingency Theory of Policy Making Behavior," *Academy of Management Proceedings*, 128–132.

Weir, J. E. (1981a), "Emerging Theory Building Issues in the Business Policy Field: Identifying the Theoretical Domains of the Field," working paper, SIU-Edwardsville.

Weir, J. E. (1981b), "Emerging Theoretical Imperatives in the Strategy/Policy Discipline: The Unit of Analysis Problem in Understanding General Management," working paper, SIU-Edwardsville.

Wu, F. H. (1981), "Incrementalism in Financial Strategic Planning," *Academy of Management Review, 6*, 133–143.

Wortman, M. S., Jr. (1979), "The Utilization of Qualitative Methods and Techniques in Strategic Management Research," Paper presented at AIDS, (November).

Yavitz, B. and Newman, W. H. (WIP), "Strategy Implementation," Strategy Research Center, New York: Columbia University.

VARIATIONS IN STRATEGIC DECISION-MAKING PROCESSES

Paul Shrivastava

I. INTRODUCTION

The organizational processes by which strategic decisions are made determine the content or outcome of corporate strategies. Thus, in order to understand and manage strategy formulation and implementation we need to understand the strategic decision processes that underlie these activities (Elliason, 1976; Schendel and Hofer, 1979; Simon, 1979). Strategic decision-making process refers to the set of activities performed by organizational members and their associates, from the time they identify and formulate the strategic problems until the time they make a final commitment of organizational resources for resolving these problems. These activities include a diverse set of subprocesses like planning information acquisition, evaluation, argumentation, persuasion, negotiation, training, recruitment, etc., which occur at multiple levels of the organization, through the participation of many stakeholders (Shrivastava and Grant, 1982).

Advances in Strategic Management, Volume 2, pages 177–189.

ISBN: 0-89232-409-0

The strategic decision-making process has been studied by several researchers and found to proceed in three important sequential steps of (1) problem formulation, (2) the generation and evaluation of alternative courses of action, and (3) the selection of a feasible solution. The problem formulation process involves identifying a specific set of interdependent problems that constitute the overall strategic problem and reaching a consensus on the relative importance of the subproblems or delineating the priority for solving them. The generation of alternatives involves considering a set of possible courses of action in terms of their relative merits, demerits, and implementation feasibility. The final choice of the solution entails selecting a feasible alternative which satisfies the organization's needs, and the ratification of this solution by the dominant stakeholder groups (Bower, 1970; Carter, 1971; Mintzberg et al., 1976). Once the final choice is made, the strategic decision may be implemented through the sanctioning of appropriate resources which fund the action programs implied by the decision.

This brief description of the complex strategic decision-making process is obviously too simplistic and serves more as an analytical device for viewing strategic decisions than an accurate description of complex real-life decision situations. In reality the strategic decision-making process is much more complex, involving many conflicting interests and agents, taking long periods of time to make, and plagued by numerous interruptions, delays, disruptions, etc. Despite the complexity and seemingly random variations that characterize this process, there is some evidence to suggest that it follows certain standard patterns across organizations.

In this paper we review some of the literature that supports our observation that strategic decision-making processes actually vary across organizations in standard patterns. Then, using data from a recent study of strategic decision-making processes, we describe four prototypical patterns in this process. These patterns–referred to as the strategic decision-making models—represent some important variations in the process and have implications for strategy formulation and implementation which are discussed below.

II. EVIDENCE OF VARIATION IN STRATEGIC DECISION-MAKING PROCESSES

Several studies have alluded to variations in the strategic decision-making processes adopted by organizations. The three modes of strategy making described by Mintzberg (1973) clearly reflect the pattern underlying strategic decision-making processes. The *entrepreneurial* mode refers to situations in which the organization actively searches for opportunities, takes risks, leaps into uncertain situations, and adopts rapid growth strategies. In contrast to this aggressive proactive stance toward strategy making is the *adaptive* or incremental mode. In this mode the organization incrementally changes its current strategy to adapt to the changes in its environment. These strategy changes are small, stepwise, and aimed at maintaining the current position rather than being radical departures from the current or past states (Lindblom, 1979). The third mode of strategy making is the *planning* mode, which involves synoptic, systematic, and integrated approach to strategy formulation. In this mode the strategic plans are developed by professional managers through extensive and intensive analysis of the options available to the organization. This mode of strategy making is usually implemented through a well-developed strategic planning system (Mintzberg, 1973; Mintzberg et al., 1976).

The strategic decision-making process patterns implied by these modes of strategy making are clearly indicated in the descriptions of strategic organizational types consisting of Prospectors, Defenders, and Analyzers (Miles and Snow, 1978). Prospectors are organizations which aggressively seek to enlarge their domain of operations by monitoring the environment and proactively seeking out new expansion opportunities, reflecting the entrepreneurial mode of strategy making described above. Defenders are organizations which are content with maintaining their current strategic posture. They attempt to seal off a portion of the total market to create a stable set of products and customers by producing and distributing goods efficiently and maintaining a strict control over organizational processes. Analyzers attempt to locate and exploit new opportunities but from a stable base of products. They make strategies in the planning mode referred to above, by analyzing and matching their internal resources to environmental trends.

In the context of governmental policy formulation Allison (1970) describes three models of organizational decision making, i.e., the rational actor model (Model I), the bureaucratic organizational process model (Model II), and the governmental politics model (Model III). These three models reflect alternative ways of conceptualizing the strategic decision-making process in the context of the Cuban missile crisis decision. The focus of decision making in Model I is a single person—the President of the United States, who attempts to rationally evaluate the best option in the national interest and make strategic choices after consulting with a group of experts. Model II conceptualizes decision making as a set of interacting bureaucratic procedures between government agencies like the White House, the State Department, the Pentagon, the National Security Council, etc. Information required for making critical policy decisions flows through these agencies in an erratic, bureaucratic, impersonal manner, and decisions are finally made by using well-established norms, rules, and regulations. In Model III the decision-making process is viewed as an intergovernmental political process involving the U.S. and Soviet governments as primary actors and other national governments (Cuba, Britain, France, etc.) as secondary influences. The decision-making progresses through bargaining and negotiations between these stakeholders, ending in a compromise decision outcome. While Allison's three models characterized top-level governmental policymaking processes, similar processes have been found to occur in a variety of business and public organizations (Blau and Scott, 1962; Quinn, 1980).

These studies provide insights into how the strategic decision-making processes vary systematically on such dimensions as the key decision makers and their roles, the nature of problem formulation, the means by which alternative courses of action are generated and evaluated, the types of analysis conducted, and the criteria used for making the final choices. However, these studies do not comprehensively describe the commonly occurring patterns of strategic decision-making processes. To get a better understanding of these patterns I recently studied one strategic decision in 32 business organizations in India. The strategic decision to restructure the data processing activities of the organization through the purchase of sophisticated data processing equipment was the focus of this study. This decision involves the determination of present and future informational needs of the organization, the search for alternative computer systems or data processing arrangements to fulfill these identified informational needs, technical and financial evaluation of the alternatives, and the choice of the most feasible alternative (Shrivastava, 1981). The analysis of data from this study revealed four prototypical patterns that the strategic decision-making process followed in the sample organizations.

These patterns are described as the four strategic decision-making models. They represent a more refined way of classifying the decision-making process. It is quite possible that in the same organization different decisions follow a different decision-making process model. These models are:

- Managerial Autocracy Model (MAM)
- Systemic Bureaucracy Model (SBM)
- Adaptive Planning Model (APM)
- Political Expediency Model (PEM)

The models are described here in terms of the following characteristics of the decision-making process: (1) problem familiarization activity; (2) solution development activity; (3) choice and implementation; (4) number and level of people involved in the process and their roles; (5) nature of evaluation or analysis conducted; and (6) environmental influences on decision making (Shrivastava and Grant, 1982). We summarize the characteristics of these four SDMMs in Table 1 and describe them in detail in this section.

A. Managerial Autocracy Model

Managerial autocracy refers to situations where a single manager is the key decision maker. His role and influence in every phase of decision making is significant. It is quite common to find young or small organizations (en-

Table 1. Summary of Strategic Decision-Making Models

Models *Characteristics*	*MAM*	*SBM*	*APM*	*PEM*
Decision Making Process Problem Familiarization Solution Development	Restricted number of p–s sets are generated. Apparent dominance of one p–s set from beginning. Limited amount of participation in solution development. One key manager develops the solution with aid from his assistants.	Proliferation of p–s sets generated in different parts of the organization. Procedures for disseminating & communicating p–s sets are well developed. Solution development procedure is also predefined	Problem familiarization is almost nonexistant. The plan is presumed to have incorporated the problem formulation activities. Solution development revolves around modification of plans to accomodate changed conditions.	Multiple p–s sets are generated but one set is championed by the vested interest group. Solution development is influenced by individuals or vested interests.
Decision Makers Number of People Hierarchical Levels	Usually one Top Management	Several groups of people. Middle and Top Management. Several depart. or functional areas are involved.	Single groups of people usually MIS/DP Depart. Middle or Top Management Usually data processing experts are involved.	A coalition of individuals or a single indiv. Top management

Table 1—Continued

Models / *Characteristics*	*MAM*	*SBM*	*APM*	*PEM*
Decision Making Orientation/Motivation	To improve efficiency Result oriented process	To satisfy procedural rationality Process is oriented to fulfilling organizational procedures.	Fulfillment of plans Implementation is emphasised over decision making.	To satisfy vested interests. Decision making process is manipulated to meet desired decisions.
Types of Analysis	Judgemental or Intuitive	Primarily Computational Cost benefit analysis is emphasised.	Computational Technical analysis and implementation planning are emphasized.	Bargaining and Negotiations among members. Analysis done depends on what the organization will accept as legitimate.
Role of Organizational Systems	Few organizational systems are used, decision making is highly personalized.	Every activity is guided by some system (usually a bureaucratic system).	Many types of formal learning systems are used. Strategic Planning system, and MIS play a central role.	Formal systems are side stepped and personal knowledge of individual members is used extensively.
Environmental Influences	Very limited involvement of environmental agents.	Environmental influences shape the problem & its solution.	Extensive negotiations with relevant environmental agents.	Environmental agents may be coopted to join coalitions.

trepreneurial firms) exhibiting this model. Here a large amount of power and authority rests with a single key executive, usually the entrepreneur–manager, who makes all strategic decisions himself with technical assistance from several subordinates.

The problem familiarization process is dominated by the key manager. He generates and supports the problem–solution (p–s) set that ultimately gains organizational acceptance. The key manager is usually formally put in charge of the solution-building activity. While several technical and financial experts may help him in evaluating the alternatives by providing relevant information, they typically work under his guidance and supervision. Due to the limited time available to the manager and also because of the cognitive limitations on processing information, the evaluation is not very detailed. The manager typically functions with imperfect technical information, because he is usually not familiar with technical aspects of computerization.

The final choice of alternatives is made in consultation with, or at least after informing, the relevant superiors, peers, and subordinates. All the information used in decision making is channelized and controlled by the key decision maker. The manager attempts to rationally analyze all the facts available to him and then make a decision himself maintaining full responsibility for its consequences.

The time taken under such decision-making situations is usually very short. In situations where the data being handled are sensitive or secret, this model may be the only available alternative for the organization to follow, because it effectively limits the distribution of sensitive information.

The key manager who controls the decision making is usually a member of the top-management team or a very senior middle-management person who has the confidence of the top management. He is a strong and influential individual who has proven his competence in the organization.

Organizations in which the managerial autocracy model can occur vary in size and structure. However, they usually possess rather poorly developed management systems and are therefore obliged to depend heavily on individuals for making and executing decisions. Both the decision-making process and outcome are biased by the style and preferences of the decision maker in charge and not by the systems, procedures, or accumulated learning and experience of the organization as a whole. Hence, even if such an organization has previous experience and accumulated learning in the given decision area, this knowledge may not get incorporated into the decision-making process.

B. Systemic Bureaucracy Model

As the name suggests, the decision-making process in the systemic bureaucracy model is more oriented toward systems and procedures than toward individuals. The problem familiarization phase is an ambiguous one in which many p–s sets are proposed by individuals at various levels of the organizations. These initial problem formulations are steadily documented in the official files of the organization. Over a period of time "one" statement of the problem is constructed, which is a combination of the original set of suggested problems. The problem formulation is very often influenced by environmental agencies (computer vendors in this case) which have a stake in the decision. The environmental agents attempt to speed up the organizational problem formulation process by providing relevant information and continuously urging decision makers to overcome the bureaucratic systems which delay the decision.

Once the problem is formulated, it is put into one of the many predetermined routine procedures for problem solving. There are well-defined and documented stepwise procedures for handling all decisions. These procedures may not be adequate or efficient ways of solving the problem; but, as long as they are fulfilled, the organization is content with the resulting solution. Evaluation of alternatives is extensive and detailed. Technically qualified persons from data processing or the MIS department are put in charge of developing a feasible solution. The evaluation procedure includes technical evaluation, financial evaluation, cost–benefit analysis, and implementation planning. At each step of the evaluation process, the decision makers attempt to fulfill the written policies of the organization. There is a heavy emphasis on impersonal, rational, objective, and quantitative analysis.

This analysis usually leads to the selection of one specific alternative which is presented to the top management as the best available option. The ratification of this choice by top management is a critical event. It legitimizes the decision and sanctions formal authority for implementation. In these situations formal sanctions are the basis for initiating action. Without the written sanction of the board of directors or some such powerful body, the decision cannot be finalized. Even after the sanction the organization has to go through several months of paper work formalities to complete the decision making.

The most conducive organizational settings for the systemic bureaucracy model are old, established, and large private-sector firms or public-sector enterprises. The management systems in these organizations are well developed and implemented. They are not the most sophisticated or modern systems available, but they serve functional objectives. The task forces or committees are extensively used in decision making. They are composed of technically qualified personnel from all relevant functional areas of the organization.

One interesting characteristic of the systemic bureaucracy model is that the decision-making responsibility is usually relegated to that part or member of the organization who has the most expertise and knowledge in the decision area, so organizational learning and experience are easily exploited for decision-making purposes. Organizational learning systems are usually formal and explicitly defined. Ways of information sharing, and the communication and routing of information, are predetermined by organizational procedures.

C. Adaptive Planning Model

The adaptive planning decision-making process is the practical version of what management textbooks describe as the systematic planning activity. In this model, current decisions flow from previously made decisions. Organizational plans become a point of departure for strategic decision-making.

The problem familiarization phase is almost nonexistent in such situations, because problem formulation has already occurred at the time of formulation of the plans. The problem formulation is delegated to a specialized planning cell which systematically evaluates the information and solution alternatives. It then recommends the planned development of solution activities. Familiarizing other parts of the organization with the problem is done through regular management reports or annual plans.

The alternative generation and choice of solution are conducted in a systematic manner with a consistent effort toward achieving efficient solutions to the problem. Qualified experts are usually available to evaluate the technical merits of the proposed alternatives. Multiple types of evaluation procedures which take into account technical and financial considerations and the maintenance of future growth needs are used. Typically several people from many levels of the organization are involved in all phases of the decision-making process.

The decision-making process is an adaptive and incremental one. The plans which serve as the basis for decision making are used only as guidelines. They may be adopted, modified, or completely dropped depending on the current analysis of the issues. Organizations which exhibit adaptive planning are usually progressive public-sector enterprises or large private-sector firms with good financial performance. They are fast-growing, prosperous firms with professionally trained managers and possess the resources required for the development of a planning system and culture. Subsidiaries of multinational companies often follow the Adaptive Planning model.

One limitation of the Adaptive Planning model is that it does not encourage managers to seek drastically new, different, or innovative solutions. There is an attempt to broadly follow the plans, with minor modifications to incorporate changed conditions. Hence, in situations where there is a sudden and severe change in the environmental conditions, these organizations are sluggish to respond. Sometimes they have to get permission to change their plans for purchase of capital equipment (like computer systems) from their corporate headquarters, which may be overseas. This is a cumbersome and time-consuming activity which local managers would rather avoid.

D. Political Expediency Model

Several strategic decision-making situations studied followed a very different kind of process from the ones discussed above. In the political expediency model there are several key decision-makers or groups of decision makers (departments, divisions, etc.) who make decisions for personal gain. They are primarily concerned with protecting or advancing their own interests even at the cost of organizational interests.

Most decisions made under this model of organizational decision making have to be justified by the decision makers to the rest of the organization as being organizationally rational. Hence, while the actual decisions are made quickly by a coterie of "insiders," they put up a facade of extensive rational analysis to legitimize their decision with other organizational members. Conflicts and disputes occur very commonly in such situations, and they are settled through negotiations among managers. The problem familiarization and solution development activities under this model could be patterned after those in either the systemic bureaucracy or the adaptive planning model, depending on which fits the situation better. This means that, while actual decision making is driven by interest-group concerns, the overt actions of problem formulation, and generation, evaluation, and choice of alternatives follow organizationally acceptable routines.

The decision-makers are generally senior middle-management or top-management personnel with expertise in data processing and information systems development. The organization critically depends on these people for its computerization activities. In the decisions we studied, it was found that the EDP or MIS departments typically became the center for such decision making. The heads of these departments along with senior managers formed coalitions with other departmental managers to orchestrate the process to their advantage. For example, the data processing department would solicit support for its demand of a larger computer system from, say, the materials manager, on the promise of developing a sophisticated inventory control system for him.

Coalitions may also be formed by organizational managers joining up with environmental agents such as government representatives and labor union representatives. In these cases too the decision was primarily in the interest of the individuals involved in making the decision and only secondarily in the organization's interest.

The Political Expediency Model is usually found in large organizations where power is highly dispersed among organizational managers. Management systems and procedures exist, but the managers have learned how to circumvent these systems to promote their own interests. Group decision making is a norm, and extensive use is made of committees, task forces, evaluation teams, etc.

III. IMPLICATIONS OF THE FINDINGS FOR STRATEGIC MANAGEMENT

What can managers learn from this study that will help them manage the process of strategy formulation? We outline below two areas of strategic management which can benefit from these findings.

A. Rationalizing the Decision-Making-Process

Those who are attempting to manage innovative and strategic decisions in organizations will find the present study useful for understanding their own role in the decision-making process. They can then attempt to redesign the process to make it more rational and efficient. Understanding the decision-making process can help managers to identify and reduce the influence of undesirable nonrational variables. Our study suggests that variables such as prestige, image, vested interests, organizational micropolitics, etc., distract decision makers from making rational decisions. By identifying the sources of these influences, managements can limit their significance or guide their impact. By carefully studying the decision-making process, they can identify other deficiencies in the various phases of the process and take action to rectify them.

One important way of improving decision making involves systematic participation by relevant members. The extreme complexity exhibited by strategic decisions suggests that decision processes designed to handle these problems should be of sufficient sophistication to handle this complexity. To handle the technical complexity, financial risks, organizational preparation, and environmental negotiations, it is important to use all relevant organizational resources and personnel for making strategic decisions. The design of the decision-making process should take into account the implicit need for integration of individual perspectives and pooling of individual skills which are required for managing such decisions.

Management theorists have been urging organizations to use participative methods of decision making. Their rationale for participative approaches is usually based on the social benefits that are derived from participation. Our research points out some other benefits of participative decision making. The opportunity to share and communicate information afforded by participative approaches enhances organizational learning. More individual insights and personal knowledge can be integrated and made available for organizational decision-making purposes. In other words, participative decision making could lead to better decisions by providing more information and better-quality information. Our research suggests a new focus for participation. The participation should aim at maximizing organizational learning. This new focus provides guidelines for structuring participative decision making. It suggests criteria for selection of participants, forums and modes of participation, frequency of contact, extent of procedural documentation, and other relevant variables that need to be monitored in participative approaches.

B. Design and Use of Strategic Information Systems

The description of strategic decision-making models suggests that the information required for making these decisions may come from a variety of sources.

This information resides in both formal management information systems as well as informal networks of peers, subordinates, and colleagues within the organization, and business associates outside the organization. Strategic information is characterized by its consensual nature. It is often qualitative and unstructured rather than quantitative and structured and deals with current issues rather than historical ones. Strategic information also has a large speculative or evaluative component. This means "interpretation" of data and its consensual validation by organizational members are important processes needed for generating information for strategic decisions.

The design of strategic information systems must be guided by two key criteria that emerge from this study.

1. Firstly, the strategic information system must be compatible with the decision-making processes in the organization. The four models described above lend themselves to different types of supporting information systems. For example, in managerial autocracy situations it may not be worthwhile investing in the development of a formal management information system to support strategic decision making. In this model the decision-making process needs quick responses, superficial information, a variety of financial and technical data, from a restricted number of sources. In these situations the information needed may be made available to the key manager by a few assistants who have it readily available.

The Systemic Bureaucracy model would be best supported by formalized and systematic methods of collection, interpretation, and dissemination of information. These brief examples should suffice to illustrate the design criteria that we are suggesting—that the design and use of strategic information systems must be compatible with the decision-making processes in the organization.

2. The second important consideration in the design of strategic information systems derives from the intersubjective nature of strategic information. We have found that subjective interpretation, sharing, and developing consensus are key characteristics of this type of information. The information system that is to provide strategic information must be capable of handling these requirements. The current emphasis on designing MISs which are formal, structured, and give "objective" data needs to be reevaluated in light of our findings.

A strategic information system needs to be flexible; it should be capable of picking up information from sources anywhere within or outside the organization. Besides providing the content of information, the system should be capable of providing strategic managers with personal access to sources of information, to aid them in the interpretation and validation of information. The information system must provide a forum for sharing managers' frames of reference and perspectives in order to facilitate a consensual understanding of strategic issues.

To conclude, we would like to recapitulate the central theme of this research—that strategic decision-making processes vary systematically and their pattern of variation can be identified and examined critically. These processes have important consequences for the strategic behavior of organizations and finally their success or failure. The strategic decision-making process can be rationalized and supported by designing appropriate strategic information systems.

REFERENCES

Allison, Graham T. (1970), *Essence of Decision*. Boston: Little, Brown and Co.

Blau, P. and R. Scott (1962), *Formal Organizations*. San Francisco: Chandler.

Bower, Joseph L. (1970), *Managing the Resource Allocation Process*. Homewood, IL: Irwin. 1970.

Carter, E. Eugene (1971), ''The Behavioral Theory of the Firm and Top-Level Corporate Decision'', *Administrative Science Quarterly*, Vol. 16, No. 4, (Dec.) 413–429.

Chandler, A. D. (1962), *Strategy and Structure: Chapters in the History of the American Enterprise*. Cambridge, Mass.: M.I.T. Press.

Cyert, Richard M. and March, James G. (1963) *A Behavioral Theory of the Firm*, Englewood Cliffs, N.J.: Prentice-Hall.

Elliason, G. (1976) *Business Economic Planning*. New York: Wiley.

Lindblom, Charles E. (1979), ''Still Muddling: Not Yet Through'', *Public Administration Review*, (November–December), pp 517–526.

Miles, R. E. and C. C. Snow (1978), *Organizational Strategy, Structure and Process*. New York, McGraw Hill.

Mintzberg, H. (1973), ''Strategy Making in Three Modes'', *California Management Review*, (Spring).

Mintzberg, Henry, D. Raisinghane, and A. Theoret (1976), ''The Structure of Unstructured Decision Processes.'' *Administrative Science Quarterly*, (June).

Quinn, J. B. (1980), *Strategic Change: Logical Incrementalism*. Homewood, IL: Richard Irwin.

Radford, K. J. (1978), *Information Systems for Strategic Decisions*, Toronto: Reston Publications.

Schendel, D. and C. W. Hofer (1979), *Strategic Management: A New View of Policy and Planning*, Boston: Little, Brown and Co.

Shrivastava, P. (1981), ''Strategic Decision Making Process: The Influence of Organizational Learning and Experience''. Unpublished doctoral dissertation, University of Pittsburgh.

Shrivastava, P. and J. Grant (1982), ''Empirically Derived Models of Strategic Decision Making Processes'', Working Paper #505, Graduate School of Business, University of Pittsburgh.

Simon, H. A. (1979), ''Rational Decision-Making in Business Organizations'', *American Economic Review*, (Sept.).

STRATEGIC MANAGEMENT:
INTEGRATING THE HUMAN RESOURCE SYSTEMS INTO STRATEGIC PLANNING

Charles Fombrun

ABSTRACT

This article focuses on the integrated human resource system and its link with the strategic planning system. Frameworks are presented for conceptualizing the relationship between planning and its human resource implications, and such concepts as organizational culture, operating philosophy, and dominant value are discussed in terms of their derivation from and impact on the human resource systems of the organization. Effective environmental adaptation, and hence effective strategy formulation and implementation, require a careful design of the linkages between the planning arm and the controlling function for the human dimension of organizations.

Advances in Strategic Management, Volume 2, pages 191–210.

ISBN: 0-89232-409-0

I. INTRODUCTION

American management is faced with a serious challenge. Whether from declining competitiveness, increasing employee dissatisfaction, or governmental pressure, the signals are clear: corporate executives are to be blamed for the current woes of American industry. Akio Monita, Sony's outspoken chairman, sums it up: "The trouble with a large segment of American management is attributable to two misguided attitudes: American managers are too worried about short term profits and too little concerned about their workers" (*New York Times*, January 3, 1981).

The theme is taken up quite explicitly by William Ouchi in his popular *Theory Z*. It is even more clearly articulated by Richard Pascale and Anthony Athos in *The Art of Japanese Management*. Both books stress management's role in designing the organizational systems that will support a long-run orientation to the basic business, one that recognizes its human capital as a major asset, an orientation that U.S. managers—it is often said—have been slow to adopt.

This article supports their argument by arguing that strategic management, if it is to be effective, must be predicated on a dual concern with strategic planning on the one hand, and human resources on the other. There is a strong relationship between the two, one that must be carefully managed if we are to avoid faddish swings in popularity between the two extremes. Specifically, this article:

- Presents a set of tools for conceptualizing the strategic planning and human resource systems;
- Discusses the role of management in carefully linking the strategic planning system to the human resource system.

In the process, such popular concepts as "operating philosophy" and "corporate culture" are discussed in terms of their relationship to the strategic planning and human resource systems.

II. STRATEGIC PLANNING SYSTEMS

The development of sophisticated planning systems largely dominated the concerns of corporate executives in the late 1960s and early 1970s. Most large corporations recognized the importance of planning as a means of coping with increasing technological complexity, diversification, and systematic growth (Warren, 1966). Unfortunately, in many cases, the output of these planning systems has been a voluminous bureaucracy of paperwork, with little impact on either managerial behavior or performance. One major reason for the past failure of planning systems may have been their overwhelming stress on the formulation of strategy, with little systematic attention paid to its implementation. In fact, this article argues that effective implementation involves inducing organizational processes through the design of the human resource system to support the strategic thrust. Thus sound strategy formulation must from the outset include implementation concerns in the early iterations of the planning process (Newman, 1975).

Strategic planning is a process through which the basic mission and objectives of the organization are set and its resources allocated to achieve those objectives. It involves:

1. An environmental assessment of threats and opportunities;
2. An internal assessment of strengths and weaknesses;
3. Competitive analysis and a formulation of the distinctive competence of the organization; and
4. Choice of a dominant value consistent with the organization's distinctive competence.

Through these four steps the organization chooses its competitive domains and the means it will use to navigate within each domain (Andrews, 1972; Steiner, 1969; Peters, 1980; Hofer and Schendel, 1978). Three levels of strategy are typically distinguished: the corporate, business, and functional levels (Lorange, 1981; Bourgeois, 1980).

Corporate strategy applies to diversified firms. Its primary concern is with balancing the needs of a set of different businesses in the corporate portfolio and managing the resource flows to and from the businesses.

Business strategy is concerned with developing the distinctive competence of the specific business, its basic stance in the product/market environment. It is a task that largely devolves to division management.

At the functional level, strategic planning involves the formulation of programs that require the cooperative efforts of different functions within the business. It also refers to the planning activities required for the separate functions themselves. Balancing functional and programmatic needs is a critical strategic concern at this level (Lorange, 1980).

Exhibit 1 diagrams the strategic planning process. Each of the three levels of the strategic plan embodies the complete strategic process and should reflect a coherent thrust, supportive of the distinctive competence and dominant value of the organization. Thus, strategic programs at the functional level must support the business strategy. In turn, the business strategy must reflect a risk/return evaluation that fits into the corporate portfolio. They are all linked through a clear articulation of the organization's competitive stance and supportive value orientation. And they are all designed to capitalize on the firm's strengths in the pursuit of environmental opportunities.

While strategy must be formulated at each of the three levels, effective implementation requires a supportive set of control systems for both the financial

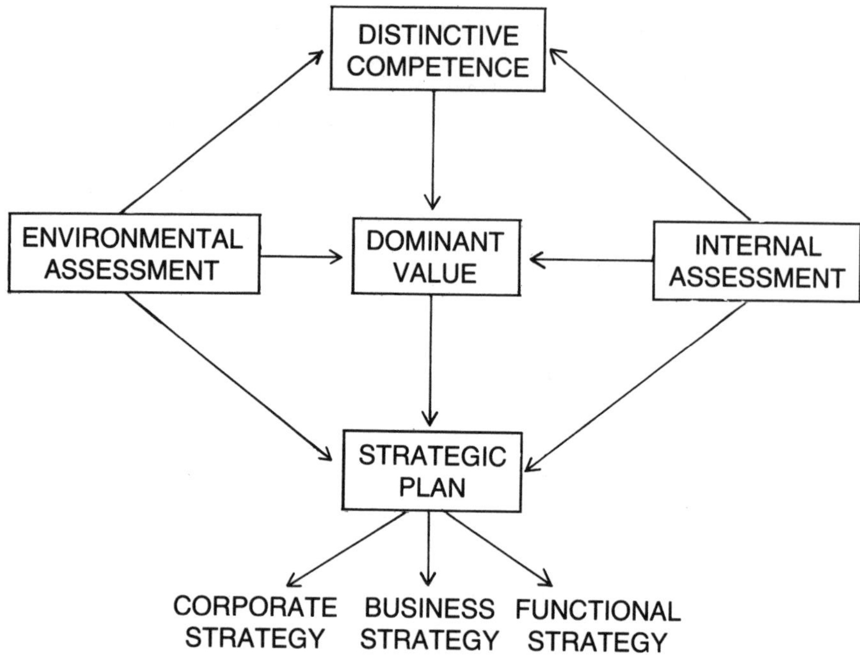

Exhibit 1. Strategic Planning.

resources and human resources of the organization. The control system for the financial resources of the organization is the budgeting process. This is a well-documented cycle of activity which involves an allocation of funds to specific activities and programs consistent with overall corporate objectives (Vancil and Lorange, 1975; Steiner, 1969).

The control system for the human resources of the organization is typically far less systematic, and research suggests that it is perhaps a critical stumbling block in the implementation process (Levinson, 1976; Guzzo, 1979). While it is typically administered by the personnel function, it is largely under the control of the line, which has typically shown little concern for understanding its dynamic or managing its impact on the organization (Devanna et al., 1981; Tichy et al., 1982).

Paralleling the three levels of strategy, a human resource strategy can be defined which describes the thrust of the organization in terms of its approach to the acquisition, use, and disposal of its human resources. At the corporate level, the human resource strategy explicitly trades off between complete integration of all the human resources systems and their total differentiation. Conglomerates and holding companies typically rely on a human resource strategy of complete differentiation. Thus, no personnel are transferred across businesses in the portfolio, and vastly different evaluation and incentive systems may be in effect. At the other extreme, a company like General Electric homogenizes its systems across all businesses (Fombrun, 1982). Developing the corporate-level human resource strategy is a vital complementary activity to sound strategy formulation at the corporate level.

The human resource strategy at the business level must support the competitive orientation of the business strategy and encourage performance in line with it. Its critical concern is with designing an integrated set of systems that will drive the desired performance. More specifically it entails developing an operating philosophy with respect to the human resource of the business. Consistent with this philosophy, a dominant value guides the design of the human resource systems. For instance, Japanese organizations are said to be paternalistic in their stress on loyalty rather than performance. Such a dominant value has strong implications for the human resource systems: they will stress attitudes rather than skills, compensate seniority, and promote collective activity rather than individualism. Developing a coherent human resource strategy at the business level is a means to the integration of the different functions and the implementation of business-level strategy.

Finally, at the functional level, the human resource strategy must design distinct human resource systems to support both departmental activities and the interfunctional strategic programs that were formulated out of the business strategy over and above the functional plans. Thus R&D will require different systems of evaluation and compensation than manufacturing or sales. Yet all three must be activated in a common direction if such an interfunctional strategic program as bringing a new product to market is to succeed. Exhibit 2 depicts the relationship between the human resource strategies and the strategic plan.

The strategic management task, altogether, involves not only careful formula-

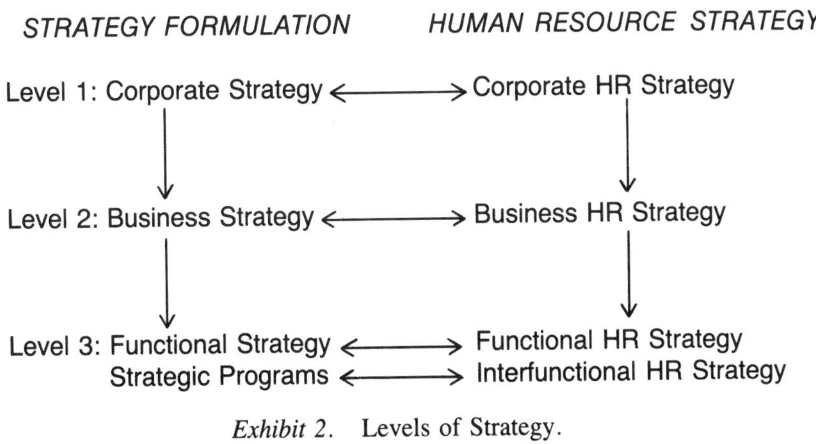

Exhibit 2. Levels of Strategy.

tion but judicious implementation through well-designed human resource components and an overarching philosophy. The net result of these human resource systems is a corporate culture which should support the strategic plans of the company as a whole (Ouchi, 1981; Pascale and Athos, 1981).

III. THE HUMAN RESOURCE SYSTEM

There are four generic processes or functions performed by a human resources system in all organizations: selection, evaluation, reward, and development. These four processes reflect a sequential managerial activity and Exhibit 3 represents them in terms of a Human Resource Cycle (HRC). At the core of the HRC is the dominant value the organization is stressing. Thus, an organization whose dominant concern is the bottom line stresses short-run outcomes, and its employees are hired on the basis of demonstrable skills, evaluated on measurable performance, and given job-relevant skills training and extrinsic compensation. An organization stressing citizenship in the organization will, on the other hand, reward loyalty and promote interaction and joint activity. These are the processes Ouchi (1981) reports for such well-known firms as Hewlett-Packard, Intel, and Eli Lilly.

A. Selection System

The selection, promotion, and placement process includes all activities related to internal movement of people across positions and external hiring into the organization. The essential process is one of matching available human resources to jobs in the organization. It entails defining the organization's people needs for particular positions and assessing the available pool of people to determine the best fit. Selection is typically naive and idiosyncratic, and there are no fail-safe systems for identifying successful candidates in low-level positions, let alone for senior executive positions (Walker, 1980).

B. Reward System

Rewards vary from pay in its various forms, through promotion, job security, and career opportunity, to such informal incentives as praise, recognition, respect, and friendship. Most organizations do not do a very good job of inducing desired behaviors through the judicious use of rewards. Organizations tend to over-rely on pay and promotion, as a result of which other rewards remain underutilized managerial tools (Lawler, 1976).

The key factor in designing the reward system is that rewards should be made contingent upon desired behavior. Desired behaviors, in turn, should follow

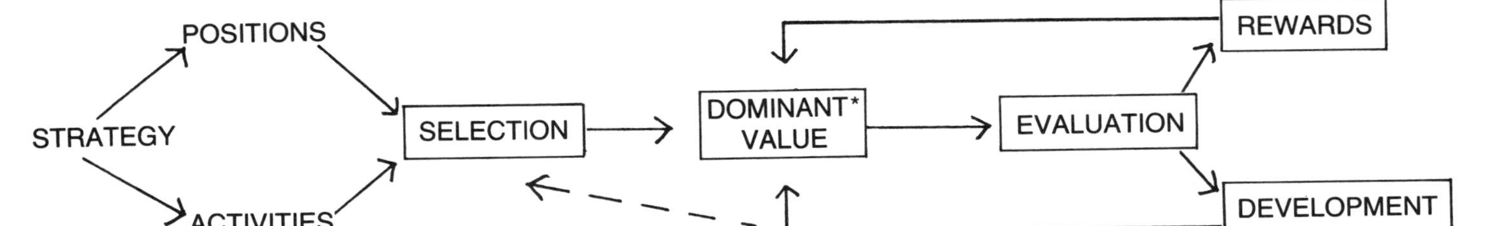

*Any dominant value can be used as the core of the human resource system, e.g. performance, loyalty, client service, etc. All the processes are then designed to support the dominant value.

(Adapted from Tichy, N., C. Fombrun, M. A. Devanna. "Strategic Human Resources Management," *Sloan Management Review,* Winter 1982.

Exhibit 3. The Human Resource Cycle.

from the business philosophy or dominant value needed to support the business strategy (Peters, 1980).

C. Development System

Development involves activities designed to ensure that individuals are properly equipped with skills and knowledge to carry out their jobs. These activities range from simple job training to the long-term development of senior executives. The longer-term strategic developmental process includes such activities as management education, the use of mentor relationships, job assignments, and life experiences. The three major areas of the developmental process are: (1) job improvement, the development of specific job skills and competencies; (2) career planning, a longitudinal focus on individual growth and development in relation to organizational opportunities; and (3) succession planning, the organizational focus on ensuring an adequate supply of human resource talent for projected needs in the future based on the strategic plan (Schein, 1979).

D. Appraisal System

Perhaps the least-liked managerial activity is doing performance appraisals. Most of the time the activity is a perfunctory paper exercise bearing little relationship to either compensation or development. As a colleague once pointed out, performance appraisals are like seat belts: everyone agrees that they are important, yet no one uses them.

There are many reasons for problems with appraisal systems, ranging from poorly designed procedures to the psychological resistance of managers to giving negative evaluations (Latham and Wexley, 1981). The important point is that the appraisal process is central to the human resource cycle and plays a vital role in linking the three other human resource systems.

E. Organizational Context

The staffing, appraisal, reward, and development subsystems do not function in a vacuum. They are designed to support specific activities, jobs, and positions. Ideally, each and every activity the organization wants its employees to engage in should be supported by a customized human resource cycle of its own designed to channel the motivations of the appropriate individual into the desired activity. Obviously this would be too idiosyncratic and complex to administer effectively. At the other extreme, organizations could choose to entirely homogenize their human resource systems across all activities and positions—in which case the system suffers from averaging and is typically full of contradictory cues.

The preferred solution of most organizations is to tailor a human resource

Human Resource Systems / Time Frame	Selection/ Placement	Appraisal	Rewards	Development
LONG RUN	—Characteristics of people needed to run business in long run	—Long term values of workforce —Early identification of potential	—Long run rewards of workforce	—Developmental mental experiences needed for people to run business of the future
INTERMEDIATE RUN	—Internal and external systems needed to reflect future	—Means needed to appraise future dimensions	—Designing compensation system	—Career paths
SHORT-RUN	—Staffing plans —Recruitment plans	—Annual or more frequent appraisal system —Assessment Centers	—Wage and salary administration —Benefits packages	—Specific job skill training —On the job training

(Adapted from Devanna, M. A., C. Fombrun, N. Tichy. "Human Resources Management: A Strategic Approach," *Organizational Dynamics,* Winter 1981.)

Exhibit 4. Human Resource Subsystems.

cycle and its subsystems to specific subpopulations within the organization. Two internal boundaries are frequently used (Schein, 1972):

1. Functional boundaries: varying the systems across functions, for instance, a different incentive structure for the sales function than the production function; and
2. Hierarchical boundaries: a different set of systems and philosophy of management between, say, support staff, technical professionals, managers, and senior executives.

Through judicious use of these boundaries, the organization attempts to create and maintain distinct subcultures that energize and channel behaviors in directions consistent with strategic objectives and which capitalize on internal strengths.

F. Balancing Long-Run and Short-Run Concerns

Each of the human resource processes can support a time orientation that stresses either the long-run or short-run component of the dominant value. For instance, the appraisal system may measure short-run performance in terms of yearly costs, profits, or sales. It could also tie compensation to such long-run measures as strategic objectives by embedding it in a Management-by-Objectives system. Similarly, the developmental system can train for immediate job-relevant performance skills, or prepare individuals for more challenging assignments in the long run through job rotation and managerial development.

Exhibit 4 diagrams the distinction between systems supporting a short-run orientation and those supportive of a long-run orientation. The criticisms aimed at American industry suggest that the human resource systems in American organizations have tended to drive a short-run orientation in business strategy through a philosophy that largely stresses bottom-line performance. Japanese organizations emphasize loyalty as the dominant value in the human resource cycle, and encourage it through a set of subsystems that are tied to long-term concerns (Pascale and Athos, 1981).

IV. TOWARD STRATEGIC MANAGEMENT: DESIGNING THE LINKAGES

Strategic management requires building an effective link between the strategic planning system and the human resources system at each of the three levels of strategy: the corporate, business, and functional levels. Each level must be attended to in terms of administrative staffing and resources as well. This section discusses in greater detail the nature of the link between the two systems and the design of the human resource arm of the organization.

A. Corporate Level

A major tool for corporate management is the proper balancing of a portfolio of products each at a different stage of the product life cycle (PLC) (Fombrun and Tichy, 1983). Exhibit 5 presents some of the implications of the PLC for the human resource systems appropriate at each stage.

Thus, a business in the start-up stage of the PLC should use different criteria to hire new employees and assess their performance than a business in the mature stage of the PLC. Similarly, the kinds of rewards valued by those employees should differ, and the organization will want to tie its reward systems to different kinds of outcomes in each case. Altogether, the corporate-level human resource strategy must decide on the basis of the mix of businesses in the corporate portfolio the degree to which the organization will attempt to homogenize its human resource systems across businesses and provide a coherent organizational umbrella for the flow of personnel. As Exhibit 6 suggests, a highly integrated set of systems is consistent with a corporate strategy designed around a single or dominant product firm. A large corporate human resource function is vested with the resources required to coordinate the human resources and manage the staffing, compensation, and career paths of employees across the organization.

The benefits of the highly integrated corporate form is its ability to draw on a large pool of employees and move them into positions that can best capitalize on their skills. Such an organization is able to function as a large internal labor market and will frequently show characteristics analogous to the Japanese *zaibatsu*. Exxon and IBM are dominant business multidivisional firms that display these characteristics. General Electric is a highly diversified multidivisional organization which nonetheless has developed a highly integrated set of human resource systems across its businesses (Fombrun, 1982).

B. Business Level

At the business level the critical concern is with designing a unifying theme for the business, an operating philosophy. As Exhibit 5 suggested, the business stage in the PLC is a valuable tool for determining the dominant value. In the early stage the innovative business wants to stress a philosophy centered around innovation, product development, and entrepreneurship. Later, as growth begins, a stress on aggressive marketing and competitiveness will drive the human resource systems. Growth, however, can be pursued through different business strategies which may involve, for instance, price competition, product quality, or customer service as a way of increasing market share. Exhibit 7 diagrams the relationship between business growth strategies and the dominant value that human resource strategy at the business level should stress. The implications of the dominant value and strategic thrust are sketched in terms of their impact on each of the four human resource subsystems.

STAGE IN LIFE CYCLE OF BUSINESS PORTFOLIO

HUMAN RESOURCE FUNCTIONS	Start-up Businesses	Growth Businesses	Mature Businesses	Declining Businesses
Selection/Placement	—Recruit for new activities —Recruit Entrepreneurial Style	—Recruit for future business needs	—Lateral transfers —Recruit cost control and efficiency orientation	—Transfers to different businesses —Outplacement —Early retirement
Appraisal	—Appraise milestones linked to plans for the business	—Linked to growth criteria, e.g., market share volume unit cost reduction	—Evaluate efficiency and profit margin performance	—Evaluate cost savings
Rewards	—Salary plus large equity positions	—Salary plus bonus for growth targets, plus equity for key people	—Incentive plan linked to efficiency and high profit margins	—Incentive plan linked to cost savings
Development	—Minimum until a critical mass of people in business—then job related	—Good orientation program for fast start-ups —Job skills —Middle management development	—Emphasis on job training —Good supervisory and management development program	—Career planning and support services for transferring people

→ Organization and design of the human resource functions within businesses

↓ Corporate Human Resource Staff, Policies Designed to integrate Human Resource Functions Across Businesses

(Adapted from Fombrun, C. and N. Tichy "Strategic Planning and Human Resources Management: At Rainbow's End", in R. Lamb (Ed.) *Recent Advances in Strategic Planning*, McGraw Hill, 1983)

Exhibit 5. Corporate Human Resource Strategy.

Following Hofer and Schendel (1978), four growth strategies can be distinguished.

1. *Share-Increasing Strategy (research-based):* the pursuit of market share through process innovations is consistent with a dominant value of "product quality." The organization stresses engineering skills and the ability to implement novel techniques that will successfully differentiate its products from those of competitors.
2. *Share-Increasing Strategy (marketing-based):* the pursuit of market share through a strong client orientation is supported by a dominant value of "service." The human resource systems stress interpersonal skills and interaction with clients.
3. *Profit Strategy:* stresses business growth through a dominant value of cost control and "efficiency." The human resource systems are quantitative in orientation, and employees are given on-the-job training.
4. *Diversification-from-Within Strategy:* the organization promotes new product development, internal "creativity," and entrepreneurship. The human resource systems reward through recognition and opportunity and encourage individual development.

While these overarching growth strategies define the operating philosophy guiding the design of each of the human resource subsystems, they also define the activities of different groups within the organization. Following Anthony's

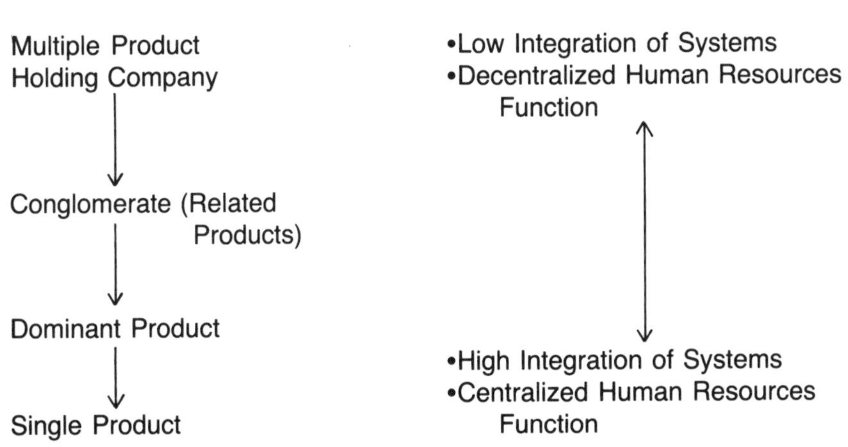

Exhibit 6. Corporate Level Human Resources Strategy.

BUSINESS STRATEGY ↕ HUMAN RESOURCE STRATEGY	Share Increasing Research-based	Share Increasing Marketing-based	Profit	Diversification From Within
Dominant Value	• Applied Development (Process Innovation) • Product quality	• Client Relations • Service	• Cost control	• Product Innovation
Selection	• Technicians • Engineers	• Appearance • Interpersonal Skills	• Skills based	• Entrepreneurial
Evaluation	• Based on successful implementation	• Based on client feedback	• Quantified • Based on objective setting	• Group based
Reward	• Promotion	• Promotion • External Representation	• Monetary	• Recognition • Opportunity to implement
Development	• Skill-building in technical areas • Job rotation	• Interpersonal skills • Career path via marketing	• On the job training • No outside development • Career path via Finance	• Conferences, travel, broad skills • Dual career ladders technical/managerial • Career path via New Ventures

Exhibit 7. Business Level Human Resource Strategy.

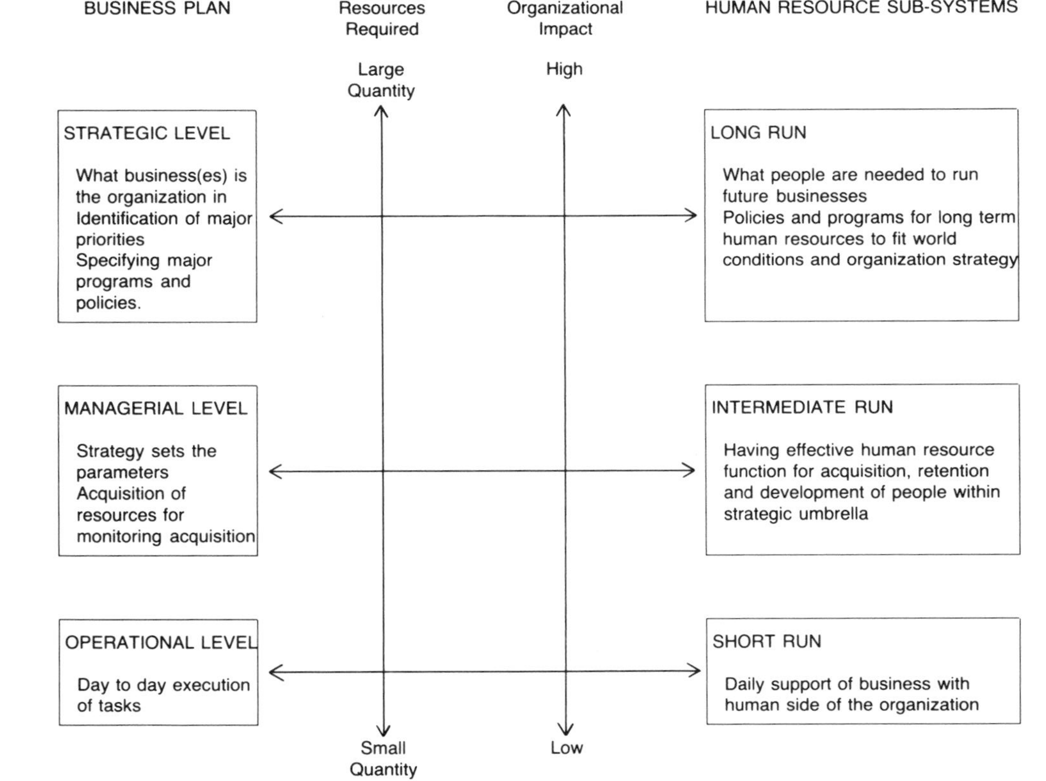

Exhibit 8. Matching Business Strategy to Human Resource Sub-Systems.

(1965) distinction between the strategic, managerial, and operational levels of control, Exhibit 8 diagrams the link that must be forged between the business plan and the human resource side of the organization (Devanna et al., 1981).

For the business-level human resource strategy to support the business plan, there must be significant dialogue between business planners and human resource staff at the business level. Human resource staff must be involved at the formulation stage of the business plan. This means empowering the traditional personnel function.

C. Functional Level

As the lowest level of strategic concern, the design of the functional human resource strategy involves:

1. tailoring the human resource systems for each function of the business, and
2. designing systems across functions to support the strategic programs of the business-level strategy.

The primary tool of the functional human resource strategy is the human resource cycle. Each set of goals identified in a functional plan must be driven by all the human resource systems, and each interfunctional strategic program must also be motivated by carefully crafted appraisal criteria, rewards, and training seminars. This is possibly one of the most difficult tasks of all since functional goals are frequently encouraged at the expense of program goals, or vice versa (Lorange, 1980).

The constant negotiation between functional and program goals suggests that, in organizations with multiple strategic programs crosscutting the functions in the business, decentralization of the business-level human resource function may be an effective means of tailoring the activities to the local population of a strategic program, while the division-level staff formulates policy and interacts with business planners.

V. OBSTACLES TO EFFECTIVE STRATEGIC MANAGEMENT

While we have been largely concerned with formulating conceptual frameworks for strategically linking planning and control, it is probably true that the most critical managerial task will involve the implementation of these linkages. There are many reasons why these systems could fail in practice. They principally fall into four categories:

1. *History*. Human resource systems have traditionally been administered through the personnel function and as a result suffer from perceptions of inefficiency, inaccuracy, and irrelevance, as a result of which the function and its activities have been largely relegated to the periphery of organizational concerns (Devanna et al., 1981).

2. *Structure*. Partly for the historical reasons just mentioned, the function is frequently structurally isolated from the planning activities of the organization. This makes dialogue between them difficult and any significant degree of influence virtually impossible since the function is not "on the scene."

3. *Staffing*. Accustomed to operational servicing and powerlessness, the personnel function has tended to attract few "superstars." Human resource activities are typically administered by competent specialists largely unfamiliar with either planning jargon or quantitative analysis, with backgrounds in psychology, education, and counseling (Stanton, 1975). The lack of common experience, education, and orientation is undoubtedly a stumbling block in integrating the human resource system into mainstream strategic planning.

4. *Resources*. Effective involvement in a reciprocal relationship with the planning side of the organization requires discretionary control over the allocation of a significant pool of resources for hiring and training human resource staff, as well as the development of programs and projects uniquely designed to support the strategic thrust of the organization. Personnel functions have traditionally faced highly circumscribed budgets and lacked the quantitative ability to show a bottom-line ROI on its activities. This is especially important at the business level, where financial ratio evaluations dominate strategic analysis.

Exhibit 9 presents a brief sketch of the kinds of structures, staff, and resources required to operate the human resource function at each level of the organization. The size of the corporate staff will largely depend on the degree to which the organizational culture supports an integrated set of systems across businesses. Nonetheless, to be effective, the function should be staffed with highly visible executives reporting to the CEO on a par with the planning group, and with enough of a broad business background to effectively dialogue with them.

At the business level the function must be responsive to business trends and concerns and is responsible for designing the basic systems to support the business strategy within the corporate guidelines. As such, it should be staffed with individuals capable of conversing about the dominant activities of the business.

Finally, on-site field offices (in larger organizations) are responsible for service delivery according to the policies designed at the business level (themselves consistent with corporate-level guidelines). As entry-level human resource positions, they largely require the expertise of specialists in the traditional areas of industrial relations. Through field rotations across subdisciplines, they come to qualify for business-level involvement, and with rotations and managerial train-

	CORPORATE LEVEL	BUSINESS LEVEL	FUNCTIONAL LEVEL
STRUCTURE	• Direct report to CEO • Equal level with planning group • Member of planning group • Sets business level guidelines for design of systems	• Direct contact with division management • Dialogue with planning group • Sets policy for field service groups • Constant internal interaction among sub-areas	• Field offices for on-site service delivery • Implement programs designed at business level • Refer unusual cases to business staff
STAFFING	• Generalists with rotations across businesses and functions • Ability to speak in business language	• Some business training for promotion • Rotation across sub-areas (e.g. compensation, recruitment, etc.)	• Specialists in sub-areas • Part of field rotation
RESOURCES	• Varies with degree of integration across businesses	• Discretionary Funds to initiate programs • Allocations to field staff	• Budgets set through business plan

Exhibit 9. The Human Resource Function.

ing may qualify for corporate positions. A key responsibility of field staff at the functional level is the identification of systemic contradictions between the systems as they are implemented to support cross-functional programs born of the strategic business plan.

VI. CONCLUSION

Overall, this article has stressed the importance of integrating the human resource element into the strategic planning function of organizations. In an increasingly competitive and turbulent environment, effective strategic management will call for systematic mobilization of the human resources of organizations for the achievement of strategic goals. The sooner organizations work to integrate the human resource systems that implicitly constrain and motivate organizational behavior, the more likely they are to meet the challenges before them. This paper presented some preliminary frameworks for conceptualizing the linkage between the strategic planning and human resource systems of organizations, and discussed the role of the personnel function across the corporate, business, and functional levels of the organization.

ACKNOWLEDGMENTS

Noel Tichy (University of Michigan) and Mary-Anne Devanna (Columbia University) contributed through collaborative research in helping to develop many of the thoughts and frameworks discussed in this article.

REFERENCES

Andrews, K. (1972), *Corporate Strategy*, Harvard Business School.

Anthony, R. (1965), *Planning and Control Systems*, Harvard Business School.

Bourgeois, L. J. III. (1980), "Strategy and Environment: A Conceptual Integration," *Academy of Management Review*, *5*, 25–40.

Devanna, M. A., Fombrun, C., and Tichy, N. (1981), "Human Resources Management: A Strategic Approach," *Organizational Dynamics*, (Winter), 51–67.

Fombrun, C. "A Conversation with Frank Doyle and Reginald Jones," *Organizational Dynamics*, Winter 1982.

Fombrun, C. and Tichy, N. (1983), "Strategic Planning and Human Resources Management: At Rainbow's End." In R. Lamb (ed.) *Recent Advances in Strategic Planning*. McGraw-Hill, forthcoming.

Guzzo, R. (1979), "Types of Rewards, Cognitions, and Work Motivation", *Academy of Management Review*, *4*, 75–86.

Hofer, C. and Schendel, D. (1978), *Strategy Formulation: Analytical Concepts*, St. Paul, Minn.: West Publishing Co.

Latham, G. and K. Wexley (1981) *Increasing Productivity Through Performance Appraisal*. Reading, Mass.: Addison-Wesley.

Lawler, E. E. (1976) ''New Approaches to Pay: Innovations that Work,'' *Personnel,* (September–October).

Levinson, H. (1976), ''Appraisal of *What* Performance?'' *Harvard Business Review,* (July–August).

Lorange, P. (1981), *Corporate Planning.* Englewood Cliffs, NJ: Prentice-Hall.

Newman, W. (1975), *Constructive Control.* Englewood-Cliffs, NJ: Prentice Hall.

Ouchi, W. (1981), *Theory Z.* Reading, Mass.: Addison-Wesley.

Pascale, R. and Athos, A. (1981), *The Art of Japanese Management.* Simon and Schuster.

Peters, T. (1980) ''Putting Excellence into Management,'' *Business Week,* (July 21,).

Schein, E. (1979), *Career Dynamics.* Acdison-Wesley.

Schein, E. (1972), *Organizational Psychology.* Addison-Wesley.

Stanton, E. (1975), ''Lost Chance for Personnel to Come of Age,'' *The Personnel Administrator,* (November).

Steiner, G. (1969) *Top Management Planning,* MacMillan.

Tichy, N., Fombrun, C. and Devanna, M. A. (1982), ''Strategic Human Resource Management,'' *Sloan Management Review,* (Winter).

Vancil, R. and Lorange, P. (1975), ''Strategic Planning in Diversified Companies,'' *Harvard Business Review,* (Jan–Feb).

Walker, J. (1980), *Human Resource Planning.* McGraw Hill.

Warren, E. K. (1966), *Long-Range Planning: The Executive Viewpoint.* Prentice-Hall.

THE BUSINESS POLICY PROBLEM AND INDUSTRY RECIPES

J.-C. Spender

I. IS POLICY A COHERENT FIELD?

Debating the changing directions of policy research should remind us how poorly defined our field is. Under the loose umbrella of "relations between the enterprise and its environment" we each research our own version of the policy problem. But just how often do another's research results have any impact on our thinking? Do we need even more alternative views? My basic argument is that we must do more to define our field before we can know whether it is the subject or the method of inquiry that is changing or whether the field is progressing or digressing.

This paper is at two levels. At one we discuss field-definition in general. At the other we discuss the business policy field in particular, differentiating it from its close neighbors, organization theory and the theory of the firm. The discussion moves between these levels and is unashamedly epistemological for two

Advances in Strategic Management, Volume 2, pages 211–229.

ISBN: 0-89232-409-0

reasons. First we need to understand that a field is defined by its practitioners' conceptual commitments. Current work in the philosophy of science illustrates both how to identify these, and what happens when they change. Second, we must see that we are caught within an epistemological conundrum—theories of policy making do not deal with well defined phenomena, they are about managers trying to make rational decisions in an uncertain world. Hence the variety of ideas about what policy is and about the problems it solves. Some see policy making as evidence of leadership, others see it as the pursuit of competitive advantage, yet others see it as the intentional response to an organization's environment.

The first sections of the paper explore the notion of a discipline. We tentatively define a field in terms of the structured body of knowledge that we have about some class of phenomena. Our knowledge is limited by this structure's defects as well as by its contents. Following Simon (1952), we can define our lack of business knowledge, our uncertainty, as the difficulty of fitting organization theory and micro-economics together—even though these are the two principal kinds of knowledge that we have of organizations. This, in turn, lets us define the business policy problem more generally as that of coping with uncertainty. In Sections VI, VII and VIII we present and elaborate a more rigorous treatment of uncertainty, and look at the implications for policy makers. In the paper's final sections we present an entirely new notion, the industry recipe. Empirical research has already endorsed the usefulness of this analytical device. It implies that policy makers cope with uncertainty by adopting the recipe which encapsulates the specialized knowledge that evolves within and is shared by firms within an industry. Recipe knowledge is part of the industry's stock of knowledge and is reflected in its idiosyncratic culture. The holism implied raises important methodological questions. We conclude that policy research can be usefully framed within a disciplinary matrix that focuses on uncertainty. But researchers working within the matrix must have an unusually broad set of social science techniques at their disposal.

One way of analyzing the coherence of the business policy field is to identify its leading paradigms. Unfortunately, the term "paradigm" is now so widely and variously used that it embraces too much. Excluding so little, it loses most of the meaning Kuhn wishes it; indeed, he is presently apologizing for the confusion he feels he has caused (1977). However, Kuhn's thesis is important and can help us get to grips with our field. His first point is that scientific research stands on a set or system of shared commitments. These include agreement among the field's practitioners about appropriate research topics, data collection methods, concepts of validation, and so forth. this is the part of Kuhn's epistemology that asserts that science is not about The Truth but about the disciplined communication of scientific experience. Shared commitments make communication possible. This becomes science when it takes place within a shared structure whose logic forces other scientists to accept conclusions that go beyond their own experience. Defining a field of research means eliciting this structure. When this is done we can abandon the term paradigm and use Kuhn's far stronger and operational term "disciplinary matrix" (1977, p. 297).

The second part of his thesis is that research activity shows two historical patterns. One, "normal science," is the internal development and elaboration of a stable disciplinary matrix. It is the unfolding of the potential implicit within the matrix. Such change is coherent and conceptually continuous. The other is "critical" science. This is the adoption of another disciplinary matrix in some way inconsistent with the one previously used within the area. Such change is discontinuous. It follows that critical science is only possible when there is some higher level of continuity. Without debating Kuhn's position on this we can see that policy research seems coherent only at this higher level; an agreement displayed, for instance, by the community of interest that draws us together today.

This may explain how a disciplinary matrix develops, but it does not say much about what it is. Kuhn's thesis is built on the practical difficulty of comparing one matrix with another without an abstract "overarching" concept. The holistic togetherness or match of the research topic and the methods of enquiry seems more important. Ultimately, a disciplinary matrix is a structure of demarcations between what is considered and what is ignored that feels right to those in its field. At this point, of course, we recognize the sociology and metaphysics of that research community, and begin to analyze its higher-level commitments.

II. THE COMMITMENTS IN A DISCIPLINARY MATRIX

A disciplinary matrix is a carefully chosen set of commitments which make scientific research and communication possible. Explanations of how research works often begin with the distinction between the positivist or a priori method and the inductive or a posteriori methods. The first is widely thought to comprise the scientific method, sufficient on its own for inquiry into both social and physical phenomena. The second is a less coherent group which stresses the primacy of individual experience and focuses on its reconstruction and interpretation. It embraces phenomenology, interpretive sociology, ethnomethodology, cultural anthropology, and many others. Although these two methods of inquiry are distinct within epistemology, I have argued elsewhere that they can become complementary within empirical science (Spender, 1979). As they are mapped into a field which is bounded at the higher level by a shared concern with a single class of phenomena, so they support each other in the dialectical process of progressive scientific thought. The point here is that a shift from one method to another within a single field does not necessarily constitute critical science. We need much more pertinent demarcating concepts before we can be confident of defining policy research or its changes.

A disciplinary matrix also stands on ontological commitments. The most obvious are its correspondence rules. These establish the units and levels of analysis. In our field they define what we mean by "firm," "environment," "goal," "policymaker," and so forth. In this paper, incidentally, the terms "policy" and "strategy" have the same meaning.

Empirical research requires something to exist, a commitment to reality or observability at some level of the analysis. Debating whether this is a table or a cloud of particles is meaningless without a theory of matter embracing both possibilities. Only at that point does it stop being a confusion of levels of analysis, of different disciplinary matrices focused on different fields of inquiry. The argument is about "reification," and when we assert "organizations do not make decisions, people do," we reject the reification of the organization. Psychologists, of course, may reject the entailed reification of the person and reify in turn, perhaps, the ego and the id.

In business policy we are concerned with many levels of economic activity: the nation, international markets, competitive firms, divisions, and so on. But the implication of our commitment to "the top-management view" or "thinking about the firm as a whole" is clearly a commitment to the organizational level of analysis, a decision to reify the firm. That this is complicated by a firm's relationships with its holding company or its shareholders, with legislators or unions, etc. indicates how committed we are to treating the organization as a free agent in an economic universe. To use an analogy, business policy decisions give the ships of commerce their course and speed—after due consideration of the hazards and benefits of voyaging. We are only concerned indirectly with relations between the engine room and the deckhands, and with the causes of hurricanes—when we know they bear on the specific policy decision being made.

Our field is bordered by others which stand on rather different ontological assumptions, and so develop different disciplinary matrices for their different areas of enquiry. Within organization behavior, we might argue, micropolitical theorists such as Pettigrew, or social psychologists such as Argyris, ignore our concept of the organization entirely. They reify the individual and investigate its behavior in loosely defined organizational contexts. Similarly, macroeconomists reify the economy or its sectors. The organization becomes an undifferentiated member of a population whose aggregated behavior is the phenomenon to be analyzed.

III. ORGANIZATION THEORY AND THE THEORY OF THE FIRM

Policy only becomes a real problem when we define the organization as a free agent wandering the economic universe under its policy commanders. Before exploring what analyzing or researching policy means within this concept, it is important to note that two academically legitimate disciplines have already made the same commitment i.e., organization theory and the theory of the firm. We must settle whether policy is simply a section of either's true territory.

This is not mere wordplay, it affects us most powerfully. Andrews remarks, in Taylor & Macmillan (1973), that doctoral students were actively discouraged from researching policy because no one knew what the field was or how to be sure of an academic career within it. To be able to move between schools, a policy person would have to be academically legitimate in some other field. Policy people are less often microeconomists than they are organization theorists, but, as the divisions of our professional body attest, they are more often neither. We may be able to understand policy better if we examine what, if anything, these two disciplines have in common.

Perhaps they are both parts of the same discipline. Many theorists, such as Simon and Cyert & March (1963), consider the possibility of integrating them. Both are derived from the political economics of democratic capitalism and should, therefore, be compatible. But there are other theorists, such as Coase (1937), who seem to deny this, doubting whether such integration is possible.

For the purposes of this analysis, we can take Adam Smith's work as the point at which the discipinary matrix of the theory of the firm begins to emerge clearly. His starting point is the independent enterprise. He then brings in two concepts which, taken together, begin to set up his analytic field. They are the social division of labor, with its attendant flux of exchanges, and the technological division of labor within the production process. The first gives us the beginnings of microeconomic theory, the second the beginnings of organization theory. The relations between these theories are as the relations between these two divisions of labor. Without such relations we have no theory of economic society. The divisions of labor involve specific ontological commitments or, to put it the other way around, the theories are only useful if the divisions of labor are reasonably representative of economic society.

It is generally agreed that one of Smith's objectives is to show that the freedom to make policy within the enterprise leads to greater wealth at the level of the economy. He achieves this by showing that the two divisions of labor interact to produce a developing economic society. But every division of labor makes order among the now separate elements problematic, so Smith must identify the source of this society's order. Rejecting the mercantilist's command economy, he shows that the social order produced by the invisible hand of market forces is in the interest of both enterprise and State. But, since he uses two divisions of labor, he must also deal with the problem of order within the enterprise. This is where his theory of moral sentiments comes in. His answer, in brief, is an appeal to a shared morality. The resulting sense of enlightened interdependence, the logical correlate of enlightened self-interest, completes Smith's theory of an economic society of citizens. The same moral sentiments, of course, reappear to solve the problem of organizational order in all organismic thinking, e.g., Durkheim, Follett, and Burns & Stalker, and are enjoying new popularity today.

But what Simon and Cyert & March mean by organization theory stands on quite different commitments. These grow out of the work of Weber, Fayol, Church, and others. Both Weber and Smith ground their thinking in historical analyses of economic society, yet they draw different conclusions. Weber, effectively rejecting the relevance of Smith's moral order, argues that organizational order is imposed. However legitimated, all organization depends on the exercise of power. The result is a contradiction of commitments that puts most of contemporary organization theory beyond Smith's disciplinary matrix. At the same time, Smith's concept of emergent free-market order beyond the enterprise is not the only possibility. It could be a command economy, organized by the exercise of power from some higher level of analysis—hence Aron's comment that Weber devoted his life to analyzing whether markets are natural and value-free or the value-laden artifacts of particular group or class interests.

When we compare organization theory and the theory of the firm, we see that they provide solutions to two different problems, those posed by Smith's two different divisions of labor. Organization presumes the relevance of power while the theory of the firm rejects it. Theoretical integration is obviously impossible until these commitments are changed or, following an Einstein of political economy superseding the work of the Newton-like Smith, both are subsumed under a new set of commitments.

IV. RELATIONS BETWEEN DIFFERENT LEVELS OF ANALYSIS

Every theory with empirical content bridges ontological commitments at different levels; there must be both parts and wholes. Organization theory brings roles at the level of the individual together with goals at the level of the enterprise. The theory of the firm brings profit-maximizing enterprises together with a market in equilibrium. The ontological commitments cannot be inconsistent between levels. So neo-Weberian organization theory treats goals, resources, technologies, and markets as givens, the consequences of external power over the enterprise. Its offers no solutions if the firm is a political force with power over its environment, able to alter these givens. Similarly, as Cyert & March point out, the theory of the firm takes the firm as a given, the integrated outcome of a coalition-generating mechanism at the individual level. We see that both theories are consistent in the ways social order is produced within and without the organization. Thus Parsons argues that organizations are societies writ small, while laissez-faire politics is individual self-interest writ large.

There is another important feature of our levels of analysis commitment. We also identify the level where we expect to find an explanation. One way of illustrating this is to differentiate between intentional and unintentional behavior. If an actor's behavior is wholly intentional, it is explainable at that level, in terms of his understanding, beliefs. and interests. Irrational behavior is that which cannot be explained. Unintentional behavior, on the other hand, is that which can be explained but only at some other level of analysis, the psychological or the sociological perhaps.

It is the notion of unintentionality that gives sociology, for example, its point. Parsons remarks that the possibility of a science of society, as opposed to a science of individuals, begins with the unintended consequences of human action. Sociology explains aspects of behavior of which individuals are unaware and about which they plainly cannot make decisions. Our basic commitment to the enterprise as the appropriate level of analysis means that we are focusing expressly on intentional activity. To avoid reification we assume the top manager is the decision-making part of the firm. As a result, the firm is a wholly intended pattern of activity, entirely understood and decided upon. In policy research we are only indirectly concerned with managerial irrationality or the unintended consequences of interdepartmental competition.

V. THE ORGANIZATIONAL BOUNDARY AND THE POLICY PROBLEM

Organization theory does not regard the enterprise's boundary or its policy as problematic. Both are necessary givens to any analysis within its language. Both are also givens within the theory of the firm. Since the social order within and without both theories is consistent, the boundary has no ontological significance. It simply indicates the analytic level where the givens apply. But why, then, do we so frequently argue that the organization is beyond definition? It is because neither theory is adequate to the task of creating and managing firms, as we define them at the higher level. We actually choose commitments which are consistent with parts of both theories but inconsistent with other parts. We regard power-induced order within, and emergent order without, as more representative than either theory on its own. It is the mutual inconsistency of these solutions to the problem of order created by Smith's divisions of labor that gives us the demarcating characteristic of our field. The policy problem is to create order within the organization in one way and order its external relations in another. The difference gives the internal and external domains their radically different flavors. It also makes the concept of the organizational boundary so problematic and so crucial. We are committed to two quite different concepts of social order which meet at this boundary. This gives it a special ontological significance which can only be analyzed with a theory that integrates organization theory and the theory of the firm. As Coase notes, to bound the organization analytically is to solve the problematics of both theories simultaneously.

We should also note that this two-domain analysis is a simplified version of Barnard's richer four-domain analysis. In his work, leadership acquires new meaning. It is not the leadership of men but of the organization, the ability to integrate his three subsystems into a single organizational system (1938, p. 240).

VI. ALTERNATIVE STRATEGIES FOR POLICY THEORIZING

It seems policy-research means inquiring into an insoluble problem. But it only appears so because of the way we describe it. Practicing policymakers are not concerned with our description. They get on with their job, generally with considerable success. How are we to capture this, and reason and generalize about it? One option is to build a new disciplinary matrix, with its attendant new language. This option leads to the proliferation of jargon and loose theorizing for which our field is infamous. It also leads us to think that our theorizing is preliminary, not attachable to what has gone before. We treat the business policy problem as entirely new; as if Defoe, for instance, had not written of "projectors" 200 years ago. Perhaps we do this because we find policy theorizing so difficult. Another option is to build new theories in some corner of a foreign field, say psychology or politics, which seems less obviously inconsistent with our disciplinary commitments.

A quite different option, to which the rest of this paper is devoted, opens up as soon as we deal directly with uncertainty. Immediately there are two issues to be settled: What is uncertainty, and what does it mean to "deal with it"? Necessarily, positivist approaches to these issues involve seeing uncertainty as a positive and measurable attribute of something. The possibilities of this position are illustrated in Gifford et al. (1979). There is a conundrum here, for such uncertainty cannot be measured without a knowledge of "certainty." This too severely limits the usefulness of both terms. We do better to think of uncertainty in negative terms, as an unmeasurable information defect. All we can say about it is that it arrests logical thought, i.e., we cannot draw valid conclusions so long as we are uncertain in any part of our analysis.

A theory is part of a universe of wholly certain discourse which embraces all possible mutually consistent theories. An empirical theory is one that structures and makes scientific an area of empirical discourse. It is attached to this lay language by correspondence rules. The positivist position is that all correct scientific theories are mutually consistent parts of the single universe of true knowledge—Popper's Third World. Consequently, if theories appear to be inconsistent, their competing truth claims can be resolved by a "crucial experiment."

These epistemological remarks show that we can imagine, so long as we have no access to certainty, several different types of uncertainty. Simon merely alludes to the limitations of individual decision makers. As a result, his theory of administration needs a philosopher–king to implement it. We can be analytically precise and point to information defects which would stop the most perfect decision maker:

1. Ignorance—a lack of data or empirical discourse about the thing to be analyzed;
2. Illogicality—defects in the logic of the theoretical discourse;
3. Irrelevance—defects in the correspondence rules;
4. Incommensuracy—theories that are logical and relevant but only qualitatively related, and so cannot be brought into a crucial experiment; and
5. Indeterminacy—theories that appear both logical and relevant to a single area of empirical discourse but are inconsistent.

The first applies to theory-neutral notions of reality. The second applies to the empirically empty notions of logic. The third applies to the relation between theory and reality. The final two apply to the relations between different theories. Broadly speaking, a disciplinary matrix becomes complete when it wholly "scientizes" an area of empirical discourse, both bounding it and mapping its internal territory. The philosophy of science is about the various strategies for doing this, and their weaknesses. Ultimately, it is about the uncertainty in our knowledge of reality and whether it can ever be dealt with.

VII. POLICYMAKING AS DEALING WITH ORGANIZATIONAL UNCERTAINTY

In this paper we are concerned with smaller questions. Even so, it is valuable to clarify the epistemological activity of "dealing with uncertainty" because the different types of uncertainty give us exemplars of the policymaker's responses to organizational uncertainty.

The theoretical structure of an analysis dictates precisely what inputs are necessary before wholly logical decision making can proceed. Defects which prevent this must be removed—coped with. Ignorance, for instance, is dealt with by getting more data. If the data is costly, other types of uncertainty arise, and the first strategy may need to be supplemented by a second. An alternative strategy is for the decision maker to invent the data—and most of us have experience of doing this. Actually, the two strategies are not so different so long as we have no knowledge of certainty. How can we know that our data is complete or correct, that the theory in use is relevant, or what the value of the unknown data is? Our deliberations are always strewn with such uncertainties. In practice, when decisions are being made, the residual uncertainties are being coped with by adding the missing data. By definition, the addition cannot be justified theoretically. The defects are being resolved by the decider's judgment alone. In general, coping with ignorance means adding judgment to the available data, so completing whatever is necessary to meet the decision structure's logical demands.

Illogicality is dealt with by reanalysis and, ultimately, appeals to the theory of logic itself. Godel's work, of course, implies that logic itself may be incomplete and so still uncertain. Thus even illogicality, an issue well removed from empirical discourse and its defects, may require a decision maker to make judgmental additions. Irrelevance is dealt with by gathering additional empirical data through prediction and experiment. This may involve crucial experiments to test the relative relevance of theories; but it always involves, as Popper shows, the judgments sedimented in the disciplinary matrix. Only these make an infinitely lengthy program of assumption testing unnecessary.

Kuhn's analysis is clarifying because he distinguishes indeterminacy and incommensurability from ignorance, illogicality, and irrelevance. Normal science is coping with the defects in the relationship between single theories and an area of empirical discourse. As the theories develop, so their scope extends and a more penetrating analysis becomes possible. For Popper, scientific progress is logical: the development of new theories which explain all that the old theory explained but also something new that was beyond the old theory's grasp. Critical science gives progress a different meaning. New theories seem to supplant old ones, and the relations between them are, at best, qualitative. They are linked only by the higher-level concerns which stand behind the disciplinary matrix. Crucial experiments are impossible, and new theories are preferred on the grounds of judgment rather than logic.

I have argued elsewhere that data is neither quantitative nor qualitative (Spender, 1979). It is the use we make of it that determines which. Information is quantitative inasmuch as we can bring it into a single theory's discourse. It is qualitative when it cannot be brought in without significant meaning loss. This happens when there is some unresolved inconsistency between the theory which gives the information its meaning and the theory into which we are trying to bring it. Even when we say a thing has or has not a certain quality, we still have the choice of regarding it as quantitative binary information or as as-yet-unanalyzed qualitative information. To bring in qualitative information, we must make it quantitative. Sometimes we can achieve this by normal science, by extending the scope of a theory to embrace previously inadmissible empirical discourse. At other times, the decision maker may be forced to construct an ad hoc theory whose status and relationship with the previous theory remains highly uncertain. Either way, the decision maker is adding structure rather than content to complete the inputs, and so enable the decision process.

Without considering the deeper epistemological questions raised here, we can describe the process of dealing with uncertainty as one of adding the judgments necessary to eliminate it.

The practicing policymaker faces a complex of uncertainties. All inhibit the logical decision making which complete intentionality requires. He must sort them out and develop different strategies for the different defects. Thus one kind of policy theory—get more data—follows from judging the uncertainty to be the result of ignorance. Another kind—do research—follows on irrelevance. Similarly, indeterminacy may suggest a nonzero-sum game situation calling for something which can shift the balance of power. The point, of course, is that since the uncertainties are analytically distinct, no one of these strategies can claim to be the exemplar of a complete theory of policymaking.

VIII. REFRAMING THE POLICY PROBLEM

In the analysis of the relationship between organization theory and the theory of the firm we were, in fact, discussing a particular type of uncertainty. We were using the incommensurability of their respective disciplinary matrices to frame the policy problem. Plainly, we need to generalize this notion so that it embraces the other types of uncertainty. But, in the absence of certainty, we cannot do this analytically because we do not know how the various types of uncertainty are related. In practical policymaking, when we deal with more than one type, we hold the argument together with our higher-level appreciation of the firm as a single intentional, and presumably coherent, actor. But we cannot put our disciplinary matrix on such poor foundations. Thus every piece of research must make, in addition to the methodological and ontological commitments discussed earlier, a commitment on the type of uncertainty being investigated.

Together, these commitments attach the formal certainty of logical discourse to the ill-structured empirical discourse bounded by the higher-level concerns. They also define the researcher's problem. The theorist's objective is to generate new statements which pull this into the logical discourse. The result is a single coherent and analyzable picture of all the issues he considers empirically significant.

But the policymaker faces exactly the same situation. Before he can choose a strategy for dealing with his situation he must judge the type of uncertainty present. Now we begin to see how closely policymaking and policy research are related. Scientific progress is always about coping with uncertainty. When we define policymaking th same way, we define the policymaker as a scientist trying to research the firm's external and internal domains so that he can make wholly intentional decisions about them. Our research tries to generalize about his process. Ultimately, we are looking for a theory which will make policy more powerfully and generally than any individual policymaker. But we do this by making a different trade-off, one which reflects how our interests differ from theirs. The policymaker must synthesize the multiple uncertainties of a specific situation so that he grasps it completely. The theorist focuses on a specific type of uncertainty in many situations.

IX. LIMITING THE POLICYMAKER'S OPTIONS

As a result, we bound the research problem with further assumptions. From our point of view, these simply limit the theory's scope. Thus organization theory only addresses goal-directed activity; uncertainty about goals cannot be admitted. But from the empirical point of view—which perceives the relevance of such uncertainty—these assumptions simply shift the burden of coping from within the policymaking process to somewhere beyond it. Sometimes we assume the goal is given by the owners' legally protected rights to direct the firm, sometimes by a coalition process at some other level, sometimes it results from legal or social constraints. In other words, we imply that the practitioner's world contains, in addition to the decision maker, and ourselves theorizing about him, an owner, a group of interested power holders, some legislators, some society—whom might limit all of his options.

We see that a disciplinary matrix often attaches a universe of theorizing to a universe of uncertain empirical discourse by assuming the existence of others besides the decision maker. They also are sources of uncertainty-resolving judgments. They can help the policymaker deal with the total uncertainty of the organizational situation. They become part of a pattern of external influence which must be realistic if the subsequent theory is to seem relevant to practitioners. It spells out how the entrepreneurial task is bounded and how the labor of creating economic activity is divided among the economy's actors.

As the theory's scope increases, so the policymaker needs less help from people other than the theorist. At one extreme there is a perfect division of labor between the theorist, who copes with all the uncertainty, and the decision maker, who works out its implications in specific instances. There is no longer even doubt about which theory to use. The decision maker has perfect knowledge. At the other extreme, he has no help whatsoever. Without a comprehensive theory, able to cope with the uncertainties of both external and internal domains, the policymaker must resolve the residual uncertainties himself. He may be helped by using the theory of the firm, but he must cope with the uncertainties that fall beyond it. These are only describable as its imperfections. Similarly he is left to deal with the other imperfections seen from within organization theory. Finally, in this Barnardian analysis, he must cope with the incommensurability of these two theories.

This notion of "outside help" separates the entrepreneurial and managerial tasks. Advice accepted is, within its own framework, certain. Drawing conclusions from it is an instrumental or managerial task. Dealing with the uncertainties that the decision maker cannot get advice on requires entrepreneurship. Thus the real objective of policy theorizing is to eliminate the entrepreneurial task, reducing it to one that can be done by any analytically competent manager. We are trying to produce a theory so powerful and extensive that nothing significant to the organizational world is beyond its grasp.

X. EXAMPLES OF POLICY THEORIZING

It seems there are three different strategies for developing such a theory. We can seek to extend either organization theory or the theory of the firm, or we can try to develop policy theories which integrate them with their relevant imperfections. As we have seen, this can only be done—in the absence of certainty—specific types of uncertainties. Thus policy theories are necessarily contingent.

Although Barnard gives us a way of posing this version of the policy problem, we get a better sense of what theorizing in this area means when we look at the work of (Chandler, Ansoff, Burns & Stalker, Hayes & Wheelwright, Thompson) and others. To take Chandler's enormous contribution, the spread of diversification and divisionalization has been noted by many writers. Indeed, Holden et al. (1941) deal with many of the issues Chandler later analyzes. But Chandler offers more than historical description, because he integrates his characterizations of market and organization through their respective imperfections. We have the external imperfections revealed when firms with excess funds engage new markets, because their existing markets cannot prudently be further enlarged. We have the internal imperfections revealed by top managers unable to retain complete effective control of diversified operations. Chandler's solution, although a generalization of what his four principal companies did, conceptually matches management's internal and external options (1962).

His solution is advisory and contingent in the sense that it is not a complete answer to the policymaker's problem. Top management is still left with the pricing and volume decisions of each market segment, and with coping with whatever imperfections occur there. It is also left with the problems of designing the functional organizations, and with deciding the appropriate basis of structural aggregation at each organizational level (process, product, or geography). Also, as Berg's work clarifies, it must decide what kinds of uncertainty will be resolved centrally and what will be delegated.

The value of Chandler's advice is contingent on the relevance of his characterizations. Strategic change necessarily leads structural change, because of the way these are defined. Strategy is the firm's response to encountering the external imperfection. Stopford and Wells show the advice is less relevant when the firm has the power to influence its markets. Similarly, Bower shows the weakness of the division of managerial labor so central to Chandler's solution. Despite these limitations, the diversification/divisionalization argument stands on its own as important advice to policymakers considering diversification for whatever reason.

Ansoff (1965) also deals with policymaking, as we have defined it here. While Chandler focuses on the problem of sustaining the firm's efficiency as its complexity increases, Ansoff tries to make sure that every market engagement is efficient. Although his analysis is quite different from Chandler's, and he merely alludes to the administrative and financial strategies that are necessary to complete a strategy, he still sketches a solution to our policy problem. It is partial in that top management must still deal with the uncertainties of the competence and competitive profiles, the resource inventory, and with their overall relationship.

The general nature of policy theorizing is now clear. It is about business judgment. Its objective is to relieve the policymaker of part of his entrepreneurial burden—systematically. Without uncertainty there would be no policy problem, nor would judgment be necessary for its solution. By generalizing the process, policy theory systematizes the generation and application of this judgment.

XI. THE POLICYMAKER'S OTHER HELPERS

As we have noted, policy theory assumes the existence of people other than the policymaker. In fact there are those who give him more than advice, who relieve him of part of his responsibility to look after the entire firm. For instance, the uncertainties of implementing strategy are delegated to implementers. They must also look after the consequences of imperfect forecasting. Alternatively, the policymaker is sometimes able to off-load his problem into the insurance market, or, by imaginative contract making, share it with customers or suppliers. In this way he moves the boundaries of the organization, and of his policy problem, with a complex of make-or-buy decisions. The firm becomes bounded by the complex of relations with actors who have a stake in it.

But there still other actors who are generating advice unintentionally. Although, as Leavitt and others note, much important new knowledge comes from outside an industry, the average policymaker gains considerable understanding from the antics of his competitors. He recognizes that their experiences often test his own notions and suggest new generalizations. We expect this because competitors are dealing with some of the same uncertainties of market and organizational behavior as he is. While many uncertainties are firm-specific, others are more generally shared. The way others respond to the shared uncertainties may influence his policymaking, even though they have no direct stake in the firm.

Because of these complex external influences, policy theorizing is more than simply bounding the policymaker's problem. It means specifying the knowledge which he employs as well as its sources. When he acts on his own, without accepting any advice, he is the pure entrepreneur about whom there can be no policy theory. When he either acquires or is forced to accept knowledge from some external source, he is a manager. Policy theorizing is only effective when it makes the source, utilization, and generation of such knowledge clear.

XII. INDUSTRY RECIPES AND SHARED PATTERNS OF JUDGMENT

Given the diversity of external influences, policy researchers have an enormous range of research topics. The territory is huge. Indeed, one of the most delightful aspects of our work is our freedom to homestead in such virgin, yet fertile, lands. But that freedom is also a burden. It becomes even more necessary to demonstrate the relevance of what we produce, to show why we theorists can generate knowledge which the policymaker cannot get elsewhere.

One way of dealing with the problem of relevance is to employ an a posteriori method and start off with the policymaker's perceptions. My empirical results have been presented elsewhere, though without being clearly related to the definitions being suggested here (Spender, 1980, 1981). The paper's final pages will sketch out this connection and, thereby, one possible disciplinary matrix for research in our area. Since it is only relevant to one particular source of judgment, I would not recommend its use for any other type of policy research.

There are at least two ways of analyzing imperfections. We can try to extend existing theory, so embracing them by relaxing the disciplinary matrix; this is the positivist strategy. Or we can approach the field directly, phenomenologically. Presuming that practicing entrepreneurs act intentionally, we can elicit their pattern of perceptions and treat it as their theory of the situation. Here we assume they too are making theory in order to embrace what they see as the important uncertainties. Their immediate perception of these may well lead to better grounded and more powerful theories than ours. While this certainly opens up an alternative research strategy, whether or not it is more productive is still uncertain. Though, in this respect, we might ask whether the substantial contributions of Chandler, Ansoff, and Burns & Stalker really grew from normal science or whether they sprang from entrepreneurs' speculations.

To argue that the policymaker can solve his problems by watching his competitors is not in itself very informative. The implied theory of policymaking—do what your competitors do—merely replaces the policy problem with another one of deciding whom to imitate and which of their actions to note. But it raises more important questions about the structure of the knowledge the policymaker is using. We justify our truth claims by referring to populations of events or actors. These populations can be constructed historically or cross-sectionally. Thus Mintzberg argues that policy becomes manifest as the pattern in a historical sequence of decisions; Hatten or Porter argue it is the pattern evident in the decisions of members of a group—pattern here meaning lack of randomness. Pattern could imply a group of firms acting in concert. Hence, given our commitment to the firm as a free agent, pattern needs explaining. Many writers, such as Unwin and Florence, have noted firms' propensity to imitate or "swarm," but without explaining it. Our hypothesis, that competitive firms are somehow influencing one another's policies as part of a common process of coping with uncertainty, becomes a researchable question.

If we assume that all organizational behavior is intentional, we are driven to explain such patterning in one of two ways. Either it is the result of shared knowledge about how best to reach a shared goal, or it is a reflection of a common lack of strategic choices. The first focuses on the policymakers' uncertainty-resolving activity, the second on their role as managers interpreting the imperatives of an unambiguous environment. If we pursue the first possibility, we must also explain how the group obtains this knowledge. It could be generated by one firm and consciously shared with the others, it could be the outcome of conscious cooperation, or it could be the unintentional consequences of the individual firms' activity. The first two possibilities raise the question of how such a purposive group comes to be formed, offending our presumption of free policymaking.

The disciplinary matrix I use, therefore, presumes intentionality on the part of the firm and examines unintentional patterning across a group of firms. To bring this pattern out, I use "focused interviewing," developed during World War II by Merton and others. It is basically a verbal projection technique which depends on keeping the respondent's language attached to a particular context of experience. It elicits the respondent's perception and reconstruction of that experience.

By presuming an identity of policymaker and firm, I attach this pattern of judgment to the level of the firm. Inasmuch as the data reveals sharing, it suggests that we should analyze these firms' policies at the group level, above that of the firm. Here, the group becomes an analytic unit with the same kind of ontological status as a "society" or "market." To differentiate such an unintended group from a purposive group such as a cartel, with its clear group entry and maintenance procedures, I use the term "recipe." Schutz, especially, uses this term to denote a shared pattern of perceptions when investigating what people take to be "common-sense" knowledge of their environment (1972). Simon also uses this term, though in a rather different way, when exploring the integration of organization theory and the theory of the firm (1952). Whether or not the concept is useful is a purely empirical question.

XIII. RELATING THE RECIPE TO POLICYMAKING

Finding a recipe is empirical evidence that it is a significant source of external judgment for individual policymakers. The extent to which it dominates their thinking is a practical measure of where each policymaker stands on our entrepreneur–manager scale. Analyzing any firm's strategy must begin with an assessment of where its policies are being made and where, therefore, the policymaking process is to be found. If the policies are shared, they may be being made outside the firm being studied. If, as often proves to be the case, the recipe is significantly different from the judgments available from other external sources, we can measure its relative significance as a source. When it dominates the policymaking, the policy—imitate your competitors—becomes operational as the policy—apply the recipe. Of course, the recipe's usefulness is contingent on the relevance of the group's characterization of its internal and external environments. This shows the indirect and advisory nature of the recipe, for it can only apply to what is common to the firms of the group. This can still dominate, as when businessmen equate their firm's situation with the industry's, explaining their policies in terms of the industry's responses to changing circumstances.

The concept of a recipe also introduces a potentially vicious circularity around how to define group membership. This can be contained, rather than resolved, by treating the recipe as dynamic, the group's collective response to its changing uncertainties. The firm is now being redefined as a member of a species-group which is evolving in an uncertain environment. The self-perceived grouping which my research reveals has much in common with E. A. Robinson's and Triffin's discussions of the concept of industry membership. It seems sensible in that, although the firms are competing among themselves, they are generally using similar methods of production to produce similar products for a shared market. The unintended evolutionary mechanism is the unexplained, i.e., random, variations in the individual firm's characterizations. As these prove successful and, by imitation, are drawn into the group's recipe, the recipe adapts. The crucial point, of course, is that although unsuccessful variations may annihilate particular firms, they still add materially to the group's knowledge. In this way, the recipe carries the sedimented experiences of the whole species-group, it is its folk-memory.

When the recipe dominates, it attacks our commitment to the firm as the appropriate level for policy research. In the same way that psychologically inclined theorists, and we should include Shackle here, say, "Look at the entrepreneur, not the firm," the recipe is saying "look at the group, not the firm." Integrating the concept into a theory of policymaking depends, as we have seen, on the commitments made at the theory's various levels. This is quite easy when both company and industry group levels carry the same disciplinary implications. Thus the concept of "strategic group," as introduced by Hunt (1972), fits so well that it can be interpreted two ways. It can be the researcher's perception of strategic similarity between different firms. So long as the similarity is not explained, the researcher is not discussing policymaking. Alternatively, the pattern reflects the firms' common knowledge of how to maximize their performance. The problem with this framework is that it is impossible to explain how an individual firm's strategy can differ from the common strategy which now defines group membership without also implying that it is irrational or deviant. As the recipe is unintentional, we do not have this difficulty. But the relationship between the recipe and an intentional firm's policy is now problematic.

One way of dealing with this, and so completing a theory of policymaking, is to locate both the recipe and the residual entrepreneurial activity within a dialectical framework. This is held together at the higher level by the empirical content behind the phrase "the firm as a whole." A dialectical frame lets us treat the recipe as the analysis of what the group members share, leaving the unresolved entrepreneurial element to reflect the sense of each firm's uniqueness. The policy analysis is partial, covering only that part of the policymaking process which relates to the external advice. The process as a whole presumes an unspecified entrepreneurial synthesis of the shared and the unique. Although we cannot generalize about the latter, the dialectical frame lets us appreciate the differences between the group's firms, and their varied resources and goals. The policies generated are unique, reflecting each firm's unique set of constraints—even though all are heavily influenced by the shared recipe.

The disadvantage of using a dialectical frame is that we can no longer predict the firm's policies, only their shared features. Because the recipe's details are grounded in what the group perceives to be the most significant situational imperfections, each carries implications about the appropriate resources and expectations that a firm should have. Thus the recipe limits its range of relevance with implicit entry and exit barriers.

In spite of these obvious shortcomings, the recipe makes the theorist's contribution unique as external advice. It is not simply the codification of best practice, nor of a particular firm's heuristics. Because it explains unintentional behavior it adds new knowledge. As with psychology or sociology, moving to another level of analysis lets the policy theorist uncover a different kind of policy analysis. This has considerable practical significance. Without being clear about the recipe themselves, policymakers cannot know whether their policies are actually being made beyond their grasp, nor how securely they are attached to the industry group's accumulated experience. The recipe concept lets us identify, analytically, a completely new strategic question: whether the policymaker should succumb to the "herd instinct." As Cyert & March point out, policy is about uncertainty avoidance too. Going along with the industry is part of making sure its experiences help to reduce the individual firm's uncertainties. The cost of doing this, of course, is that the firm gets "locked" into the industry, and will go the way it goes. Being clear about the recipe, that aspect of the firm's industry membership that has policy significance, is the basis of any thoroughly professional decision to break away into a new kind of business. The alternative is pure entrepreneurship, with its considerable potential—and its huge exposure.

The detail of researching, structuring, and employing the recipe is discussed in Spender (1981). The resulting theory may lack simplicity, but it does cast the recipe as an advisory culture or pattern of meaning rather than as a prescriptive formula which displaces the entrepreneur entirely. It involves a disciplinary matrix which makes good use of a posteriori methods and yet relates them to the more familiar a priori methods. It suggests the usefulness of closer relations with industrial anthropology and with business history. But perhaps its strongest point is that it defines policy as a distinctive field by sketching out one possible disciplinary matrix.

PRINCIPAL REFERENCES

Ansoff, H. (1965), Corporate Strategy, McGraw-Hill, New York.

Barnard, C. (1938), The Functions of the Executive, Harvard U.P., Cambridge, Mass.

Chandler, A. (1962), Strategy and Structure, M.I.T. Press, Cambridge, Mass.

Coase, R. (1937), "The Nature of the Firm" Economica. November: 386–405.

Cyert, R. & March, J. (1963), A Behavioural Theory of the Firm, Prentice-Hall Inc., Englewood Cliffs, N.J.

Gifford, W. et al. (1979), "Message Characteristics" Academy of Management Journal. XX n.3:458–481.

Holden, P. et al. (1941), Top Management Organization, Stanford U.P., Stanford.

Hunt, M. (1972), Competition in the Major Home Appliance Industry 1960–1970, Ph.D. Dissertation, Harvard University.

Kuhn, T. (1970), The Structure of Scientific Revolutions, University of Chicago Press, Chicago.

______ (1977), The Essential Tension, University of Chicago Press, Chicago.

Schutz, A. (1972), The Phenomenology of the Social World, Heinemann, London.

Simon, H. (1952), "A Comparison of Organization Theories" Review of Economic Studies. XX n.1:40–48.

Spender, J-C. (1979), "Theory-building and Theory-testing" in Schendel, D. & Hofer, C. (Eds.), Strategic Management; A New View, Little Brown, Boston: 394–404.

______ (1980), Strategy-making in Business, Ph.D. Dissertation, Manchester University.

______ (1981), "Strategy-making in Business" Academy of Management National Conference, San Diego.

Taylor, B. & MacMillan, K. (Eds.) (1973), Business Policy: Teaching and Research, Bradford U.P., Bradford.

THE ROLE OF STRATEGY IN THE DEVELOPMENT OF A GENERAL THEORY OF ORGANIZATIONS

Charles C. Snow and Raymond E. Miles

I. INTRODUCTION

This is an exciting and pivotal period in the study of organizations. A number of recent developments seem to be moving the field toward a theoretical convergence, and the outline of a general theory of organizations may be emerging. This confluence of ideas appears to be developing not so much from conceptual breakthroughs as from imaginative attempts to synthesize existing knowledge.

The source of this growing synthesis lies primarily in the area of strategic management. Strategy is a key concept because it encompasses a variety of organizational decisions, focuses on both the internal and external environment, and highlights the notion of a fit or equilibrium both within an organization and between an organization and its broader societal context. Thus strategic manage-

Advances in Strategic Management, Volume 2, pages 231–259.

ISBN: 0-89232-409-0

ment scholars appear to be well positioned to understand and integrate the various concepts and frameworks relevant to the design and management of complex organizations.

This chapter seeks to advance organization theory by describing an approach that offers a systematic means of generating and classifying knowledge of organizational behavior. The first section describes briefly how organizational knowledge has accumulated historically—a process referred to as "context inclusion." It is argued that the context-inclusion approach is not likely to produce much useful knowledge about strategic management (i.e., management of the organization as a complete system in interaction with its environment), nor of the pattern of interaction of the main internal components of the system.

The second section describes a central idea that appears to pervade theories of organization and management: the ongoing search for fit in the alignment and arrangement of organizational resources. By examining several widely known studies, each of which used different perspectives, samples, and methodologies, it is argued that the process of search for alignment–arrangement fit represents the fundamental dynamic of managerial behavior.

The third section describes an alternative research approach to that of context inclusion. Relying on the notion of "contextual overlays"—broad categories of personal, organizational, and environmental characteristics that circumscribe identifiable patterns of organizational behavior—it is argued that theory development should first describe and explain major types of organizational form and behavior, then examine managerial actions and member responses within the various types. Three key overlays—industry, strategy, and management philosophy—are described, and these are related to the core concept of fit in the alignment and arrangement of organizational resources.

The fourth section presents an illustration of the contextual overlays framework, and the final section is the conclusions.

II. ORGANIZATIONAL RESEARCH: THE CONTEXT-INCLUSION APPROACH

In the 1960s it was popular among those who studied organizations to proclaim that "little is known . . . and nothing for certain." At the time, this skeptical attitude served a useful function: it helped to unshackle both academics and practitioners from the chains of simplistic, universal principles of organization and management. In response to attacks on unsupported, generalized, prescriptive theories, a predictable swing occurred in the direction of tightly specified but limited contingency models of organizational behavior that were more suited to rigorous empirical analyses. In rapid succession, numerous contingency theories were developed, each of which offered its own set of concepts and a framework for analyzing relations among them.

Today, almost 20 years of scholarly investigation have produced a diverse collection of theories and a large but unorganized body of empirical research. Not surprisingly, this effort has had only a small impact on the practice of management. In a period in which the world of organizations has become more complex and interrelated, attempts to build broader and more integrated theories of organization have been discouraged or diverted by attention to issues of specification and measurement. Overall, it is tempting to agree with today's cynics who proclaim that the field has now managed to prove with certainty that little is known. Further, it seems safe to say that the field of organization and management is dominated by micro contingency theories: narrow, tightly integrated theories of individual and group behavior.

Unfortunately, the current thrust of contingency thinking is inconsistent with attempts to achieve an understanding of strategic management. The body of knowledge about organizations has been developed primarily from a research process that might be called "context inclusion." Early theories of organization and management were based almost entirely on the individual and group as units of analysis. Gradually, these theories incorporated peripheral or contextual variables as they appeared to be relevant. However, many of these contextual variables are, in reality, system characteristics and processes of a fundamentally different magnitude, and it is unlikely that these systemic phenomena can be understood by incrementally attaching them to available micro models through the context-inclusion process. For example, present theories of leadership are focused largely on patterns of interaction between supervisors and subordinates. Moreover, the supporting evidence for these theories consists mostly of observations of lower- and middle-level managers. As it became clear over time that additional contextual variables were needed in order to explain variations in behavior, performance, and satisfaction, investigators extended their models to include departmental characteristics like organizational climate and organizational characteristics like mechanistic–organic or, most recently, corporate culture. These contextual characteristics, often narrowly defined and/or mere aggregates of individual characteristics, have simply been grafted onto theories of interpersonal processes. Generally speaking, the addition of these variables has added little to the explanatory power of interpersonal leadership models and has not helped at all in building theories of leadership at the top of organizations.

The cumulative result of research conducted in the context-inclusion vein will not be a theoretical integration of systemic with individual/group phenomena but rather continued fragmentation and irrelevance. Instead, an understanding of the systemic properties and behavior of organizations—which in turn provide the context for individual and group behavior—requires concepts that are defined and operationalized at the appropriate level (Roberts et al., 1978; Daft and Wiginton, 1979). Furthermore, these concepts need to be based on a widely agreed-upon core idea that will permit theory development to proceed logically and systematically.

III. ALIGNMENT AND ARRANGEMENT OF ORGANIZATIONAL RESOURCES

Most academic disciplines, especially those in the natural and life sciences, have been built upon a set of elements or concepts that serves to keep theory development focused. By contrast, in the field of organization and management, there is no widespread agreement on an element (or set of elements) that should pervade organizational and managerial theories. It is proposed that a core concept does exist—that the search for fit in the alignment and arrangement of resources is the basis of organizational behavior. Andrews (1971) discussed the alignment problem as "matching" organizational resources with environmental opportunities and constraints. Other theorists (Drucker, 1954, 1974; Chandler, 1962; Thompson, 1967; Weick, 1969, 1977; Child, 1972; Miles et al., 1974; Miles and Snow, 1978) have argued in a similar fashion that organizations (i.e., their managers) in large part choose the domains, or portions of the environment, in which they wish to operate. This alignment task, as Thompson (1967, p. 148) pointed out, is dynamic and never-ending—the organization is continually "shooting at a moving target of coalignment." Thus the ideal alignment is seldom achieved by any organization, but every organization is in search of it.

Alternatively, other theorists have focused on the internal arrangement of organizational resources. Burns and Stalker (1961), Woodward (1965), Lawrence and Lorsch (1967), Perrow (1967), Galbraith (1977), and others have developed frameworks and criteria for making choices about internal structures and processes, given the nature of management's choices about environmental alignment. Here, too, the solution to the arrangement problem involves the idea of fit (Galbraith and Nathanson, 1978; Aldrich, 1979; Van de Ven, 1979). Just as the organization must be continually fitted to its environment, internal structures and processes must be fitted to each other in ways that support environmental-alignment mechanisms.[1]

In sum, there is a substantial body of literature that has examined various aspects of the process of search for alignment–arrangement fit. Specifically, this basic phenomenon has been consistently observed in several different settings: (1) across populations of organizations viewed historically (Chandler, 1962); (2) in organizations during short-run periods of technological transition (Burns and Stalker, 1961), (3) across industries at a given point in time (Lawrence and Lorsch, 1967), and (4) within industries at a given point in time (Miles and Snow, 1978).

A. An Historical Perspective

Chandler's (1962) study of the evolution of strategy and structure among 70 of the largest U.S. corporations was perhaps the first to portray the alignment–arrangement problem clearly. Writing about the period from approximately 1850 to 1960, Chandler described the major changes that occurred in the U.S. economy. Broadly speaking, these changes offered opportunities for many companies to expand by diversifying their product lines and/or dispersing geographically. Chandler's specific focus, however, was on how the top executives of four of the largest and most complex American firms at the time accepted this challenge and changed their organizations' strategies and structures in order to take advantage of these product and market opportunities.

Until these pioneering companies, duPont, General Motors, Standard Oil of New Jersey (now Exxon), and Sears, Roebuck, began to experiment with new environmental alignments in the 1920s and 1930s, the usual alignment was that of the "single-line" business. The typical firms of that period was a manufacturing entity that made a single product or a very limited product line. Compared to the organizations and environments of today, the alignment problems of these companies were relatively homogeneous and straightforward. Therefore, those firms that attempted to grow through product and market diversification were developing a form of environmental alignment that had virtually no precedent.

As these organizations grappled with their diversification strategies, it became apparent that the common internal arrangement for the allocation of resources, a functional organizational structure, was not well suited for this type of growth. Therefore, the top managers of these companies also began to experiment with new organizational structures and management processes that might better support a diversification strategy. In each of the four cases, the executives responsible for identifying and pursuing the new strategic direction initially paid little attention to the required organizational structure. In those instances where structure was not appropriately modified to fit strategy, "executives throughout the organization were drawn deeper and deeper into operational activities and often were working at cross purposes to and in conflict with one another" (Chandler, 1962, p. 315).

The development of new structure–process configurations proceeded at a different pace and displayed different features in each of the four companies. Executives in each organization shaped the structure to fit the requirements of the industry in which the organization operated; there was no deliberate imitation of structural characteristics across firms or industries, though the leaders of GM and duPont were obviously influenced by their frequent contact. Nevertheless, even though it took over 20 years and was largely accomplished independently, these four firms arrived at essentially the same structure–process arrangement (the product or multidivisional structure) to support the new form of environmental alignment (a diversified product–market domain).

Chandler's (1962) study addresses at least three important aspects of the alignment–arrangement problem, characteristics that have tended to recur in subsequent studies by other investigators. First, using the broad sweep of the historian's brush, Chandler was able to show how companies in different industries were presented with the challenge of developing new alignment forms.

Some of the companies in each industry accepted this challenge, others did not. The chosen form for most of the organizations studied by Chandler was growth through diversification in products and markets, but the development of this type of alignment did not come easily. As indicated, the pioneering companies took 20 years or more to reach a satisfactory equilibrium with their new environments. Second, Chandler clearly demonstrated that a new alignment required a new, or at least different, arrangement of internal structures and processes. Essentially, a strategy of diversification seemed to require a product form of organizational structure with its accompanying general manager role, some decentralization of planning and decision making, and so on. This structure–process configuration represented a major shift from the functional structures and processes used by other organizations at the time. Finally, this study highlighted the important role that top-management philosophies and expertise play in the adaptive process. As Chandler noted, most of the top executives in these companies were "empire builders" rather than "organization builders," and this orientation presumably delayed the development of the structure–process arrangements required by new alignment choices. Subsequent theory and research have confirmed that top-management's philosophies and capabilities play an important role in resolving the alignment–arrangement problem (Forrester, 1965; Argyris, 1973; Beer and Davis, 1976; Miles and Snow, 1978).

B. Technological Transition

Two British researchers, Burns and Stalker (1961), examined a set of strategy–structure issues that overlapped the research by Chandler (1962). However, the Burns and Stalker studies differed from Chandler's research in two major ways. First, the period of observation was considerably shorter, involving organizational behaviors over a period of only a few years. Second, the research was confined largely to a single industry (electronics). But despite these differences, the research by Burns and Stalker both confirmed and extended the findings of Chandler.

Burns and Stalker (1961, p. vii) described and explained "what happens when new and unfamiliar tasks are put upon industrial concerns organized for relatively stable conditions." The focus of their study developed in an interesting way. Burns had studied a rayon mill in which research and development was "impotent," but nevertheless the company was successful in its industry. He next studied an engineering concern that was structured much differently than the rayon mill and which was managed along quite different lines. This firm was also a successful participant in its industry.

Intrigued with the notion that organizations with different structures and management processes could be equally successful, Burns (and now Stalker) began a more systematic study of how different types of organizations respond to environmental change (defined as the technological basis of production and the market characteristics of the industry). This investigation, which the authors called the Scottish Study, involved a number of companies in Scotland. With the encouragement and assistance of the Scottish Council, a voluntary body supported financially by industrial firms, several Scottish companies attempted to get into electronics development work and, eventually, into the manufacture of electronics products.

Most of the Scottish companies failed to realize the expectations of the Council. The primary reason for this failure, according to Burns and Stalker, was that many of these companies had "mechanistic" management systems: structures, processes, and management philosophies that were appropriate for organizations operating under relatively stable conditions but inappropriate for conditions of change. Under conditions of environmental change, the appropriate management system appeared to be "organic," that is, one which contained enough flexibility to accommodate new and unfamiliar tasks.

The last study reported by Burns and Stalker was the English Study, a survey of eight electronics firms conducted by Burns. The findings from this study were in marked contrast to those of the Scottish Study in that the English firms were much more able to incorporate new and unfamiliar tasks into their operations. The authors attributed this successful adaptive response largely to the fact that the English companies had more organic management systems. But elsewhere, Burns and Stalker (1961, p. 8) noted that "the eight English firms . . . were not only much larger but much more committed to electronics development and manufacture than were the firms of the Scottish Study, which were in the earliest stages of their careers in electronics." Thus, whether or not the Scottish firms had organic management systems, it is possible that their top executives simply were not committed to pursuing new forms of environmental alignment.

The study by Burns and Stalker confirmed one of Chandler's key findings: there must be a fit or congruence between strategy and structure. If structure and process are not well suited to a particular strategy, then this strategy cannot be pursued effectively. In addition, this study added two other dimensions to the alignment–arrangement problem (although their importance was not entirely evident at the time). First, it is now clear that different forms of environmental alignment can occur within the same industry. That is, mechanistic, organic, and other types of organizations may coexist within an industry provided that each organization's strategy–structure relationship is appropriately designed. Second, the Burns and Stalker findings emphasized the fact that industries experience different rates of technological and market innovation, and, in order to understand fully the alignment options available to a given organization, industry factors must be taken into account. Thus, the rayon mill observed by Burns and Stalker could survive with an "impotent" research-and-development function, but the British electronics firms could not.

C. Interindustry Behavior

A study by Lawrence and Lorsch (1967) viewed the alignment–arrangement problem from an interindustry perspective. Starting with a general objective that was strikingly similar to that of Burns and Stalker—an attempt "to gain an understanding of the organizational characteristics which allow firms to deal effectively with different kinds and rates of environmental change"—Lawrence and Lorsch (1967, p. v) addressed industry factors directly. They noted that:

> managers have long recognized that different industrial environments have particular economic and technical characteristics, each of which calls for a unique competitive strategy. A set of marketing, manufacturing, and research policies that works well for a firm in the chemical industry will not meet the needs of a corporation producing steel. (1967, p. 1)

In these authors' view, a "unique competitive strategy" can be achieved by (1) differentiating the organization into subunits, each of which deals in a specialized manner with a segment of the firm's environment, and (2) employing the integrating mechanisms needed to bring about a state of high-quality collaboration among the various subunits. Thus, Lawrence and Lorsch focused on the characteristics of major organizational subunits as well as on the total system.

This study involved 10 companies in three different industries. The industries were selected to provide a wide range of environmental uncertainty (unpredictable changes in market and technological conditions). Six of the firms operated in the highly uncertain plastics industry, two in the somewhat less uncertain consumer foods industry, and two in the highly certain standardized container industry. In each firm in each industry particular attention was paid to three organizational subunits: research and development, marketing, and manufacturing.

In general, Lawrence and Lorsch found that managers in the marketing, manufacturing, and R&D subunits of the two firms in the standardized container industry all perceived their relevant environments to be as certain as, or more certain than, similar organizational subunits in the plastics or consumer foods industries. Therefore, according to Lawrence and Lorsch, it appeared that these three industries indeed did vary in terms of environmental uncertainty, and this variation required more differentiation in the plastics and foods companies than in the container companies. Presumably, also, the uncertainty associated with the plastics and consumer foods industries presented the firms in these industries with more alignment options than those available to companies in the standardized container industry.

With respect to integration, there was no difference in the amount of integration required among the different subunits in all 10 organizations; in every case, a high degree of integration was viewed as necessary. However, the types of mechanisms used to achieve integration varied considerably between firms in the container and the other two industries. In the former, integration occurred primarily through the managerial hierarchy, was less frequent and less complicated, and was largely confined to the top-management group. In the plastics and consumer foods industries, integrating mechanisms were more numerous and complicated, and often they were placed at much lower levels in the managerial hierarchy. Thus, according to Lawrence and Lorsch, a complex (differentiated) alignment required a set of complex integrating mechanisms (internal arrangements).

The study by Lawrence and Lorsch reaffirmed the importance of fitting strategy to structure, and it showed that complex alignment strategies required complex structure–process arrangements. Even more importantly, however, this study showed that industry characteristics had a significant impact on organizational strategy, structure, and process.

D. Intraindustry Behavior

The studies by Chandler (1962), Burns and Stalker (1961), and Lawrence and Lorsch (1967) assumed or demonstrated that the environment was changing, and they showed how successful organizations developed the structure–process mechanisms needed to cope with environmental change. A series of studies reported by Miles and Snow (1978) approached the alignment–arrangement problem from a somewhat different perspective. Building on the concepts of strategic choice (Child, 1972) and enactment (Weick, 1969, 1977), Miles and Snow argued that organizations, in large part, choose the environments in which they wish to operate. They select or "enact" their domains of operation by focusing only on certain conditions, events, and trends in the environment. Those factors that go unnoticed or are deliberately ignored are not part of the organization's enacted environment and thus do not affect managerial decision making and action.

Within each of the industries studied (college textbook publishing, electronics, food processing, and health care), organizations exhibited a wide range of alignments with their environments, which Miles and Snow called strategies. A fourfold strategic typology was developed, of which three were viable (Defenders, Prospectors, Analyzers) and one generally unworkable (Reactors). The Defender exhibited the simplest environmental alignment by choosing a narrow, relatively stable product–market domain. This type of alignment was supported by a set of structure–process mechanisms that typically included a functional structure, a mass-production technology, centralized planning and control, and other management processes consistent with a stable form of alignment. The Prospector, on the other hand, enacted a much more complex environmental alignment in that this type of organization chose to operate in broad, changing domains. Because of the fluid nature of the Prospector's alignment, the structure–process mechanisms used to support it included a product (or program) structure, flexible production technologies, decentralized planning and control processes, and so on. Analyzers attempted to develop and maintain an environmental alignment that contained elements of both the Defender and the Prospector alignments, and, as a result, these organizations frequently exhibited the complex characteristics associated with matrix structures. Finally, the Reactor was a type of organization that, for one reason or another, had not completely solved its alignment problem. In many cases organizations found themselves temporarily functioning in this mode when they were unwilling or unable to develop a consistent set of structure–process mechanisms that would permit a clearer, more acceptable environmental alignment. Frequently, as will be explored in more detail later, this unwillingness or inability to develop or maintain an effective alignment–arrangement relationship was due to top executives' philosophies about how to manage human resources. Specifically, some strategies appeared to require more participative management philosophies, and, if these were not forthcoming, the strategies could not be fully implemented (Ansoff and Stewart, 1967; Argyris, 1973; Beer and Davis, 1976).

E. Summary

As suggested, these and other studies appear to have investigated different aspects of the same phenomenon. Successful organizations exhibit systemic consistency in that they have forged operational alignments with their environments and have developed internal structure–process arrangements to fit these alignment choices. Thus, it is argued here, the alignment–arrangement concept portrays a fundamental feature of organizational behavior. Viewed from the alignment–arrangement perspective, a comprehensive theory of organizations might be constructed using the following key ideas:

1. *Industries offer particularistic alignment demands and possibilities.* Industries differ considerably in their attractiveness due to growth possibilities, regulatory constraints, barriers to entry and mobility, and a host of other factors. For a given organization, the configuration of such industry characteristics is highly important to the type of alignment sought. Moreover, certain industry factors may dictate, or at least constrain, arrangement options.
2. *Within an industry, organizations are typically able to develop a variety of competitive strategies.* Some strategies involve a relatively simple environmental alignment, and, therefore, only relatively simple structure–process arrangements are required to pursue them. Other strategies bring the organization into a complex alignment with the environment, and they require correspondingly complex internal arrangements. But in all cases, a fit or congruence must exist among strategy, structure, and process.

3. *Every strategy requires continuous management, but currently available management philosophies are not equally well suited for all strategies.* Although industry and strategy influence greatly an organization's alignment–arrangement options, they do not fully determine these options. Management philosophy, beliefs about how human resources should be directed and controlled, also affects the shape of internal structure-process arrangements and may inhibit or facilitate the development of a given type of environmental alignment.

Together, industry, strategy, and management philosophy constitute a general framework for the analysis of organizational design and behavior. These are not the only factors affecting the design, behavior, and management of an organization, of course, but they are clearly major influences that could provide the starting point for a comprehensive theory. Furthermore, factors associated with these broad sets of variables largely define the organizational context in which individual and group behavior occur. In the next section, a way of examining the impact that industry, strategy, and management philosophy have on the alignment and arrangement of organizational resources is described.

IV. THE CONTEXTUAL OVERLAYS APPROACH

One means of conceptualizing how industry, strategy, and management philosophy affect an organization's alignment–arrangement options and choices involves the notion of overlay: broad categories of personal, organizational, and environmental characteristics that circumscribe identifiable patterns of organizational behavior.[2] As used here, an overlay is intended to increase understanding of organizational behavior by highlighting key contexts or boundaries within which behavior occurs. By successively superimposing on the alignment–arrangement process one important context (overlay) after another, an increasingly specified pattern of behavior is observable.

None of the contextual overlays is, of course, unidimensional; each may take a variety of forms. Therefore, it would appear that the first requirement for the specification of an overlay is the development of an appropriate typology, a description of the different forms the overlay may exhibit. Generally speaking, the development of typologies is not a popular activity among organizational scholars, despite the fact that in other disciplines it is viewed as an essential first step before more refined research can take place (Carper and Snizek, 1980).

Typologies are simply schemes for classifying information about organizations.[3] The major benefits of typologies are codification and prediction (Tiryakian, 1968). Codification refers to the ordering of heterogeneous elements into distinct groupings; therefore, valid and comprehensive typologies of major organizational elements would "allow large amounts of information about various forms of organizations to be collapsed into more convenient categories that would then be easier to process, store, and comprehend" (Carper and Snizek, 1980, p. 73).

Typologies also can aid in predicting organizational characteristics and behavior. Because a given organizational type is defined as a cluster of attributes that are internally consistent and occur commonly, the presence of some attributes logically permits the reliable prediction of others (Miller and Mintzberg, 1980). McKelvey (1975, p. 523) describes the predictive possibilities of typologies thusly: "If a usable classification existed, there would be no need for contingency theory. Biologists do not need contingency theories because their taxonomy and classification scheme makes it clear that one does not apply findings about reptiles to mammals unless one is dealing broadly with the subphyla level of vertebrates. Organization and management researchers need contingency theories because there is no taxonomy to make it clear that one does not, for example, and only for example, apply findings from small British candy manufacturers to large French universities."

The contention here is that typological development, as a fundamental building block of science, is more likely to lead to a general theory of organizations than the current approach associated with contingency theory, which generally can be characterized by narrowly defined relationships among a few variables, cross-sectional analyses, and heavy emphasis on measurement issues. As Schein (1980, p. 188) maintains: "It should be recognized that we are in a very early stage of organizational science where careful observation and the building of appropriate taxonomies is just as important as testing hypotheses or attempting to develop precise theory."

The three key overlays of industry, strategy, and management philosophy are discussed below. A rationale is presented for the importance of each of these overlays to theory development, and special attention is paid to the impact of each overlay on the alignment and arrangement of organizational resources.

A. Industry Overlay

For most private-sector organizations, industry is the fundamental arena in which behavior occurs. This broad overlay circumscribes organizations in ways that are both theoretically and practically meaningful. First, industry is a proxy for a number of important characteristics of an organization's environment. For example, simply knowing the industry in which an organization operates allows one to know something about product life cycles, required capital investments, long-term profit prospects, types of production technologies, regulatory requirements, and so forth. These are the sorts of environmental factors that affect managerial decision making, and thus an industry overlay is useful for determining the "feasible set" of alignment–arrangement options available to organizations within a given industry.

Second, industry is an environmental context that is rooted in reality. Unlike other environmental dimensions presumed to affect organizational behavior, such as uncertainty, munificence, or hostility, industry factors are concrete and frequently externally verifiable. For example, it is possible to collect relatively objective data on the degree of competition in an industry, barriers to entry, average profitability of major firms, and growth projections, and to relate these factors to the behavior of organizations within the industry (Porter, 1980, 1981). Moreover, such data can be used to make needed interdisciplinary linkages between the study of organizations and other relevant sciences (e.g., economics). Current conceptualizations of organization–environment relations, which are based largely on artificial constructs, have sparked little interest among scholars in other fields and have influenced practitioners hardly at all.

A third reason for regarding industry as a crucial context of organizations is that a substantial amount of knowledge about this overlay already exists (Chandler, 1962; Caves, 1972; Schoeffler et al., 1974; Caves and Porter, 1977; Hatten and Schendel, 1977; Porter, 1979). From the standpoint of theory building in the area of strategic management, this presents a considerable opportunity for synthesis.

1. *Impacts on Alignment*

Every industry provides a host of alignment demands and possibilities that vary both in scope and complexity. For example, numerous researchers have alluded to, but seldom have studied systematically, an industry's dominant environmental requirements. Such requirements are industry factors that must be addressed by organizational participants if they wish to enter or remain in the industry. In the study discussed earlier, Lawrence and Lorsch (1967) specified the dominant environmental requirements as product and technological development in plastics, product development and market research in consumer foods, and customer service and product quality in standardized containers. But despite the apparent importance of dominant environmental requirements, only one study has attempted to catalog these requirements by industry (Steiner, 1969). Therefore, there is very little evidence about the number and types of environmental requirements by industry, the extent to which industry requirements change over time, or the relationships between requirements and other industry characteristics such as age of the industry, point in the product life cycle, degree of competition, and so forth.

Considerably more is known about the range and nature of alignment options presented by a given industry. In some industries, alignment options are relatively few. For example, the major home appliance industry is rapidly becoming the exclusive province of companies that compete only on a high-volume, low-cost basis (*Business Week,* 1979). On the other hand, the tobacco industry supports a much broader range of alignment possibilities, so companies may compete on a manufacturing, marketing, or product development basis (Miles, 1982). Recently, Prescott (1983) developed a taxonomy of competitive environments, some or all of which could be found in a particular industry. Analyzing a diverse set of industries, he found that the vast majority contained multiple competitive environments. Within each of these competitive environments, one or more competitive strategies were feasible.

In addition to the range of alignment options, industry characteristics may affect the nature of an organization's environmental alignment even for organizations pursuing generally similar strategies. For example, Miles and Snow (1978) found organizations that they called Prospectors in both the college textbook publishing and electronics industries. However, Prospector behavior was not exactly the same in each industry. Textbook publishing has undergone relatively few product, market, or technological innovations in the past two decades. Prospector firms in this industry, therefore, tend to focus on locating new markets for their basic product and to a lesser extent on technological innovations (such as the use of computerized typesetting and printing). By contrast, over the past 20 years, Prospectors in the electronics industry have developed a much larger and wider array of new products, markets, and technologies. Differences in the implications for Prospector firms' structure, process, and types of personnel in the two industries are large.

In sum, the impact that industry has on the alignment options and processes of organizations has received a considerable amount of research attention. In the main, this research has been in the form of industry and/or case studies (de Chazeau and Kahn, 1959; Peck, 1961; Hunt, 1972; Brock, 1975; Hatten and Schendel, 1977). Recently, however, there have been a few encouraging attempts at systematic theory development in this area (Porter, 1976, 1979, 1980; Caves and Porter, 1977; Prescott, 1983).

2. *Impacts on Arrangement*

In addition to its effects on alignment possibilities, industry has direct and indirect impacts on certain internal arrangements of the organization. Perhaps the strongest and most direct impact is on the organization's core production technology. In most industries, there exists a "technological imperative" in the sense that the nature of the product (Rushing, 1968) and available technical knowledge determine the essential nature of the production process. Organizations within the industry are obliged to adopt this core technology, for if they operate outside these technological norms they will be unable to enter or remain in the industry.

Production technologies must be coordinated and controlled, and the mechanisms for doing so vary according to whether the system is unit or small batch, mass, or continuous process (Woodward, 1970; Van de Ven et al., 1976).

Different technologies require different forms of coordination and control, and these in turn create some demand for, but do not precisely determine, a particular organizational structure. Thus industry may have an indirect impact on organizational structure and management processes via its effect on production technology. However, those investigators who have isolated technology's effects at different organizational levels, such as Hickson et al., (1969), Hrebiniak (1974), and Comstock and Scott (1977), have not yet examined closely the role that industry factors play in the technology–structure relationship.

In sum, industry appears to be an important overlay influencing both the alignment and arrangement choices made by managers of organizations. A particular industry type, in the hands of a skilled consultant or other industry analyst, would immediately offer a good deal of information about an organization's strategic options, its core production technology, its coordination and control mechanisms, and, to some extent, its structure. Obviously, however, industry factors do not completely circumscribe an organization's behavior, requiring more specific overlays to be superimposed on a particular organization.

B. Strategy Overlay

Because of its position at the interface between organization and environment, strategy interacts with industry to suggest additional, more specific features of the organization. Strategy has been variously defined, but the most useful definitions for the organization as a whole are those that include management's broad objectives with respect to environmental alignment as well as the major means used to achieve the desired alignment. Strategic decision making is a complex, ongoing, and often dynamic process, and thus it has resisted attempts at specific definition. Furthermore, organizational strategies sometimes are formulated in an emergent rather than premeditated fashion (Quinn, 1977, 1978; Mintzberg, 1978) making it difficult to monitor an organization's strategic actions using standard planning models. For these reasons, Mintzberg (1978) and Miles and Snow (1978) suggested that strategy be viewed as a *pattern* in the organization's ongoing stream of important decisions and actions. Typically, these decisions will be directed at (1) maintaining or improving the organization's alignment with its environment, and (2) managing its major internal interdependencies. Defining strategy in this manner allows researchers to move beyond the abstract and normative aspects of strategy toward those decisions that actually involve organizational objectives and the allocation of resources necessary to achieve objectives.

1. *Impacts on Alignment*

As described earlier, every industry offers a range of alignment options. Whether, in a given industry, the range of options is broad or narrow, every participant in that industry must choose its own preferred form of alignment. The formulation and implementation of an organizational strategy seek to operationalize and solidify this alignment choice.

Strategy appears to be an important overlay for two major reasons. First, when top executives develop an effective strategy—when a logical pattern exists in their decisions over time—the organization has a clear direction and a means of responding consistently to environmental change (Andrews, 1971). In past decades it could be argued that strategy was not as crucial to organizations as it is today. Prior to World War II, most companies produced only one or a few products, so the direction of growth was straightforward. Also, the required integration of functions such as manufacturing, marketing, and finance could be performed centrally by the top-management group. Today, however, this is no longer the case for many organizations. As numerous industrial environments have become increasingly complex, well-conceived strategies are required by organizations wishing to operate in these environments. Thus, in the 1980s and beyond, strategic planning apparently will become absolutely essential to the majority of organizations (*Business Week,* 1978), and strategy consulting will continue to be a high-growth industry (Kiechel, 1979).

A second reason for regarding strategy as an important contextual overlay is its enduring quality. Most organizations prefer to apply familiar solutions to new problems and are, therefore, generally reluctant to change their strategies (Cyert and March, 1963; Cohen et al., 1972). The investment in time, people, money, and other resources required to develop the distinctive competences, technologies, structures, and management processes needed to pursue a particular strategy is large. In addition, the managerial stress associated with planning and executing strategic change is often a deterrent to major and/or frequent changes in strategy. Perhaps the greatest hurdle to strategic change stems from the fact that over time a given strategy attracts and fosters a set of managerial values and philosophies that are wedded to the strategy (Guth and Taguiri, 1965; Beer and Davis, 1976; Miles and Snow, 1978). Thus, if at all possible, organizations, when faced with external change or pressure, tend to adjust their current strategies rather than change to new strategies (Snow and Hambrick, 1980).

If, as suggested, strategy is an important mechanism for achieving environmental alignment, is it possible to identify and classify different types of strategy? The studies by Chandler (1962), Burns and Stalker (1961), and Miles and Snow (1978) represented attempts to describe various strategic patterns. Chandler (1962) described essentially two types of growth strategy, market penetration and diversification. Burns and Stalker (1961) described two types of organizations: the mechanistic, which was suitable for a stable environment, and the organic, which was required by a changing environment. Miles and Snow (1978) identified four organizational strategies that they called Defender, Prospector, Analyzer, and Reactor. It is quite probable that these studies, in the aggregate, do not encompass all of the strategies used by organizations to achieve environmental alignment. However, to this point, research on strategy has not been conducted with the aid of a broad and explicit theoretical perspective nor a purposeful effort toward typological development and classification. Future research needs to be undertaken with the clear intent of systematically exploring strategic patterns in a variety of industrial environments.

2. *Impacts on Arrangement*

The primary impact that strategy has on the arrangement of organizational resources concerns the number and types of major resource-allocation points in the organization. As new forms of organizational structure have evolved, these decision points have become more numerous and decentralized. For example, the role of the general manager, developed during the 1950s and 1960s to facilitate pursuance of diversification strategies, represented a major innovation in the way organizational resources were deployed. General managers, in effect, managed their own ''businesses'' within the confines of a larger organizational structure (Chandler, 1962). Only a decade or so later, various matrix-manager roles were developed (Sayles, 1976; Davis and Lawrence, 1977). These managerial roles enabled organizations to pursue ''mixed'' strategies combining a set of both stable and changing businesses into a single system (Miles and Snow, 1978).

Evolution in alignment options and strategies has required a similar evolution in structure–process arrangements. Until the product or divisionalized structure was developed, a diversification strategy could not be pursued effectively (Chandler, 1962). Until the matrix structure was developed, mixed strategies could not be pursued. And so on. Thus, strategy broadly determines the form of the organization's structure and accompanying management processes. However, in most cases, strategy does not shape structure and process beyond key decisions such as the choice between a product or a matrix structure, whether or not to utilize the general manager role, and so forth. A final overlay, management philosophy, must be combined with the industry and strategy overlays to complete the broad framework for analyzing the systemic behavior of organizations.

C. Management Philosophy Overlay

In any except the most completely deterministic models, the values, beliefs, and skills of top managers must be taken into account in order to understand fully the functioning of an organization. It would be easy to construct a lengthy list of the personal and/or demographic characteristics of top managers that might influence their decisions about the alignment and arrangement of organizational resources, but two characteristics seem most relevant to this overlay: (1) managers' philosophies of management and (2) managers' problem-solving styles and orientations.

1. *Impacts on Alignment*

A sizable body of literature indicates that managers develop beliefs about themselves and others in organizations to explain how and why employees are motivated, directed, and controlled (Miles, 1975). Although managerial philosophies would appear to be most closely related to decisions concerning organizational structure and management processes, they also can and do influence strategic choices. For example, Chandler (1962) described how at DuPont and Sears plans for divisionalized structures were delayed for long periods or even vetoed because of arguments about whether managers had the capability to operate decentralized divisions. While it seemed clear that the new diversification strategies demanded new internal arrangements, beliefs about the efficacy of existing functional structures and processes were strong. In the old system, top managers felt as if they were in control of all segments of the business, even though evidence was mounting that centralized decision making was impeding the development of new strategies (Chandler, 1962).

One would expect that careful histories of most organizations would find similar instances of managerial philosophies influencing, directly or indirectly, organizational strategies. Where incompatibility exists between strategy and management philosophy, top managers' attachment to current structures and processes limits the strategic options considered or chosen. In other cases, however, managerial philosophies have prompted new and innovative strategies. For example, the founders of one prominent electronics firm believed that operating units should remain small enough to allow an informal, face-to-face, professional atmosphere in which the ideas and talents of managers could flourish. The firm now has approximately 35,000 employees arranged in 35 or more (the numbers grow yearly) operating divisions, each of which is aligned with a distinct segment of the industry. In this firm, top managers' strong beliefs about the management of human resources has created a successful strategy emphasizing product innovation (Miles and Snow, 1978).

Preliminary cross-sectional research suggested that management philosophies, defined as Traditional, Human Relations, or Human Resources, were associated with different organizational strategies (Miles and Snow, 1978). Combined with Chandler's (1962) historical descriptions, the general nature of the association seems to be that diversification strategies are unlikely to be pursued by organizations whose top managers hold Traditional (or Theory X) management philosophies.

2. *Impacts on Arrangement*

Chandler's (1962) research suggested strong and direct links between top managers' philosophies and the types of structural arrangements, planning and control systems, and decision making they are likely to prefer or adopt. Other research indicated that managers' beliefs about their own and others' capabilities were strongly associated with the nature and quality of their relationships with their subordinates (Miles and Ritchie, 1970). Finally, managers' beliefs about employee capabilities were associated with the design and operation of organizational reward systems (Ruh et al., 1973; Kerr, 1983). In all cases, the relationship was primarily inhibitory: participative systems could not succeed in organizations whose managers held Traditional (Theory X) management philosophies.

On the other hand, strongly held beliefs by top managers about the creativity of organization members have led some firms to develop what may amount to a new organizational form centered around a venture capital committee (Hutchinson, 1976). A venture capital committee provides funding for product and other innovations brought to the committee's attention by any organization member. In a fully developed system of this sort, most organization members can be viewed as having both scanning and operating responsibilities, that is, to be involved in both alignment and arrangement processes.

In sum, an overlay reflecting types of management philosophies could be expected to help explain top managers' alignment and arrangement decisions. Clearly, a well-developed management philosophy overlay would have considerable practical use in that top managers considering various strategic options would be encouraged to examine the management philosophy implications associated with each.

3. *Problem-Solving Orientation and Style*

In addition to management philosophy, top managers' problem orientations and problem-solving styles appear to be an important part of the systemic behavior of organizations. It is clear that many managers develop patterns of problem-solving behavior that are clear enough and well enough known that they may serve as the basis for selection or placement. For example, in World War II, General George Patton's orientation and problem-solving style appeared to make him an ideal person to spearhead a major offensive. Similarly, corporate executives are frequently sought out for particular posts because of their reputations for being innovative, tough-minded, or some other orientation presumably demanded by a given situation.

Chandler (1962) described major differences in the outlook and style of such "empire builders" as William C. Durant (of General Motors), Richard Sears, and Coleman DuPont, and such "organization builders" as Alfred Sloan (of GM) and General Robert E. Wood (of Sears). The first group tended to focus their attention on new products, markets, and acquisitions—the accumulation and alignment of resources—while the second group tended to be adept at rationalizing the huge enterprises their predecessors had put together—creating and refining administrative structures and processes suited to the emerging strategies.

While there is little agreement at present concerning whether or how problem-solving style and orientation may be measured or codified (Hellriegel and

Slocum, 1975), an exploratory study conducted in the college textbook publishing industry is suggestive of a possible approach. In this study two of the overlays in the present framework were already available. Earlier research had provided evidence of the strategies of most of the major firms, and an industry analysis had clarified technological alternatives, market growth patterns, types of product innovation, and so forth (Miles and Snow, 1978). It thus seemed useful to explore the fit between organizational strategy and top managers' problem orientation within a known industry context.

Six organizations were selected based on agreements about strategy among a panel of industry experts. Because they represent polar opposites in strategy, three of the chosen organizations were Defenders and three were Prospectors. The top-management team (president or general manager, editor-in-chief, national sales manager, financial officer, production head) in each firm completed the Kirton Adaption–Innovation Inventory, a short instrument that measures the extent to which managers focus on problems associated with "doing things better" (adaptors) or "doing things differently" (innovators) (Kirton, 1976). Predictably, the chief executive of each of the three Prospector firms scored higher on innovation while the three top managers of the Defender firms scored higher on adaption. In addition, there were differences among managers from different functional areas that appeared to reflect not only the expected problem orientation of their department but also the importance of that department to the organization's strategy. For example, in the Prospector firms, the critical roles of editor-in-chief and national sales manager were consistently held by innovators, whereas in the Defender companies these same roles tended to be held by adaptors (though not as consistently). Alternatively, two of the three financial officers in Defenders were innovators (consistent with this cost-oriented strategy), whereas in Prospectors two of the three financial officers were adaptors.

Although this study was too small to warrant detailed interpretation or generalization, it did suggest the possibility of categorizing important aspects of top managers' predispositions and relating these to major alignment and arrangement decisions. However, though a close fit between an organization's strategy and its top managers' philosophy and problem-solving orientation would be expected when considering the system as a whole, this relationship would also be expected to attenuate as one moves down the hierarchy into the middle- and lower-management levels.

V. AN ILLUSTRATION OF THE CONTEXTUAL OVERLAYS FRAMEWORK

A short example, based mostly on consulting experiences, may help to illustrate the kind and degree of system specification possible through knowledge of industry, strategy, and top-management characteristics.

A. Industry

Suppose, for simplicity's sake, that an industry overlay is available that groups industries into three categories on the basis of two key dimensions: (1) capital requirements for entry and (2) product innovation rates. Using such a categorization scheme, the basic metals industry (e.g., steel and aluminum) represents a class of industries with high entry capital requirements and low product innovation rates (Type A). At the other extreme, the electronics industry would be a prime candidate for a class of industries with relatively low entry capital requirements and a high rate of product innovation (Type B). The consumer packaged goods industry might represent a middle category of industries in terms of entry capital requirements and product innovation rates (Type C).

Using only industry information (Type A, B, or C), what organizational characteristics can be predicted? Within Type A industries (e.g., steel) one would expect to find a relatively small number of vertically integrated firms, tending toward departmentalization by function and stage of production. High entry capital requirements would limit the number of firms in this type of industry, and these requirements, coupled with relatively stable products, would make vertical integration possible and profitable. Large, vertically integrated organizations usually operate according to a central plan, with appropriate buffers between the stages of operation. Environmental alignment options characterized by rapid shifts in products and markets would generally not be associated with industries of this type.

At the other extreme, in Type B industries (e.g., electronics) one would expect to find a large number of firms of predominantly medium or small size, with a clear tendency toward departmentalization by product or project. High product innovation rates limit the benefits of detailed, centralized operating plans and push the system toward an arrangement emphasizing flexibility through the use of autonomous divisions. Lower capital requirements permit more rapid entry into the industry, and the range of feasible alignments is much broader than in Type A industries.

Finally, Type C industries (e.g., consumer packaged goods) would be expected to have a number of medium to large firms with essentially functional structures, integrated largely by coordinating mechanisms in the form of product or brand managers. Scale economies discourage departmentalization by product, but periodic product innovations required to maintain market share demand that resource allocation within the basic functional structure be influenced by individuals with specific product responsibility.

Obviously, an industry overlay of this sort does not fully describe or explain the shape of organizational systems within a particular class of industries. Instead, it suggests a feasible set of alignment options and structure–process arrangements out of which specific choices will likely be made.

B. Strategy

Again, for ease of illustration, suppose that the strategy overlay is composed only of Defenders and Prospectors, two contrasting but viable strategies identified by Miles and Snow (1978). By overlaying patterns of strategy over industry characteristics, it is possible to specify consistent organizational systems.

Although most firms in a Type A industry (e.g., steel) will tend toward a centralized, vertically integrated, functional structure, those pursuing the Defender strategy would be expected to be strongest in this tendency. Defenders attempt to protect a particular market niche against encroachment through careful attention to the price and/or quality of a limited set of products or services. This strategy serves to further stabilize an organizational system already constrained by technological imperatives, limit the requirement for environmental scanning, and increase the benefits to be gained by centralized planning. On the other hand, Prospectors in a Type A industry would be likely to broaden their alignment by integrating forward into a wide range of end products. Some divisionalization by product might well be required to support this strategy, and some market mechanisms to control the lateral flow of raw materials (e.g., transfer pricing) would be expected to emerge. Thus, though most firms in a Type A industry would appear to be similar in technology, structure, and process, a limited though important set of characteristics could be predicted with the strategy overlay.

In a Type B industry (e.g., electronics), Defender firms attempting to protect their narrow domains might still be forced to arrange some segments of their system in project form to pursue prototype development of new models of their existing products. Prospectors, on the other hand, would be expected to move furthest toward decentralized, divisionalized structures. Thus, while virtually all firms in a Type B industry would be less mechanistic than those in a Type A industry, predictions concerning just how organic a given firm's structure and process are likely to be will be improved through knowledge of its strategic orientation.

Finally, in a Type C industry (e.g., consumer packaged goods), most firms would tend toward functional structures, laterally integrated by product or brand managers (large firms in this type of industry may first be divisionalized by major classes of products). In such an industry, key structure–process differences would be expected to turn on the amount of influence built into the product or brand manager position. Therefore, Prospectors would be likely to have relatively more powerful brand or product managers than would Defenders. Again, while most firms in the industry might have similar structures and processes, predictable differences would occur consistent with strategic orientation.

C. Management Philosophy and Problem-Solving Style

To complete the illustration of increasing system specification through successive application of contextual overlays, three consistent patterns of top-management characteristics, identified in the textbook publishing study mentioned above and in a study of hospitals (Miles and Snow, 1978), can be defined: (1) Prospector organizations in Type B industries (e.g., electronics) would be expected to have top managers who, on average, tend to be innovators in their problem orientation and who hold the Human Resources philosophy of management; (2) Defender organizations in Type A industries (e.g., steel) would be expected to have top managers who lean toward an adaptor problem orientation and problem-solving style; and (3) problem orientation and problem-solving styles among top managers in Type C industries (e.g., consumer packaged goods) would tend to be mixed, with product managers tending to exhibit innovator characteristics (especially in Prospector firms) and functional managers adaptor characteristics. Note that no attempt has been made to specify management philosophy in any other than Prospector organizations. Based on the limited evidence to date (Miles and Snow, 1978), a Human Resources management philosophy appears to be a necessary condition for the effective pursuit of a Prospector strategy in most industries; there do not appear to be any industry–strategy combinations that demand Traditional or Human Relations philosophies.

The major value of a management philosophy/style overlay may well be to alert organizational analysts to possible sources of system ineffectiveness or inefficiency. For example, in one insurance organization there was general agreement concerning the need to move away from a Defender strategy into an Analyzer or perhaps even a Prospector strategy. Industry characteristics made such a move feasible, and technological and other requirements appropriate to the new strategy were well understood. However, it was apparent from managers' descriptions of the difficulties the system was incurring as it attempted to shift its strategy that the problem-solving orientation and management philosophy of key top managers were not well suited to the desired market alignment. While it may be premature to begin detailed measurement of top managers' characteristics in situations like these, further development of an overlay that would mesh with the industry and strategy overlays seems useful both for theory building and practice.

VI. CONCLUSIONS

The central argument of this paper has been that more comprehensive, systematic, and relevant theories of organizational behavior can be developed by using the contextual overlays approach. This approach, which relies heavily on the development of appropriate typologies of key environmental, organizational, and individual/group characteristics, not only serves to synthesize present knowledge but also provides a means for generating new knowledge about organizations and management. The obvious question to pose at this point is: How feasible is this approach? Do we in fact have, or can we construct, typologies for use in each of the three key overlays of industry, strategy, and management philosophy? The answer, we believe, is mixed. In our view, the strategy overlay is furthest along toward operational usefulness, followed by the management philosophy overlay. In the cases of both the industry and decision-making style overlays, we are less comfortable—not because typologies in these areas do not exist but because there are so many competing categorizations.

With regard to the strategy overlay, there is today a convergence among work in several areas toward a categorization of the sort used in the lengthy example presented above. We drew the example's strategic types from our own empirical research, but there are obvious links between the Defender, Prospector, and Analyzer types and the three generic strategies identified by Porter (1980). These generic strategies are cost leadership, differentiation, and the use of either or both strategies within a specific or "focused" environment. The reader can easily see cost leadership as the usual distinctive competence of the Defender, differentiation (through innovation) as the key competence of the Prospector, and the ability to be both efficient and innovative in a limited arena as a defining characteristic of an Analyzer. In addition to the convergence from economics (and marketing) suggested in Porter's work, there is also apparent convergence from biology and sociology. It is not uncommon for biologists to use business and/or military language in describing specie's behavior and for behavioral scientists to draw on biological analogies in explaining organizational phenomena. Recently, sociologists such as Hannan and Freeman (1978) have made direct applications of biological concepts to explain birth and death within populations of organizations. In general, the concepts borrowed from biology describe the "strategies" which species employ in obtaining and utilizing environmental resources. Some species appear to be particularly adept at surviving in new arenas (a Prospector competence) while others fare well in competition with other species for increasingly scarce resources (a Defender competence). Also, biologists categorize species by their ability to apply their strategies generally or narrowly within particular niches. By combining these two dimensions of resource acquisition and use, one can approximate all the characteristics of the strategic types identified by Miles and Snow (1978) and those of Porter (1980). Thus, given that (1) the strategic typology employed here has historical roots (in the work of Chandler described earlier), (2) the typology was empirically based and has been widely used, and (3) related but independently developed typologies are emerging, we believe the Miles–Snow typology can be used with some confidence as the principal component of the strategy overlay. An improved typology may well emerge from future research, but theory development need not wait.

In our opinion the management philosophy overlay is also easily specified, but the support for our chosen typology is not as solid as with strategy. For example, the historical roots of the typology employed here (Traditional, Human Relations, and Human Resources philosophies) are less clearly developed than those of the strategic typology. The source and time of emergence of the Traditional and Human Relations philosophies have been well documented by Bendix (1974), but the origins of the Human Resources philosophy are less clear (in part because it is so recent). Similarly, while there are convergent typologies, they are not independently verifiable. That is, though related typologies such as McGregor's (1960) Theory X and Theory Y or Likert's (1967) Systems 1–4 flow from the same general body of research and writing, there are no similar typologies drawn from other fields or disciplines. Nevertheless, the Traditional, Human Relations, and Human Resources typology has been widely used, and there is a rather consistent body of research which suggests that the key characteristic (managers' beliefs about the capabilities of those below them) of the three philosophies is correlated with aspects of organizational performance and subordinate satisfaction. Moreover, these beliefs have been reliably measured and compared over time and across a variety of settings (Miles, 1975).

In sum, we believe a useful, though perhaps not yet thoroughly operational, typology of management philosophy exists which can serve as the main component of a management philosophy overlay. Recall, however, that in the example we also included a categorization of management decision-making style in this overlay. In our judgment there is not widespread agreement supporting any particular set of alternative decision styles and thus, for purposes of theory development, effort should be concentrated on management philosophy. If further research on decision styles and their possible links to major organizational issues (e.g., strategic choice) is forthcoming, one may argue for inclusion. At the moment, the payoff associated with management philosophy is likely to be higher, since this factor is a major correlate of an organization's strategy and management processes.

Finally, there are many industry typologies, ranging from simple descriptions such as heavy and light to the complex multidigit codifications used by economists and government statisticians. A recent attempt to characterize industries has been made by Lawrence and Dyer (1983), who employ the dimensions of resource scarcity and information complexity. This categorization approach is somewhat more complex than necessary for the purpose of typological construction, but the key dimensions are obviously important. It may in fact be the case that more than one industry typology—and therefore perhaps more than one industry overlay—may be required. At the moment, however, we would opt for the sacrifice of some accuracy in the search for simplicity and generalizability (Weick, 1979). In the example above, we suggested that a useful typology might be built using only capital requirements for entry and product innovation rate. These two characteristics are in turn highly correlated with industry age and market structure, and quite probably with several other relevant dimensions. It may well be that an industry typology will emerge which, like that for strategy, captures a particularly salient set of interrelated characteristics. We and others are continuing this search.

If one agrees that the contextual overlays approach is both sound and feasible, then the final question becomes: So what—where will this approach lead us? It is our view that even a rudimentary general framework, employing no more than the three overlays described here, provides a very powerful diagnostic tool. For example, in our consulting experience, many planning and control failures in organizations flow from poorly coupled strategy and structure (as research and theory have frequently predicted). If we know an organization's industry and the strategy it is enacting, we can usually pinpoint the two or three most crucial planning and control mechanisms. These mechanisms can then be examined to see if the ways in which they are structured and managed fall into the feasible set. If not, the solution to the organization's problems may be obvious, providing the required structure and process do not directly contradict the managerial philosophy of the executives involved. Proceeding as if one were applying a series of overlays can both direct and accelerate the diagnostic process.

For theory construction the overlay approach is especially helpful. The process of examining each organizational behavior issue within the context of the salient industry, strategy, and management philosophy contexts brings a rigorous and operational level of validity to bear. For example, issues of reward system design and effectiveness may hinge not only on individuals' need structures but also on the fit between the reward system and the organization's strategy and management philosophy (Kerr, 1983). Other issues such as leadership, structure, climate, etc., should also be examined within their appropriate context.

As we claimed at the outset of this paper, efforts at synthesizing the literature on organizations and management appear to be increasing. Clearly, in our view, these efforts should be encouraged, and we hope the arguments presented here serve to speed this process.

NOTES

1. Van de Ven (1979) has identified four different conceptual meanings of fit. As used here, fit means "that characteristics of environmental niches and organizational forms must be joined together in a particular configuration to achieve *completeness in a description of a social system*—like pieces of a puzzle must be put together in certain ways to obtain a complete image" (p. 323, author's italics).

2. A version of the material in this section, and the example that follows, appeared in a different context in Mariann Jelinek et al., *Organizations by Design: Theory and Practice* (Plano, Texas: Business Publications, Inc., 1981), pp. 548–62.

3. Theoretical schemes usually are called typologies. Empirically derived schemes usually are called taxonomies.

REFERENCES

Aldrich, Howard E. (1979), Organizations and Environments. Englewood Cliffs, NJ: Prentice-Hall.

Andrews, Kenneth R. (1971), The Concept of Corporate Strategy. Homewood, IL: Irwin.

Ansoff, H. Igor and John M. Stewart (1967), "Strategies for a Technology-based Business." *Harvard Business Review, 45:*71–83.

Argyris, Chris (1973), "On Organizations of the Future." In Administrative and Policy Study Series, Vol. 1, No. 03-006. Beverly Hills, CA: Sage Publications.

Beer, Michael and Stanley M. Davis, (1976), "Creating a Global Organization: Failures Along the Way." *Columbia Journal of World Business, 11:*72–84.

Bendix, Reinhard (1974), Work and Authority in Industry. Berkeley, CA: University of California Press.

Brock, G. W. (1975), The U.S. Computer Industry. Cambridge, MA: Ballinger.

Burns, Tom and G. M. Stalker (1961), The Management of Innovation. London: Tavistock.

Business Week (1978), "The New Planning," December 18:62–68.

______ (1979), "White Consolidated's New Appliance Punch," May 7:94–98.

Carper, William B. and William E. Snizek (1980), "The Nature and Types of Organizational Taxonomies: An Overview." *Academy of Management Review, 5:*65–76.

Caves, Richard E. (1972), American Industry: Structure, Conduct, Performance. 3rd ed. Englewood Cliffs, NJ: Prentice-Hall.

Caves, Richard E. and Michael E. Porter (1977), "From Entry Barriers to Mobility Barriers: Conjectural Decisions and Contrived Deterrence to New Competition." *Quarterly Journal of Economics, 91:*241–261.

Chandler, Alfred D., Jr. (1962), Strategy and Structure. Garden City, NY: Doubleday.

Child, John (1972), "Organizational Structure, Environment, and Performance—The Role of Strategic Choice." *Sociology, 6:*1–22.

Cohen, Michael D., James G. March, and Johan P. Olsen (1972), "A Garbage Can Model of Organizational Choice." *Administrative Science Quarterly, 17:*1–25.

Comstock, Donald E. and W. Richard Scott (1977), "Technology and the Structure of Subunits: Distinguishing Individual and Workgroup Effects." *Administrative Science Quarterly, 22:*177–202.

Cyert, Richard and James G. March (1963), A Behavioral Theory of the Firm. Englewood Cliffs, NJ: Prentice-Hall.

Daft, Richard L., and John C. Wiginton (1979), "Language and Organization." *Academy of Management Review, 4:*179–191.

Davis, Stanley M. and Paul R. Lawrence (1977), Matrix. Reading, MA: Addison-Wesley.

de Chazeau, M. G. and A. E. Kahn (1959), Integration and Competition in the Petroleum Industry. New Haven: Yale University Press.

Drucker, Peter F. (1954), The Practice of Management. New York: Harper & Brothers.

______ (1974), Management: Tasks, Responsibilities, Practices. New York: Harper & Row.

Forrester, Jay W. (1965), "A New Corporate Design." *Industrial Management Review, 7:*5–18.

Galbraith, Jay R. (1977), Designing Complex Organizations. 2nd ed. Reading, MA: Addison-Wesley.

Galbraith, Jay R., and Daniel A. Nathanson (1978), Strategy Implementation: The Role of Structure and Process. St. Paul: West.

Guth, William and Renato Taguiri (1965), "Personal Values and Corporate Strategy." *Harvard Business Review, 43:*123–132.

Hannan, Michael T. and John H. Freeman (1978), "The Population Ecology of Organizations." *American Journal of Sociology, 82:*929–964.

Hatten, Kenneth J. and Dan E. Schendel (1977), "Heterogeneity Within an Industry: Firm Conduct in the U.S. Brewing Industry." *The Journal of Industrial Economics, 26:*97–113.

Hellriegel, Don and John W. Slocum, Jr. (1975), "Managerial Problem-solving Styles." *Business Horizons, 18:*29–37.

Hickson, David J., D. S. Pugh, and Diana Pheysey (1969), "Operations Technology and Structure: An Empirical Reappraisal." *Administrative Science Quarterly, 14:*378–397.

Hrebiniak, Lawrence G. (1974), "Job Technology, Supervision, and Work Group Structure." *Administrative Science Quarterly, 19:*395–410.

Hunt, Michael S. (1972), Competition in the Major Home Appliance Industry. Doctoral Dissertation, Harvard University.

Hutchinson, John (1976), "Evolving Organizational Forms." *Columbia Journal of World Business, 11:*48–58.

Kerr, Jeffrey L. (1983), An Examination of the Relationship Between Corporate Strategies and the Design of Control and Reward Systems in Large Industrial Organizations. Doctoral Dissertation, The Pennsylvania State University.

Kiechel, III, Walter (1979), "Playing by the Rules of the Corporate Strategy Game." *Fortune,* September 24:110–115.

Kirton, Michael J. (1976), "Adaptors and Innovators: A Description and Measure." *Journal of Applied Psychology, 61:*622–629.

Lawrence, Paul R. and Jay W. Lorsch (1967), Organization and Environment. Boston: Harvard Graduate School of Business Administration.

Lawrence, Paul R. and Davis Dyer (1983), Renewing American Industry. New York: Free Press.

Likert, Rensis (1967), The Human Organization. New York: McGraw-Hill.

McKelvey, B. (1975), "Guidelines for the Empirical Classification of Organizations." *Administrative Science Quarterly, 20:*509–525.

McGregor, Douglas E. (1960), The Human Side of Enterprise. New York: McGraw-Hill.

Miles, Raymond E. (1975), Theories of Management. New York: McGraw-Hill.

Miles, Raymond E. and J. B. Ritchie (1970), "An Analysis of Quantity and Quality of the Participative Decision Making Process." *Personnel Psychology, 23:*347–359.

Miles, Raymond E., Charles C. Snow, and Jeffrey Pfeffer (1974), "Organization-Environment: Concepts and Issues." *Industrial Relations, 13:*244–264.

Miles, Raymond E. and Charles C. Snow (1978), Organizational Strategy, Structure, and Process. New York: McGraw-Hill.

Miles, Robert H. (1982), Coffin Nails and Corporate Strategies. Englewood Cliffs, NJ: Prentice-Hall.

Miller, Danny and Henry Mintzberg (1980), "The Case for Configuration." Working Paper, McGill University.

Mintzberg, Henry (1978), "Patterns in Strategy Formation." *Management Science, 24:*934–948.

Peck, M. J. (1961), Competition in the Aluminum Industry, 1945–1958. Cambridge, MA: Harvard University Press.

Perrow, Charles (1967), "A Framework for the Comparative Analysis of Organizations." *American Sociological Review, 32:*195–208.

Porter, Michael E. (1976), "Please Note Location of Nearest Exit." *California Management Review, 19:*21–33.

Porter, Michael E. (1979), "How Competitive Forces Shape Strategy." *Harvard Business Review, 57:*137–145.

Porter, Michael E. (1980), Competitive Strategy. New York: Free Press.

Porter, Michael E. (1981), "The Contributions of Industrial Organization to Strategic Management." *Academy of Management Review, 6:*609–620

Prescott, John E. (1983), An Empirical Analysis of Competitive Environments, Strategic Types, and Performance. Doctoral Dissertation, The Pennsylvania State University.

Quinn, J. Brian (1977), "Strategic Goals: Process and Politics." *Sloan Management Review, 18*:21–37.

——— (1978), "Strategic Change: 'Logical Incrementalism'." *Sloan Management Review, 18*:7–21.

Roberts, Karlene H., Charles L. Hulin, and Denise M. Rousseau (1978), Developing an Interdisciplinary Science of Organizations. San Francisco: Jossey-Bass.

Ruh, Robert A., Roger L. Wallace, and Carl F. Frost (1973), "Management Attitudes and the Scanlon Plan." *Industrial Relations, 12*:282–288.

Rushing, William A. (1968), "Hardness of Material as Related to Division of Labor in Manufacturing Industries." *Administrative Science Quarterly, 13*:229–245.

Sayles, Leonard R. (1976), "Matrix Management: The Structure With a Future." *Organizational Dynamics, 5*:2–17.

Schein, Edgar H. (1980), Organizational Psychology. 3rd ed. Englewood Cliffs, NJ: Prentice-Hall.

Schoeffler, Sidney, Robert D. Buzzell, and Donald F. Heany (1974), "Impact of Strategic Planning on Profit Performance." *Harvard Business Review, 52*:137–145.

Snow, Charles C. and Donald C. Hambrick (1980), "Measuring Organizational Strategies: Some Theoretical and Methodological Problems." *Academy of Management Review,* 5:527–538.

Steiner, George A. (1969), Strategic Factors in Business Success. New York: Financial Executives Research Foundation.

Thompson, James D. (1967), Organizations in Action. New York: McGraw-Hill.

Tiryakian, Edward A. (1968), "Typologies." *International Encyclopedia of the Social Sciences, 16*:177–186.

Van de Ven, Andrew H. (1979), "Review of Howard E. Aldrich, Organizations and Environments." *Administrative Science Quarterly, 24*:320–326.

Van de Ven, Andrew H., Andre L. Delbecq, and Richard Koenig, Jr. (1976), "Determinants of Coordination Modes within Organizations." *American Sociological Review, 41*:322–338.

Weick, Karl E. (1969), The Social Psychology of Organizing. Reading, MA: Addison-Wesley.

——— (1977), "Enactment Processes in Organizations." In Barry M. Staw and Gerald R. Salancik (eds.), New Directions in Organizational Behavior. Chicago: St. Clair Press, 267–300.

Weick, Karl E. (1979), The Social Psychology of Organizing. Second Edition. Reading, MA: Addison-Wesley.

Woodward, Joan (1965), Industrial Organization: Theory and Practice. London: Oxford University Press.

Woodward, Joan, (ed.) (1970), Industrial Organization: Behaviour and Control. London: Oxford University Press.

Research in
Personnel and Human Resources Management

Edited by **Kendrith M. Rowland**
Department of Business Administration, University of Illinois
and **Gerald R. Ferris**
Department of Management, Texas A & M University

This series will serve as a forum for the presentation of conceptual and methodological issues in the field of personnel and human resources management. It will seek to encourage the development of improved theory and research. The papers in each volume will attempt to critically analyze and challenge traditional views and move beyond mere state-of-the-art discussions of current topics. Additionally, papers dealing with statistical and methodological issues of concern will be included.

Volume 1, 1983
ISBN 0-89232-268-3